AC/DC
FAQ

AC/DC
FAQ

All That's Left to Know About the World's True Rock 'n' Roll Band

Susan Masino

Backbeat
Books

An Imprint of Hal Leonard Corporation

Published in 2015 by Backbeat Books
An Imprint of Hal Leonard Corporation
7777 West Bluemound Road
Milwaukee, WI 53213

Trade Book Division Editorial Offices
33 Plymouth St., Montclair, NJ 07042

Except where otherwise noted, all images in this book are from the author's personal collection.

The FAQ series was conceived by Robert Rodriguez and developed with Stuart Shea.

Every reasonable effort has been made to contact copyright holders and secure permissions. Omissions can be remedied in future editions.

Printed in the United States of America

Book design by Snow Creative Services

Library of Congress Cataloging-in-Publication Data

Masino, Susan, 1955–
   AC/DC FAQ : all that's left to know about the world's true rock 'n' roll band / Susan Masino.
      pages cm
   Includes bibliographical references and index.
   ISBN 978-1-4803-9450-6
1. Progressive rock music—Miscellanea. I. Title.
   ML3534.R676 2014
   781.66—dc23

                                                            2014027918

www.backbeatbooks.com

For Malcolm

Contents

Foreword

I prefer my rock bands to be the dangerous type. The music that thrills me—that keeps my attention and makes me feel the most alive—is the kind that teeters on insanity. The bands that play their guts out every time—and you can feel that in the grooves of the vinyl or the digits of the download. Those are the bands that inspire me to play, and that is why I fucking love AC/DC.

No band rocks harder than AC/DC. Malcolm and Angus are the evil bastard sons of Chuck Berry. Their music may seem simple and pedestrian to some, but I prefer a hypnotically relentless pummeling groove that never lets up.

If you have this book in your hand, you may remember the first time you heard that sound. Mine was the fall of 1978. I visited my older brother's college campus. He took me to a dorm room that had blankets tacked above the windows so it was dark 24/7. The only light on was a coned single bulb over the turntable, as well as a cabinet speaker stoner light—the kind that pulsated colors in time to the music. I took a slug from my second underage beer. They dropped the needle on "Whole Lotta Rosie," and my induction commenced. "*And you could say she's got it allllll.*" BAM! The sound, the power, the tone, the tempo, THE CONVICTION TO THE BEAT! There was no escaping this one. As the music continued, I heard bizarre lyrics like her weight was "19 stone," and songs with imagery of sex, and violence, and murder. WTF—is this shit legal? Add in their twisted, sick humor, and this band was my new obsession. I was hooked.

I had to see them live. Their tour stopped at Royal Oak Theater, in a suburb of Detroit, opening for Thin Lizzy. Once the downbeat hit—as you know—Angus never fucking stopped moving the entire show. Then the siren voice of Bon Scott cut through the mix and commanded me to listen to every word. Malcolm occasionally would step up for some football chorus vocals, then retreat to his comfort zone of a stack of Marshalls. Malcolm is one of rock's greatest rhythm guitarists. Right up there with Keef and Townshend. Malcolm, along with Phil and Cliff, drove that fucking train as hard as I ever saw anybody drive. This band was playing like they had no show tomorrow. They left it on stage—and they still play that way today. That changed my life.

Why does every AC/DC song feel so good? Phil Rudd. You can set your watch to him. Strippers even endorse it. That rhythmic, driving music is played in more dance clubs than any other music in the world. It's the ultimate testimony. Mike Campbell from the Heartbreakers said "their music is made for arenas." It was a revelation to me. Some music was meant to be listened to in headphones, or in a small club. AC/DC's music—the arrangement, the space, the rumble, the volume—was made to be played in arenas. Like it's one large cavernous speaker cabinet, where the sound and the rhythm are in perfect harmony. It works!

I had the honor to watch AC/DC record a song in the studio. Those guys laid down each track with every fucking cell in their body. They played like it was a live show. Moving and banging, determined to make that song soak into the machine and come out into your ears like they mean it. They are not a multiple take, "let's fix it in the mix" kind of band. That impressed me. I always strive to approach recording the same way. Every great recording has that element. You should feel the sweat, the pain, and the joy.

Enjoy this book of stories and crazy antics. Add to your appreciation of a band of brothers who have dedicated their lives to rocking out as hard as any band on our planet. They're probably Hell's house band . . . but God bless AC/DC.

Chad Smith
Los Angeles, 2014

Acknowledgments

I would like to thank all the members of AC/DC, including Bon Scott, for being the greatest rock 'n' roll band in the world. Their friendship and support over the years mean more to me than I can express. As a journalist, and now a biographer, it has been an honor to write about them and share my love for the band with the rest of their fans around the world. A special thanks also to Ross Young, Milla, and Tuesday Rudd.

Thanks to my editor, Bernadette Malavarca, and everyone at Hal Leonard/Backbeat Books, including John Cerullo, Wes Seeley, Brad Smith, and James Barnett, for all of their help, support, and belief in me. Bernadette went above and beyond the call of duty to make this book happen, and I will always be forever grateful. A very special thank you to Chad Smith, the drummer of the Red Hot Chili Peppers, for a foreword that perfectly captures the essence of AC/DC. It is a joy to read and a true honor.

Thanks to my daughter Teal, my son Jamey, and my son-in-law Eric, who I love more than I can say. And to all my family and friends who have supported me through another AC/DC adventure. Especially my sisters Kathy and Lori; my cousin Sandy; and my soul sisters, Jennifer McNulty, Terry Bucheger, Tamara Springer Gleason, Dawnette Springer Cook, Dawn Lalley, and Ronnie Norpel.

Thanks to all my friends and fellow AC/DC fans Carl Allen; David Allen; BandX, including Igor Škoro, Darko Štefulj, Dragan Telalović, Darko Vukotić, and (Billy) Milan Živadinovič and their family and friends Lika Voli Darka, Goga Plemic, Kristina Radovic, and Biljana Vukotić; Brian and Sarah Bethke; Paulo Biggers; Bruce Blaschko; Peter Cliff; Andrew Cogan; Don Coleman; Jacquie Cooper; Renee Cooper; Tracey Cooper; Tony Currenti; Tom Danheiser; Laura Day; Kenny Dee; Darren Goulden; Veronica Handeland; Micah Hanks; Angela Yvonne Hill; Gary Karnes; Marja Ladybike; Maggie Laidlaw; Paul Ledbury; Tommy Maddox; Jaelyn Messer; George Noory; Kelsey Obrigewitsch; Smiler O Rocker; Pamela Patrou; Irene Whitehead Peterson; Mary Renshaw; Mario Rimati; Adrian Seidel; Sal Serio; Pablo Andres Sanchez; Alan Shailes; Lanea Stagg; Joel and Jenn Sturgis; Brendon Sturgeon; Fred Temps; Abdul Vas; Paolo Vermellino; Owen Wacey; Mark Waterbury; Jeff Willan; and Paul Wozniak.

A special thank you to all the fans on Facebook and on the Internet who devote their time and energy to keeping us all informed on their favorite band, and to the photographers Tom Giles, Jim Johnson (especially all the album covers!), Teal Kozel, Henri Lassander, Philip Morris, Brian Rasic, Doug Thorncroft, and Keith Wessel, who provided some fantastic images.

Thanks to the authors who have written books about AC/DC, and who are listed in the back of this book. I recommend each and every one of them, as they all contribute their own unique ways of telling the AC/DC story. Also to all the great websites out there that have helped in the compiling of information for this book, especially acdc.com, ac-dc.galeon.com, ac-dc.net, bonscott.com.au, acdcblackicetourfanblognews.blogspot.com. au, and theacdcfamily.com.

Thank you to Solo Dallas, the official "AC/DC Sound Researcher," who not only helped write the chapter on AC/DC's equipment, but was able to visit with Angus Young while he was in the studio in Vancouver in May of 2014. Together with the legendary inventor Ken Schaffer, they presented Angus with his very own Schaffer Replica, which you will no doubt hear on the latest AC/DC album.

Special thanks and much gratitude to everyone who gave me interviews or sent in their thoughts past and present, including Mike Andy, Rick Brewster, "Pyro" Pete Cappadocia, (the late) Perry Cooper, Kirk Dyer, Keith Emerson, Dave Evans, Brian Johnson, Julius Grafton, Joe Matera, Tommy Redd, Ken Schaffer, Kelly Shaefer, Barry Taylor, Bill Voccia, Andrew "Don" Williams, Raymond Windlow, and Angus and Malcolm Young.

Introduction

While I was writing this, AC/DC were back in the studio in Vancouver working on a new album—exciting news for AC/DC fans. However, it was bittersweet, considering that founding member Malcolm Young would not be able to join the rest of AC/DC due to ill health. On New Year's Eve of 2013, the band celebrated their fortieth anniversary. It was announced in early 2014 that the band would record a new album and tour through forty cities in recognition of this milestone.

Then on April 16, 2014, AC/DC made an official announcement regarding Malcolm Young. It stated that he would be taking a break due to health problems, but the band would continue to make music. Staying true to their word, on May 1, AC/DC met up with producer Brendan O'Brien at the Warehouse Studio in Vancouver to record a follow-up to their hit album, *Black Ice*. This time, for the first time ever, Malcolm's rhythm parts would be played and recorded by Angus and Malcolm's nephew, Stevie Young.

The only time Malcolm has ever taken a break from the band was when he left during the North American leg of the *Blow Up Your Video* tour, to quit drinking. For a short time, Stevie Young filled in for his uncle, and as soon as Malcolm was ready, he was back in the band. Considering Malcolm Young has been known as the "brains behind AC/DC," his absence from the studio and a future tour will no doubt be felt by everyone, especially his little brother, Angus. Knowing AC/DC, I can guarantee you that they will record and perform to the best of their abilities, especially for Malcolm—someone who they all look up to, the very person who created AC/DC and led the band for the past forty years. It was later revealed that Malcolm was suffering from dementia and would not be returning to the band. On December 2, 2104, AC/DC released their new album, *Rock or Bust*, which debuted at #1 in forty-two countries.

Personally, I have had the honor and the privilege of knowing the band since the summer of 1977, when I met them on their first American tour. They played a little club in downtown Madison, Wisconsin, on August 16, the very same day Elvis Presley died. I was just starting out writing for a local music paper, and my assignment that night was to help out the promoter with a band from Australia called AC/DC.

At the time, I had never heard of them, or any of their music. Needless to say, I had no idea what I was in for that night. Bon Scott was the first band member to speak to me, and it was one word: "Sit!" He ordered me to sit down as he walked into their makeshift dressing room, as I was quietly trying to sneak out. From what I had read in their one-page biography, they sounded like a bunch of troublemakers, and I thought it would be best to stay out of their way.

Over the course of that evening, I not only got to meet and talk to the whole band, but was able to see them perform in a small club; watching their live show is something I will never forget. I was already a huge rock 'n' roll fan, but I had never before encountered anything like AC/DC. Not only were they really sweet and polite, albeit salty, they played rock with such a fervor that it made the hair on my arms stand straight up. From that night forward, I was their biggest fan. Thirty-seven years later, I still am.

That night I also became friends with one of their roadies, Barry Taylor, who would call or write to me every week for the next three years. His friendship enabled me to hang out with the band every time they came through the Midwest, and I saw them go from playing small clubs, to opening for bands like UFO and Aerosmith, to becoming headliners in their own right.

I remember their elation over the release of *Highway to Hell* and how excited everybody was for their rising success. Just as they were taking off, AC/DC suffered the terrible loss of Bon Scott, and for a time, no one knew what they were going to do next. Encouraged to keep going by Bon's parents, Angus and Malcolm pulled the band back together, hired Brian Johnson, and recorded a new album, *Back in Black*, which is now the second-biggest selling album in music history. In the fall of 1980, AC/DC embarked on the *Back in Black* tour and kept right on rocking. Exactly what Bon would have wanted them to do.

Over the years, I watched the band replace drummer Phil Rudd with Simon Wright, Angus and Malcolm both get married, and Barry Taylor leave rock 'n' roll to become a minister. After Malcolm's short departure from the band, he came back and replaced Simon Wright with Chris Slade, and the band came back even stronger in 1990, with their album *The Razors Edge*. Five years later, Phil Rudd would rejoin the band, and for the first time in their entire career, they took a seven-year break between the release of *Stiff Upper Lip* and *Black Ice*.

In 2008, the band was back on the road supporting their new album, which hit #1 in thirty-one countries as soon as it hit the shelves. I was able to see AC/DC live four times during that tour, including a night watching them in front of 47,000 screaming fans in Udine, Italy, on May 19, 2010. That tour ended up being the second-biggest grossing tour in history, and I was lucky enough to visit with them both times they played in Chicago.

The amazing thing about the band, and their music, is that they have never forgotten where they came from. They are still so humble and genuinely sincere that it is hard to believe that they happen to be in one of the best and most successful rock 'n' roll bands to exist, ever. Angus and Malcolm both love to talk about the Bon Scott days with me, and they have been so generous and kind to me and anyone I got to bring backstage, that it's hard to describe how much I admire them and how much I truly love their music.

But if you're reading this, you know what I'm talking about. AC/DC has written some of the greatest songs in the history of rock 'n' roll. That is their legacy. Yet what sets them apart from so many other performers is that they truly love and care about their fans. Writing this book, I kept in mind how much their fans love them, and I hope you appreciate reading about their incredible accomplishments, along with memorable personal stories and some fun facts. Enjoy, and always remember to *Let There Be Rock!*

AC/DC
FAQ

Rock 'n' Roll Roots

W hole books have been written about who influenced the sound of AC/DC. True fans already know that Angus and Malcolm Young's older brother George was a rock star in his own right, and any kid with a guitar and a plan was going to follow in his older brother's footsteps. That being said, there is also a whole array of artists that influenced the Brothers Young and their bandmates.

Aside from George Young, they all grew up listening to Elvis, the Beatles, the Stones, Chuck Berry, Free, Muddy Waters, Fats Domino, and every blues record they could get their hands on. AC/DC, a straightforward rock 'n' roll band, grew their roots from an eclectic mix of individuals, including some major musical architects, Bon Scott's love for Broadway show tunes, and one older sister.

When you roll their sound together, everything from the blues to the earliest chords of rock, AC/DC managed to forge a special blend of rock/metal/blues that stands the test of time. Their hundreds of songs (some have accused all only contain the same three chords) have been listened to and enjoyed for over forty years and will continue to entertain for decades to come.

Some of those individuals who inspired the band include John Lee Hooker, Chuck Berry, Little Richard, George Young, T. Rex, the Rolling Stones, and their older sister, Margaret. That's right, their older sister Margaret. She gets a little bit of credit now and then, but here she is going to get her rightful due.

John Lee Hooker

John Lee Hooker was one of eleven children born on August 22, 1917, in Coahoma County, Mississippi. Home schooled, he grew up listening to spiritual songs sung in the church. When he was five, John's parents separated, and his mother Minnie remarried blues singer William Moore. Moore introduced the young Hooker to his first guitar and helped influence his unique playing style. Before the age of fifteen, Hooker ran away from home and ended up in Memphis in the 1930s. Taking work in factories throughout the Second World War, Hooker landed a job at the Ford Motor Company in 1948. Eventually switching from acoustic to electric guitar, Hooker spent his evenings playing his way through Detroit's east side, honing his "talking blues" style that would become his trademark sound.

Not able to read, Hooker was a talented lyricist, often coming up with original songs on his own. Because of his variance in beats, studio musicians had a hard time playing with him. Much of his early studio recordings are Hooker playing guitar, singing, and stomping the beat on a wooden pallet. His most popular songs include "Boogie Chillin'" in 1948, "I'm in the Mood" in 1951, and 1962's "Boom Boom." The first two songs made it to #1 on *Billboard*'s R&B chart.

In 1989, Hooker won a Grammy with Santana for the album *The Healer*. During his career, he recorded over 100 albums. Hooker fell ill while on tour in Europe at the age of 83, dying in his sleep on June 21, 2001, just two months before his 84th birthday. John Lee Hooker was inducted into the Blues Hall of Fame in 1980 and the Rock and Roll Hall of Fame in 1991, and received a Grammy Lifetime Achievement Award in 2000. "Boogie Chillin'" and "Boom Boom" are included in the Rock and Roll Hall of Fame's "500 Songs That Shaped Rock 'n' Roll."

If you really listen to John Lee Hooker, you can hear plenty of riffs that AC/DC plays to this day. The band has been accused of recording the same album over and over again, and Angus has always been quick to retort, "No, we haven't. They all have different titles." Angus and Malcolm Young took John Lee Hooker's three simple chords, rearranged them a few times, and made them into millions.

Angus once stated, "It's just rock 'n' roll. A lot of times we get criticized for it. But if you believe you shouldn't play just three chords then you don't understand rock 'n' roll."

Chuck Berry

Duckwalk master himself, Chuck Berry was born Charles Edward Anderson Berry in St. Louis, Missouri, on October 18, 1926. Taking an interest in music at an early age, Berry first performed at his public high school.

Quickly running into trouble, Berry served a three-year prison sentence for armed robbery. Upon his 1947 release, Berry married, settled down and found work at an automobile plant. Within six years, influenced by the sounds of blues player T-Bone Walker, Berry snagged a weekly spot on stage with the Johnnie Johnson Trio.

Two years later, in 1955, Berry traveled to Chicago and met up with Muddy Waters who sent him to Chess Records. Leonard Chess signed him immediately, and Berry recorded "Maybellene," which shot up to #1 on the R&B charts, selling over one million copies. During the mid-fifties, Berry, a true pioneer of rock 'n' roll, had hits with "Roll Over Beethoven" in 1956, "Rock 'n' Roll Music" in 1957 and 1958's "Johnny B. Goode."

As an established star and owner of his own club in St. Louis, Berry's Club Bandstand, Berry was sentenced in 1962 to three years in prison for transporting a minor across state lines. Released in 1963, Berry came back with hits "No Particular Place to Go," and "Nadine," but never saw the success he had enjoyed before his second stint behind bars. Although he wound up on the wrong side of the law, Berry's contribution to the sound of rock 'n' roll in immeasurable.

When the Rock and Roll Hall of Fame opened in 1986, Chuck Berry was one of the first musicians to be inducted. The Rolling Stones did the honors, and Keith Richards was quick to point out that he had stolen every lick Chuck Berry ever played.

In 2004, Berry was ranked #5 in Rolling Stone's 100 Greatest Artists of All Time. Berry also has three of his songs included in the Rock and Roll Hall of Fame's "500 Songs That Shaped Rock 'n' Roll," including "Maybellene," "Rock 'n' Roll Music," and "Johnny B. Goode." At the age of 88, you can still catch Berry occasionally performing live in his hometown of St. Louis, Missouri.

Not only did Chuck Berry's music have a huge impact on AC/DC, but apparently his duckwalk inspired Angus Young to add a schoolboy suit and his own twist to Berry's infamous gait. So much so that his emulation of Berry almost altered his fate. When executives from Atlantic Records first saw a video of AC/DC live, Angus' take on Berry's walk almost killed the deal. Some thought that Angus copied Berry too closely, and that would detract from the band. The late Perry Cooper, an A&R executive with Atlantic, fought in Angus' favor to let him play any which way he wanted to. Cooper convinced the suits that once fans saw the band and heard their music, Angus' nod to Chuck Berry would be widely accepted. Perry Cooper knew what he was talking about.

Angus' take on Chuck: "I remember many years ago there was a guy doing a thing about Chuck Berry and he thought, oh, Chuck Berry, he's so straight-ahead. It's the same licks. But, when he listened, he found each time it was different and then, when he started really getting into it, he started to see other pieces of the puzzle. Because in Chuck there's jazz, there's country, there's the blues element and, of course, he's got that rock 'n' roll. Then the great thing is he always knew when to play and when not to, and he'll pull back. . . ."

Regarding his own musical influences, Malcolm once stated, "As a kid it started with Chuck Berry. You can't forget Chuck Berry. I mean, just about everything he did back then was great. The first time I heard 'My Generation' by the Who, that was something. The Beatles and the Stones were the big thing and then all of a sudden this thing sounded heavier. That changed my whole thing. Later on I guess 'Jumpin' Jack Flash,' and I'll give you two more, 'Honky Tonk Women,' and these are all just tracks on their own, and then 'Get Back' by the Beatles. That's just pure rock 'n' roll as it evolved, I reckon."

Little Richard

Little Richard, who still claims to have invented rock 'n' roll, is a serious player in the sound of rock as we know it. Born the third of twelve children in Macon, Georgia, on December 5, 1932, Richard Wayne Penniman started listening to music in his mother's Baptist church and his father's juke joint, the Tip In Inn. Due to his small stature and his skinny frame, the nickname "Lil' Richard" stuck, and having been born with one leg shorter than the other, his antics on stage would soon become legendary. His ability to sing high and loudly got him screamed at more than once during his church performances.

As a student at Macon's Hudson High School, Penniman's musical prowess gained him the ability to play alto saxophone, which afforded him a place in the school's marching band. At sixteen years old, Penniman left high school and started playing with the Dr. Hudson's Medicine Show, performing a blues staple, "Caldonia." From that band he went onto Buster Brown's Orchestra and by 1950, was appearing in various vaudeville groups performing in the area. Crossing paths with one of his idols, Billy Wright, put him in touch with Wright's management, which led Penniman into the recording studio. Unfortunately those recordings got him nowhere, and Penniman wound up washing dishes for the Greyhound Lines while perfecting his boogie-woogie style of piano playing.

Eventually Penniman hit it big with "Tutti Frutti," recorded in three takes in 1955. The song went to #2 on the R&B charts and crossed over to the pop charts in the US and UK. Penniman's next hit single, "Long Tall Sally," went to #1 on the R&B charts, making it into the Top Ten on the American and British pop charts and like "Tutti Frutti," also sold over one million copies.

Little Richard Penniman was one of the first performers to bring white and black audiences together, back in the days of segregation. Quickly gaining a legion of fans, Little Richard gave dynamic performances that drove the fans into a frenzy. He was also the first to use spotlights and flicker lights to enhance his shows. He continued to record hit records throughout the fifties, including "Lucille" in 1956 and "Good Golly Miss Molly" in 1957.

Pressured by his wild ways on stage attracting white female fans, Little Richard Penniman performed at the Apollo Theater in New York City and later that month entered Oakwood College in Huntsville, Alabama, to study theology. Forming the Little Richard Evangelistic Team, Penniman traveled the country preaching, although over the years, he gravitated back to his rock 'n' roll roots.

Little Richard was inducted into the Rock and Roll Hall of Fame in 1986, and received the Grammy Lifetime Achievement Award in 1993 and the Lifetime Achievement Award from the Rhythm and Blues Foundation in 1994. Included in *Rolling Stone*'s "500 Songs That Shaped Rock 'n' Roll" are "Tutti Frutti," "Long Tall Sally," and "The Girl Can't Help It."

Mr. Penniman takes great delight in telling everyone that he invented rock 'n' roll and that the Beatles stole his "Ooooo!" Elvis must have been inspired by Little Richard's inability to stand still on stage, Jerry Lee Lewis stole his banging and playing piano with his feet and legs, and Bon Scott embraced Little Richard's command of the stage, especially over the ladies in the audience. AC/DC took Little Richard's energy on stage and turned it up a notch. I have no doubt Mr. Penniman would be proud of that.

Malcolm once said, "Chuck Berry was the master lyric writer in rock 'n' roll. He would sing about sex in the back seat in such a way that is was funny. If we came out with a song like 'Sweet Little Sixteen,' they'd probably arrest us. That and Little Richard's sense of humor with words, and of course Bon. We just try to come somewhere near the area that those guys have all been."

George Young

Older brother George was born George Redburn Young on November 6, 1946, in Glasgow, Scotland. At seventeen years old, his family immigrated to Australia, and George quickly put a band together. Their older brother Alex stayed behind in Scotland to continue his band, Grapefruit. That band was one of the few signed to Apple, the Beatles' record label.

Playing rhythm guitar, Young joined forces with lead guitarist Harry Vanda, bassist Dick Diamonde, drummer Gordon "Snowy" Fleet, and singer Stevie Wright, forming the Easybeats. Right on the tails of the British invasion, the Easybeats hit international stardom with their song "Friday on My Mind." Young and Vanda dissolved the band in 1970 and opened their own studio, writing almost all their own tunes and recording, producing, and managing other bands including Flash and the Pan, the Marcus Hook Roll Band, Rose Tattoo, and the Angels.

In 1973, George Young started Albert Productions in Sydney with Ted Albert, and their first order of business was to produce Young's little brother's band, AC/DC. George coproduced (with Harry Vanda) AC/DC's *High Voltage*, *T.N.T.*, *Let There Be Rock*, *Dirty Deeds Done Dirt Cheap*, and *Powerage*, and was the sole producer of *Stiff Upper Lip*.

George Young and Harry Vanda were inducted into the inaugural class of the ARIA (Australian Recording Industry Association) Hall of Fame in 1988. In 2007, the Australian *Musician* magazine chose the meeting of Young and Vanda in Sydney in 1964 as one of the most significant events in Australian pop and rock history. Capturing the early sounds of AC/DC on vinyl was and still is the key ingredient in George Young's genius. The boys were comfortable with them, and Young and Vanda pushed the band to their limits, often recording an album over a couple of weeks. One time Angus' amp caught on fire during one of his blazing solos, and George waved him to keep on playing!

George Young also taught his brothers to write a song and then break it down into a classical version. If they couldn't do it, they had to scrap it and try again. Moving halfway around the world and finding themselves Down Under with an older brother who became what some called "the Australian Beatles" had an insurmountable effect on Angus and Malcolm. George readied them with guitars almost before they could read, and his songwriting skills include one of the most popular songs in Australian history.

George Young and the Easybeats' "Friday on My Mind" was voted the #1 song of all time in Australia on May 29, 2001. Little brothers Angus and

Angus on Harbour Bridge in Sydney, Australia, on March 27, 1976. The band were set up on a barge beneath the bridge, and the show was sponsored by local radio station 2SM.   *Photo by Philip Morris*

Malcolm made the list with "It's a Long Way to the Top (If You Wanna Rock 'n' Roll)," coming in at #9.

George has been called the sixth member of AC/DC, helping to write, record, and produce their music. He filled in on bass whenever they lacked a bass player, and regarding his guidance over the years, some have claimed that AC/DC are as much George's band as Angus and Malcolm's.

T. Rex

Formed in 1967 by guitarist/singer/songwriter Marc Bolan, T. Rex was first known as Tyrannosaurus Rex. T. Rex rose to fame in the United Kingdom during the seventies with fourteen Top 20 hits including "Get It On," "20th Century Boy," and "Metal Guru." Bolan, together with percussionist Steve Peregrin Took, developed their vocals in the English pubs, gaining the attention of BBC's Radio One disc jockey John Peel.

Peel helped launch the band. Bolan and Took would eventually go their separate ways, and Bolan recorded with percussionist Mickey Finn, drummer Bill Legend, and bassist Steve Currie. "Get It On" was re-titled "Bang a Gong (Get It On)" and became a Top Ten hit in the US. T. Rex had four #1 hits in the UK, and by 1973, they had released four albums: *Electric Warrior*, *The Slider*, *Tanx*, and *Zinc Alloy*.

T. Rex disbanded after the death of Marc Bolan in a car crash on September 15, 1977. Bassist Steve Currie died four years later, also in a car crash. Took choked to death in 1980 and Mickey Finn died in 2003. Dino Dines, who played keyboards for T. Rex, died of a heart attack in 2004. Legend is the sole remaining member of T. Rex and welcomes talking about it on his website.

Marc Bolan is said to be the only guitar hero whose poster ever made it onto Malcolm Young's bedroom walls. T. Rex's success peaked during the glam period of rock, but the rhythm and swing of T. Rex's music certainly appealed to Malcolm's love for bluesy rock 'n' roll. Even today, it's hard not to turn up the volume when "Bang a Gong" comes on the radio—the timelessness of a simple backbeat.

The Rolling Stones

Now together for over five decades, the Rolling Stones, England's scruffier version of the Beatles with attitude, started out in 1962 with Mick Jagger on vocals and harmonica, Keith Richards on guitar, Ian Stewart on piano, Bill Wyman on bass, Charlie Watts on drums, and Brian Jones on guitar and harmonica. Jones left the band in 1969, just a month before his death. Mick Taylor replaced him, and Ronnie Wood added another guitar. Wyman eventually retired in 1993, and Darryl Jones has played bass for them since.

Rising along with the British invasion, the Rolling Stones released their first single, a Chuck Berry cover "Come On," in June of 1963. By the end of the year the Stones were opening for American acts Little Richard, Bo Diddley, and the Everly Brothers.

During their first tour of the United States, the Rolling Stones recorded two songs at Chess Studios in Chicago, meeting their idol, Muddy Waters. The band had named themselves after one of Waters' hits, and that recording session garnered their first number hit in the UK with a cover of "It's All Over Now."

In 2012, the Rolling Stones launched their *50 & Counting* tour at the London O2 Arena along with Jeff Beck. Over their career, the Stones have released over twenty albums. Their blues-based rock has spawned dozens of hits including "I Can't Get No Satisfaction," "Paint It Black," and "Start Me Up."

Their dedication and perseverance has not been lost on AC/DC, who have looked up to the Stones and earned the honor of being the only band to ever co-headline with the Rolling Stones when they played the SARS Benefit in Toronto, Canada, on July 30 of 2003. Both bands gave an amazing performance with Angus and Malcolm coming back out on stage to play with the Stones on a cover of B. B. King's "Rock Me Baby." The crowd that day was estimated to be 450,000 to 500,000 people.

"Pyro" Pete Cappadocia, who has had the honor of blowing things up for AC/DC since 1982, marveled at how relaxed Angus and Malcolm were that day. They were playing in front of one of the biggest crowds of their career, and they waited patiently on the side of the stage to be called back out to play a song with the Stones. Cappadocia and Malcolm chatted until he was called out on the stage. Judging by the pictures of that event, AC/DC gave their best to the audience and their admiration for the Rolling Stones is quite evident.

Sharing a drink with Brian Johnson in Sarasota, Florida, five days after the SARS benefit, playing with the Stones was an honor and quite entertaining for them all. Brian, always the comedian, did a dead-on impression of Keith Richards, claiming Keith had a road case with four drawers marked, "Guitar Strings," "Picks," "Guns," and "Drugs." Of course he was just kidding (I think).

When I eventually spoke with Malcolm on the *Black Ice* tour, I brought up something I had told the band the night I first met them when they played my hometown of Madison, Wisconsin, on August 16, 1977. After seeing them live for the first time, I claimed that someday AC/DC would be as big as the Stones. Malcolm and I always laugh at that comment, and when I reminded him of that backstage in Chicago on November 1, 2008, he laughed and said, "I don't know about being as big as the Stones, but I know we blew them off the stage at the SARS benefit up in Toronto!"

Margaret Young

Margaret is the second oldest Young child and the only Young daughter, and big sister to both Malcolm and Angus. Ms. Young was the lady that brought home the albums and helped introduce her brothers to the early sounds of rock 'n' roll. Margaret is also infamous for sewing some of Angus' first schoolboy outfits and suggesting that the band call themselves AC/DC, after the lettering on the back of her sewing machine. Some reports claim it came from a vacuum cleaner, but I'm sticking with the sewing machine. It makes more sense. Margaret used to watch Angus come home from school and run out to band practice without changing his clothes.

In the early days of AC/DC, disco and glam rock were dominating the airwaves. For a while, AC/DC struggled with their stage persona, going through several costume ideas including pilots, rock stars in satin, and Angus' "Super Ang(us)" outfit. Margaret was the one who suggested Angus adopt his schoolboy uniform while the rest of the band reverted back to black T-shirts and jeans.

One of the key components in influencing especially Angus' outlook on music was when Margaret took him to see Louis Armstrong live. Armstrong was an extraordinary jazz trumpeter who was known for his scat vocalizing and passionate performances. One of his timeless classics is 1967's "What a Wonderful World." When Angus went to a stadium in Australia to see Armstrong play, being in his presence made a huge impact.

Angus told *Guitar World* in 1996, "My sister took me to see him when I was a kid, and I still think he was one of the greatest musicians of all time. Especially when you listen to his old records, like these ['Basin St. Blues' and 'St. James Infirmary'], and hear the incredible musicianship and emotion coming out of his horn. And the technology in those days was almost nonexistent, all the tracks had to be done in one take. I can picture him in that big football stadium where I saw him: he wasn't a big man, but when he played, he seemed bigger than the stadium itself!"

Margaret ended up marrying the Easybeats' tour manager Sam Horsburgh, and their son Sam Jr. now works as an engineer for Albert Productions.

Brian Johnson told Greg Kot of the *Chicago Tribune* in 1996, "He (Angus) and Malcolm are the geniuses in the band, even though they'd hate to hear that word applied to them. They're basically two quiet fellows who have taken boogie-woogie, the blues of B.B. King and Muddy Waters, and electrified it. It's great, timeless stuff. The kids may not know it's coming from B.B. and Muddy, but they're tapping their feet to it just the same."

2

So Many Musicians, So Little Time

The Players Who Made the Final Cut

AC/DC were originally formed by rhythm guitarist Malcolm Young, who went through a plethora of members in the early days. Former members (some temporary) include bassists George Young, Rob Bailey, Paul Matters, Neil Smith, Bruce Howe, Larry Van Kriedt, and Mark Evans. Former drummers include Colin Burgess, Peter Clack, Noel Taylor, Ron Carpenter, Russell Coleman, John Proud, Tony Currenti, Simon Wright, and Chris Slade.

While the lineup constantly kept changing, Malcolm recruited his younger brother, Angus, to join the band. Eventually settling on drummer Phil Rudd, Malcolm replaced singer Dave Evans with Bon Scott and bassist Mark Evans with Cliff Williams. With the right mix of musicians, AC/DC were finally ready to set the world on fire.

They successfully toured for six years before the death of Bon Scott, who was replaced by vocalist Brian Johnson in 1980. The only other time AC/DC would perform with different members was when Colin Burgess filled in for Phil Rudd in 1975 after Phil broke his thumb in a bar fight, and Malcolm and Angus' nephew Stevie Young filled in for Malcolm on the north American leg of the *Blow Up Your Video* tour in 1988.

Malcolm Young

Malcolm Mitchell Young is the second youngest brother of eight children, born on January 6, 1953, in Glasgow, Scotland. Growing up in a musical household at 6 Longstone Road, the boys were encouraged to pick up instruments, especially when their family went on weekend camping trips.

Older brother Alex was first to become a professional musician as George Alexander, playing saxophone in Emile Ford's Checkmates. By the

The lineup of players that made the final cut. This glossy was sent out by Atco Records to promote the *Powerage* album.

time the family decided to relocate to Australia he was playing with the Big Six. Their claim to fame was backing Tony Sheridan after the Beatles had left him. Alex would go on to form the band Grapefruit, which was the first group signed to Apple Records, the Beatle's label.

When their father had trouble finding work, they left Cranhill, Glasgow, and took advantage of the Assisted Passage Scheme, implemented in 1947. This allowed emigrants to sail to Australia for ten pounds each, or roughly $25.

The Youngs arrived in Sydney, first moving to Villawood, and then finally settling into a bunker-style neighborhood in the suburb of Burwood in the summer of 1963. Burwood was filled with Scottish, Dutch, and English families, some with sons who owned musical gear. The neighborhood soon filled with fledging garage bands, and that's where older brother George Young met Dutchman Johannes Jacob Hendricks, better known as Harry Vanda. George and Harry recruited fellow Brit vocalist Stevie Wright, bassist Dick Diamonde, and drummer Gordon "Snowy" Fleet. Playing their first gig at the Beatle Village in Sydney in late 1964, they called themselves the Easybeats.

The Easybeats broke into the international music scene with their single "Friday on My Mind." That song made it to #16 on the US charts and #6 in Britain, which prompted the band to relocate to London.

Following in their big brother's footsteps, Malcolm had started playing around the age of four, strumming to Elvis or whatever he was listening to. By the age of eleven he was playing along to Beatles songs. When Malcolm was fourteen, Harry Vanda gave him his Gretsch guitar, which he had always admired. It was originally red with the neck and middle pickups removed. Malcolm removed the red paint and used his socks in the pickup cavity to stop feedback. Gretsch eventually produced a signature version of this guitar, with pickups included.

Malcolm attended the Sydney Ashfield Boys High School, spending much of his time defending his younger brother, Angus. Apparently the Young brothers were also at odds with their headmaster at Ashfield's Boy High School, judging from the letter he sent to their parents. Published inside their first album *High Voltage* is an excerpt: "Malcolm is certainly old enough to know that his constant humming is neither amusing nor impressive. The few times a day he puts pen to paper it turns out he is writing what appears to be poetry of some vile sort. Angus does not stop eating chocolate bars . . . his uniform is filthy, his knees are constantly bruised, his eyes blackened, and his nose running."

Luckily both Malcolm and Angus had their minds set on doing something much bigger than graduating from Ashfield. George's rise to fame was not lost on Malcolm or Angus, who once recalled coming home from school to find dozens of girls trying to do anything they could to get a look at George. Angus once joked to me that when he saw that, both he and Malcolm knew that rock 'n' roll was going to be the life for them. He said, "One day George was a sixteen-year-old sitting on his bed playing guitar, the next day he was worshipped by the whole country."

When Malcolm wasn't listening to the Beatles, he was listening to the Rolling Stones, the Yardbirds, and the Who. He also admired Eric Clapton with John Mayall's Blues Breakers, and the Paul Butterfield Blues Band, continually perfecting his own unique playing style. Once big brother George had moved to England, Malcolm used to ask him to send him music. "(George would) pick me out anything that he thought was good at the moment, and he'd send me over a parcel of albums. He was a good help to us."

Malcolm dropped out of high school and took a job working as an apprentice fitter, and then later as a sewing machine maintenance mechanic for Berlei, a brassiere factory. In 1971, at the age of eighteen, while working at Berlei, Malcolm met and joined the Velvet Underground (which was not the same Velvet Underground that was fronted by Lou Reed). This band had formed in Newcastle, England, in 1967 and had become a top dance band, playing covers by the Doors and Jefferson Airplane. After they lost their lead singer, they moved to Sydney, Australia.

The Velvet Underground included drummer Herm Kovac, guitarist Les Hall, bassist Michael Szchefswick, and singer Andy Imlah, who joined after they relocated. When they met Malcolm, they needed another guitar player, and they all wanted to get out of the factory. Once Malcolm joined the band, he added songs by his idol, T. Rex's Marc Bolan. Malcolm had been working steadily in the Velvet Underground, and by 1972, they were playing their own sets and providing backup for another Australian artist, Ted Mulry. By this time Malcolm had become disenchanted with the Velvet Underground's musical direction, and was looking to do something on his own.

Malcolm was introduced to recording through his brother George, who with the help of Ted Albert, formed Albert Productions and started recording some of Australia's biggest artists. Malcolm decided he didn't believe rock 'n' roll was meant to be overdubbed and recorded to perfection. Malcolm wanted to record rock 'n' roll like it was played, live without any studio tricks. Now he just had to find the right people to record it with. Although his future band would go through several incarnations, he eventually found the perfect combination.

A couple of decades later, Malcolm would state to Tim Henderson of *Hard Radio*, "I think it gets back to our starting days again. Working our butts off, getting covered in oil and all the shit that goes with it, and when we got to play club gigs, luckily enough, we thought, 'This is it! Don't have to work! Angus, we can make fifty bucks a week each here. We can survive without a day job.' That was the big plan. So everything outside of a club gig is a bonus to us. We made it twenty-five years ago, as far as we're concerned!"

Angus Young

Angus McKinnon Young was the last son and youngest of eight children, born on March 31, 1955, in Glasgow, Scotland. His siblings were Steven, Margaret, John, Alex, William, George, and Malcolm. Malcolm once told *Mojo* magazine, "Stevie, the oldest, played accordion. Alex and John were the first couple to play guitar, and being older it was sort of passed down to

George, then myself, and then Angus. Like when you're kids and you get all your brothers' and sisters' hand-me-downs. We never realized that we were learning guitars—they were always just there. We thought that everyone was like that. Me and Angus would just fiddle—12 bars mainly, Chuck Berry, Little Richard, Elvis."

Growing up with musical instruments all around him, Angus' earliest memory of playing was strumming on a banjo with missing strings. Older sibling and only sister Margaret had introduced the family to Chuck Berry, Fats Domino, and Little Richard—the literal blueprints of rock 'n' roll in its purest form. Angus once told me that the first time he heard "Rock Around the Clock" by Bill Haley, that that was it for him. Seeing Louis Armstrong perform in an Australian stadium also left a huge impact on Angus. By the age of four or five, he was playing anything he could get his hands on. To cut down on the sibling squabbling, their mother went out and bought Angus and Malcolm each a ten-dollar acoustic guitar.

When George's recording partner Harry Vanda gave Malcolm his Gretsch guitar, Angus received a Hofner. Soon after, in a friend's guitar catalog, Angus spotted a Gibson SG, which he switched to and has played ever since. Angus played so much that he was known to sleep with his guitar. The first two records Angus ever purchased were "Club A Go-Go" by the Animals and "I'm a Man" by the Yardbirds.

Attending the Sydney Ashfield Boys High School with Malcolm, Angus spent most of his time skipping school, although his favorite subject was art, which was the only class where he could do what he wanted. George's fame in the Easybeats had a huge impact on both brothers.

Angus recalled in the February 1984 issue of *Guitar Player*, "It was definitely an inspiration. There was a hell of a lot that came from that band; they were the forerunners of a lot of things. They were at the time of the early stages, when people didn't know how to react. Mal and me were kept away from them. In school, you got frowned upon because obviously your brother or your family was an influence to rebel. At that time, it was better for us not to be sort of pushed at it. My parents thought we'd be better off doing something else."

Angus played in two bands before joining up with Malcolm: Kentuckee, and later, Tantrum. He often ran home from school and would leave again for rehearsal without changing out of his school uniform. When his headmaster gave Angus grief over his brother George being a pop star, demanding that he cut his hair, and declaring that his older brother was now in "a profession for perverts," his parents defended him. They didn't care for

Angus being pushed around, so they didn't protest when he stopped going to school all together.

His father encouraged him to keep learning and suggested he spend some time in the library, where Angus discovered the American rock 'n' roll magazine, *Down Beat*. These were magazines you couldn't buy on the newsstands in Australia, and he loved reading about his favorite blues artists, like Muddy Waters.

At fourteen and nine months, he was officially asked to leave school. Angus stated in Clinton Walker's book, *Highway to Hell*, "If you weren't there for so many days a year, they figured you weren't worth teaching, so they got rid of you." Angus quickly found work as a typesetter at the soft porn magazine *Ribald*.

Velvet Underground drummer Herm Kovac remembered, in Clinton Walker's book, *Highway to Hell*:

> We used to go round and pick Malcolm up. The first time, this little punk skinhead answered the door. It was Angus. I hid behind Les (the guitarist); in those days you'd hear about the skinheads down at Burwood Station, Strathfield Station. Shaved head he had, big boots. He said, Eh, come in 'ere. So we follow him into his room, he straps on his SG, jumps on the bed, and goes off on this exhibition, running over the dressing table, showing off, couldn't play any chords, just lead, and when he finishes he says, "Whaddya reckon?" You had to say, "Pretty good, Angus." Every time you'd go there you'd have to go through this same ritual.

Two years younger than Malcolm, Angus was allowed to come out and see his big brother play in the Velvet Underground, where he would stand in front of the stage, awestruck. Only receiving a few formal lessons around the age of eleven, Angus became a self-taught musician. Once he was out of school, he would hang out with older musicians, and jam with any band that would let him. He quickly started catching on, and was later billed as the "Baby Guitar Star." Since he was underage and very small in stature, they often told club owners who would question his age "that (Angus) was a dwarf, which usually got him in."

Originally Malcolm had planned on adding keyboards, but changed his mind and decided a second guitar was what he was looking for. Once Angus joined the band, he and Malcolm would, for a while, alternate between playing rhythm and lead guitars.

They had tossed around ideas for a band name, and came up with Third World War. Their sister Margaret had a better idea when she noticed

"AC/DC" written on the back of her sewing machine. Some sources say it came from George Young's wife Sandra, who saw it on the back of a vacuum cleaner, but I'm sticking with the sewing machine, since Margaret would eventually make some of Angus's first schoolboy uniforms.

Regardless of who came up with it, they agreed on the name "AC/DC," because it suggested power and electricity (although for years the band would have to fend off the theory that it referred to their personal sexual preferences). Malcolm told me the first time he realized the sexual connotation was when a cab driver asked him about it, suggesting the band must "swing both ways." Malcolm quickly shot back, "What, are you trying to start a fight or something?"

AC/DC's first professional appearance was at a small club called Chequers at 79 Goulburn Street in Sydney on New Year's Eve of 1973. Much of their set was covers of songs by Chuck Berry, the Stones, Free, and the Beatles.

Angus's stage antics were encouraged by George. One night when he was still playing in Tantrum, he tripped over his own guitar cord and fell down. Instead of getting up, he used it for effect, and rolled around on the stage. It was the only applause they received all night. When George heard about that, he suggested Angus make it part of his act. His inability to stand still goes back to the way he feels about music. He just simply can't stand in one place while he's playing. Angus claims he's a rotten guitar player when he can't move around.

Angus once told Jim Miller of *Newsweek*, "An Australian audience likes to drink a lot . . . So I used to jump on tables, anything to get them to stop drinking for ten seconds. They would be throwing beer cans and I thought, 'Just keep moving,' and that's how it all started."

Angus explained the original plan in 1982 in *Circus* magazine, "The uniform was originally a one-off thing. The drummer in my previous band talked me into doing something outrageous, so I dressed up like a school kid. The idea was to become a nine-year-old guitar virtuoso who would play one gig, knock everyone out and disappear into obscurity. I'd have been a legend. But then I kept doing it. Now . . . well, I'm stuck with it."

Angus was once described in an American print ad by Albert Music as an "atomic microbe." *Australian Guitar* declared Angus the best guitar player to ever come from Australia. Putting so much energy into his performances, he was known to vomit into a trash can at the side of the stage after the first song, which the late Perry Cooper said, "Yeah, he does that every show." The funniest review of Angus was published in the October 1981 issue of *Creem* magazine in their "*Creem* Profiles":

> Home: Somewhere between Tasmania and Bad Axe. Age: As old as Angus's last leg waxing. Profession: Parlaying screaming chariots of thud into big Aussie bucks all around. Hobbies: Rendering the gray matter of rock critics *numb*, baying at the moon while mooning at the bay, pant amputation, conspicuous consumption as a way of life. Last Book Read: *The Tree of Life* by Patrick White. Last Accomplishment: Gleefully accepting 1981 dollars for 1976 music. Quote: "Basically, I just like to get up in front of a crowd and rip it up." Profile: Spawned in Oz with Friday on their minds, these Vanda-Youngkin started screeching glam rock and thudded their way to the top, the sexual inclinations of their name taking on a new meaning: the purposeful deafening of millions. One yelper lost down the *Highway to Hell*, another taking his place, and these kangaroos won't be satisfied 'til everybody hops. Have a drink on us, Angus!

Bon Scott

Bon Scott was born Ronald Belford Scott on July 9, 1946, in Kirriemuir, Scotland, which lies in the foothills of Cairngorms, in the county of Angus—the same birthplace as J.M. Barrie, the author of the book *Peter Pan*. Which is ironic, since Bon seemed to delight in never wanting to grow up.

Once Bon's father was discharged from the Army, he and his wife Isa settled in Kirriemuir, where he became a member of the local amateur light opera company and played drums in the Kirriemuir Pipe Band. Bon grew up loving music and started playing the drums by practicing on bread boards and biscuit tins. Every Saturday night, when his father's pipe band would march through town, Bon would march right alongside him.

Bon loved the pipe band, although he eventually turned his back on the kilt. As his mother said, "Once he turned seventeen, he refused to wear a skirt." Except for the one time, years later, when he appeared singing with AC/DC on the television show *Countdown*, wearing braids and a schoolgirl's dress. Even though he looked quite cute in it, his choice of wardrobe caused a complete uproar.

Also taking advantage of the Assisted Passage Scheme, Bon's family relocated to Sunshine, a suburb of Melbourne, Australia, in 1952. Quickly Bon acquired the nickname "Bonny Scotland," and the moniker stuck. Known to his family and friends as Ronnie, "Bonny" took flak from his schoolmates for having an accent. Explaining his nickname, Bon was quoted in the *Bonfire* box set: "My new schoolmates threatened to kick the shit out of me when they heard my Scottish accent. I had one week to learn to speak like them if I wanted to remain intact. 'Course, I didn't take any notice. No one railroads me, and it made me all the more determined to speak my own way. That's how I got my name, you know. The Bonny Scot, see?"

At the age of six, Bon was enrolled in the Sunshine Primary School and immediately accompanied the class on drums as they marched to school every morning. First learning how to play the recorder, Bon then tried piano. Deciding piano lessons weren't for him, Bon went back to his first love and something he had a natural talent for, the drums.

In 1956, in an attempt to ease the asthma Bon's youngest brother Graeme suffered from, the family moved 1,700 miles away to Perth. Bon's father lined up work in Perth with the firm he was with in Melbourne, and there he immediately joined the Fremantle pipe band. Bon became a student at John Curtin High and gave his first public performance at the age of twelve, playing a duet with a schoolmate at the North Fremantle Town Hall. Eventually Bon was added to his father's pipe band as a side drummer.

Bon's brother Graeme was quoted in Clinton Walker's book, *Highway to Hell*: "Before TV, we used to sit around and listen to the radio. My dad and Ron used to go out to practice for the pipe band, drumming. It was a big occasion when the bands played, the whole family used to go out, put on their kilts, strap the drums on. Me and Derek (Bon's older brother), would follow behind. Those were the big occasions, Scottish things."

Bon and his two brothers enjoyed their time together, playing by the river that was just minutes from their house. Once in high school, Bon would hang out near the water, smoking cigarettes and chasing girls. By the time he was fifteen, he had dropped out of high school.

His first job was as a farmhand on a market garden, driving a tractor. He later switched to working on a crayfish boat. Fishing was backbreaking work, so Bon quickly left the water to work as an apprentice weighing-machine mechanic for Avery Scales.

Bon was first introduced to American rock 'n' roll through the 1956 movie *The Blackboard Jungle*, which featured Bill Haley's "Rock Around the Clock." He also loved listening to Elvis Presley, Chuck Berry, Little Richard, and Jerry Lee Lewis, and at times was known to sing along to Broadway show tunes.

Fremantle, just a few miles from Perth, was a rough place to grow up and Bon learned how to be a street fighter. Bon and his friends started going to dances at Perth's Port Beach, often seeing the band the Nomads, which was fronted by Johnny Young, a future Australian pop star. Following their set, some of the local boys would get up and sing. Bon was often requested by the girls, who went wild when he would do a cover of "Blue Suede Shoes" or "Long Tall Sally."

One night after Bon returned with a girl he had stepped outside with, he was forced to fight off other boys who wanted to "take a walk with her" as well. When the local police arrived, Bon took off in a car and was later arrested for trying to steal some petrol.

The incident was reported in the *West Australian* newspaper on March 13, 1963: "A sixteen-year-old youth pleaded guilty in Fremantle Children's Court yesterday to charges of having given a false name and address to the police, having escaped legal custody, having unlawful carnal knowledge, and having stolen twelve gallons of petrol." Bon was committed to the care of the Child Welfare Department until he was eighteen, with a recommendation that he be kept in an institution of maximum security.

He could have been released to the custody of his parents, but Bon was so ashamed that he pleaded guilty and was sent to serve nine months at the Riverbank boy's home. Although his parents tried to visit, he refused to see them. He also missed an opportunity to see his grandparents, who had traveled all the way from Kirriemuir. They would go back to Scotland, and Bon would never see them again.

Bon spent his entire nine-month sentence scrubbing floors on his hands and knees, freezing, and trying to stay out of trouble with the other boys. He was released to the custody of his parents on Christmas of 1963, and the unlawful carnal knowledge charges were dropped. As soon as he got home, he set up his drum kit in front of the window in his living room, and got a job as a store man with the egg board.

By 1965, Bon formed his first band, the Spektors, with guitarist Wyn Milson, bassist Brian Gannon, and vocalist John Collins. For about a year, the Spektors played every weekend in Perth, covering songs by Them, the Beatles, and the Stones. The Spektors soon became one of the top five bands, and once they went as far as they could go in the local scene, they joined forces with another Perth band, the Winztons, to form the group the Valentines.

Bon's brother Graeme told author Clinton Walker that Bon said, "I was a drummer in those days, and I used to play half the night on drums and spend the other half singing. The singer also played the drums—but not as good as me! Then I got an offer from the Valentines as a drummer. But I wanted to be a singer so I joined as a singer. It wasn't because I wanted to be up front—it was because the singer used to get more chicks." By now Bon had left the egg company, becoming a postman, riding around on his bicycle delivering the mail.

Joining the Valentines, Bon shared the vocals with Vince Lovegrove. Vince was quoted in the local newspaper, *RAM*: "Bon was the cute little drummer with cute little eyes, pixie-like ears, a cute turned-up nose, a cute little Scottish accent, and about four very obvious cute little tattoos. In rock 'n' roll in those days, you could go a long way being cute. We became friends." Vince and Bon formed a close friendship, and Vince would play a pivotal role in Bon's musical future.

Once the Spektors and the Winztons merged, they inherited both followings, which made the Valentines the biggest band in Australia. They signed a contract with independent label Clarion Records, and went into the studio to record two songs, "Everyday I Have to Cry" and "I Can't Dance with You," a Small Faces cover, which made it to the top five on the charts in Western Australia. The "Vallies," as their fans called them, were on their way.

When George Young's band the Easybeats came back to Sydney for two shows at Her Majesty's after the worldwide success of "Friday on My Mind," the Valentines opened for them. This was most likely the first time George Young met Bon Scott. Bon in turn idolized the Easybeat's lead singer, "Little" Stevie Wright.

The two bands would get along so well that the Easybeats came up with the first of three songs they would write for them, called "She Said." After almost winning a battle of the bands in Melbourne, they decided to leave Perth, agreeing not to return until they were all big stars. The following spring they scored an eight-week stay in Sydney, and in May went into the studio to cut their second Easybeats song, "Peculiar Hole in the Sky." which wasn't as successful as they had hoped.

While the rest of the world was discovering Jimi Hendrix, Australia was more focused on bubblegum pop at the time, like the Monkees and the 1910 Fruitgum Company. This would inspire the Valentines to declare themselves as a pop group "unafraid of commercialism." They changed their image by adopting flashy clothes, shorter hair, and Bon started using makeup to cover up his tattoos.

They ended the year by recording their third Easybeats tune, "My Old Man's a Groovy Old Man," backed by "Ebeneezer." It was officially released on Valentine's Day, 1969, and was very successful. When they appeared at the disco Thats Life, a reporter from *Go-Set* wrote, "The audience screamed in unison, 'We love the Valentines!' As soon as they appeared the audience went completely berserk, and started to storm the stage. The two lead singers, Vince and Bon, were dragged to the floor and Bon's pants and jacket were completely ripped off him." This was a constant at all their concerts, and on March 10, they played in front of 7,000 at the Alexandra Gardens, which caused a riot. Vince was arrested for booting a policeman from the stage.

Their next, and perhaps strangest, release was "Nick Nack Paddy Whack," with the B-side being Bon's first writing credit, "Getting Better," which he shared with Wyn. Bands like Led Zeppelin were finally making an impact on the Australian music scene, and it was the beginning of the end for the Valentines.

As they stated before they left, the Valentines returned to Perth rock stars, being met at the airport by 4,000 screaming fans to play a New Year's Eve show at the Supreme Court Gardens for radio station 6KY. Their final recording was "Juliette," which sounded just like the Beatles' "Dear Prudence" and barely made it into the top thirty. Playing one more gig, the band broke up.

Within months, Bon was invited to move to Sydney by Fraternity leader, Bruce Howe. Fraternity was the hottest band in Australia, and included Howe, Mick Jurd, John Freeman, Sam See, John Bisset and "Uncle" John Ayers. Bon immediately became their new lead singer. Eventually making it into the studio, they recorded *Livestock*, which was released on Sweet Peach Records, a small Australian label. Much of the album features Bon playing the recorder.

Even though the album wasn't that impressive, Fraternity still appeared on the new television show GTK, and Bon was featured on the cover of the new national magazine, *Sound Blast*, with his face done up with war paint. Billed as the "Wild Man of Fraternity," Bon looked more like an aborigine than a rock singer.

By the end of the summer of 1971, Fraternity was at the top of their game, winning the Battle of the Sounds. Adelaide's Channel Nine produced a special about the band, which featured them on their farm, with Bon doing stunts on his trail bike. That September, Bon would meet his future wife, Irene Thornton. A tall blonde, she enjoyed smoking, drinking, and, especially, Bon's jokes.

Early in 1972, Fraternity decided to relocate to London. Before they took off, they went into the studio and recorded *Flaming Galah*. The record included three new songs: "Getting Off," "Welfare Boogie," and "Hemming's Farm." When their management offered to pay for wives to move as well, Bon and Irene got married on January 24, 1972. Securing a deal with RCA Records, their single "Welfare Boogie" was released in March and the entire album came out in April of 1972.

Their move to England was a giant dose of reality for Fraternity, with the British music scene being dominated by glam rock like David Bowie's Ziggy Stardust and Marc Bolan's band T. Rex. Fraternity's roots rock couldn't have been more out of place. Unable to get many bookings, the band members and wives all took day jobs, with Bon knitting wigs in a factory.

It took them until November to get their first gig, at the Speakeasy in London. By 1973, they got to open a couple of shows for a band from Newcastle called Geordie. Their lead singer was a working class bloke named Brian Johnson. Bon's brother Graeme remembers visiting Bon on tour and he told author Clinton Walker, "They had the bus, and the thing was, if they'd support a band, they'd use the other band's equipment too, and they were booked to go with Geordie. I think we went to Torquay first, and then we packed up that night and went on to Plymouth. Brian used to carry his guitar player on his shoulders too, I think that's where Ron got the idea, because when he joined AC/DC there was no one around doing that sort of thing. Angus was the perfect guy to carry around. He was so small."

Bon remembered seeing Brian Johnson perform in Geordie and was very impressed with him. Brian recalled in an interview that Bon saw him on the night he was actually suffering what he thought was an appendicitis attack, but in reality turned out to be food poisoning. Bon took Brian's passionate writhing around on the stage as one fantastic performance. Later he would tell his bandmates in AC/DC that if they ever needed to replace him, Brian Johnson would be the man to call.

Fraternity changed their name to Fang, and when their management couldn't recoup their investment in the band, they pulled the plug on the band and bailed, explaining "the real reason Fraternity failed in England was because they were too loud!" As the band fell apart, dashing their dreams of stardom in England, Bon took a job bartending in a pub. By Christmas they had all returned to Australia, with band and personal relationships in ruins. Bon took a day job loading fertilizer at a plant in Wallaroo, buying a Triumph motorbike to get around. He also started jamming with Peter Head's Mount Lofty Rangers, as his marriage to Irene fell apart.

One night, after a drunken fight with Irene, Bon went to a Lofty Rangers rehearsal. After telling the band to sod off, he climbed on his motorbike and took off down Stirling Highway in Claremont, which is a section of Perth. After driving his motorcycle directly into an oncoming car, Bon laid in a coma in serious condition in Queens Elizabeth Hospital intensive care unit for three days, suffering a broken arm, collarbone, leg, and nose. He had severe cuts to his face and a concussion, and had lost several teeth. Irene stayed by his side, and his mother Isa moved in with Bon and cared for him while Irene was at work. No matter how much he suffered, he never lost his sense of humor. Bon sent a picture of himself right after the accident to a friend, writing on it, "I left my teeth behind on the road."

Spending weeks to recover, Bon eventually went back into the studio to record two songs with Pete Head and Carey Gulley. They recorded "Covey Gully," and "Round and Round and Round," which wouldn't be heard by the public until 1996.

Always a good friend, Vince Lovegrove gave Bon odd jobs to do, like putting up posters, driving bands around, and painting. Things finally started to look promising when Vince told him about this exciting new band from Sydney, who needed a new lead singer. He persuaded Bon to check them out at the Pooraka Hotel. They were called AC/DC.

Vince Lovegrove had stayed in touch with George Young, and when George passed along the information to Malcolm and Angus, they decided Bon was too old for the job, considering he was the ancient age of twenty-eight, which made him nine years older than Angus.

When Bon saw them live for the first time in Adelaide, he knew he was right for the band. Bon himself explained how he was hired in the documentary movie *Let There Be Rock*. "I knew their manager. I'd never seen the band before, I'd never even heard of AC/DC, and their manager said, just stand there, and the band comes in two minutes, and there's this little guy, in a school uniform, going crazy, and I laughed. I'm still laughing. I took the opportunity to explain to them how much better I was than the drongo they had singing with them. So they gave me a chance to prove it, and there I was."

Years later, Vince Lovegrove told *No Nonsense* in May 1999, "One day Malcolm told me they were going to sack their singer and he asked me if I knew anyone. I told him I did, that it was Bon, and that I'd introduce him that night as they were playing at my venue. They said to me that Bon was too old, that they wanted someone young. I told Malcolm that Bon could rock them 'til they dropped, that he could out rock them anytime. When I told Bon, he told me they were too young, that they couldn't rock if their lives depended on it."

Describing his first meeting with Bon Scott, Angus told author Paul Stenning in *Two Sides to Every Glory*, "Bon first came along and saw me and

Malcolm, he sat behind the drums and started bashing away. We said, 'We know a good rock 'n' roll drummer—what we want is a great rock 'n' roll singer,' hence the song we recorded. This is what we wanted. For us it was great, he was a striking person, he did have the stuff legends are based on."

Bon Scott's first appearance with the band was actually more of a jam session at the Pooraka Hotel. They asked Dave Evans to leave after his last concert in Melbourne, and Bon's real debut with the band was at Brighton-Le-Sands Masonic Hall in Sydney on October 5, 1974.

On Bon's first performance with the band, Angus recalled, "For the first gig the only rehearsal was us just sitting around an hour before the gig, pulling out every rock 'n' roll song we knew. When we finally got there Bon downed about two bottles of bourbon with dope, coke, speed and says, 'Right, I'm ready,' and he was, too. He was fighting fit. There was this immediate transformation and he was running around yelling at the audience. It was a magic moment." The brothers endearingly called Bon "the old man."

Right after Bon joined the band, AC/DC went on a two-month tour of Australia. They also switched managers, leaving Dennis Laughlin and signing on with Michael Browning. They hadn't been happy with the way Laughlin was handling the band and their finances.

Michael Browning was the manager of the Hard Rock Café in Melbourne, not to be confused with the now-famous restaurant chain. He had previously managed the Australian rock star Billy Thorpe and his band the Aztecs, but gave up after five years of trying to break Billy overseas. George went to Melbourne to check out Browning, and was impressed with his vision for the band. His leadership abilities were going to catapult AC/DC out of Australia and into the international music scene.

Phil Rudd

Phillip Hugh Norman Witschke Rudd, née Rudzevecuis, was born in Melbourne, Australia, on May 19, 1954. Dropping out of school at fifteen, Phil started out as a painter, became an electrician's apprentice, and then an apprentice with a company that specialized in air conditioning. With his first paycheck, Phil bought a $250 Japanese drum kit from a company called Boston. Only receiving one formal lesson, and more concerned with playing, Phil claimed he didn't have the patience or the desire to learn the "traditional" way. Phil chose to play along with all his favorite albums, including the Small Faces, the Beatles, Free, Bad Company, and Mountain.

He once told Steven Scott Fyfe for *Cyber Drum* in August of 2000, "My first inspiration to play drums and to be excited about music was probably a song called 'Tin Soldier' by the Small Faces where you have a breakdown in the middle section then the guitar comes blaring in." He also told *Hard Rock* magazine, "Man, I've been admiring these crazy syncopations of Kenny Jones after the break in the middle of the song! I am also left on Simon Kirke [Free] and Corky Laing [Mountain], because of their ability to keep the pace as they thrashed like animals on the skins. They were not spectacular, but devilishly precise and effective."

Joining Mad Mole, a blues-rock band, in 1972, and then Krayne, a more progressive band in the Deep Purple vein, he wound up in the band Charlemagne, playing mostly Humble Pie covers. Leaving Charlemagne with bassist Geordie Leach, they formed Coloured Balls, adding guitarist Lobby Lloyd and featuring singer Gary "Angry" Anderson, who went on to form the popular Australian group Rose Tattoo. Coloured Balls dominated the local club circuit during the early seventies. They recorded two singles, "Liberate Rock" and "Mess of Blues."

In 1974, they changed the name of the band to Buster Brown, and Phil's first real studio experience was recording one album, *Something to Say*, for Mushroom Records. Dissatisfied with making little money, Phil left the band and went back to work at his father's car dealership, washing cars. Buster Brown had actually played some dates with AC/DC, so when a friend tipped Phil off to the fact that AC/DC were auditioning drummers, he went straight away and landed the job. His audition included playing a few rock 'n' roll standards and some songs from their upcoming debut album, *High Voltage*.

On what the band expected of him, Phil explained to *Musician* magazine, "right from the start the band kept to a basic formula where 'simplicity has always been the most important thing' . . . when I get down to business I always revert back to the style that I prefer, which is straight-ahead. Someone said once that I get to play the way that every schoolboy wishes to play. I don't know what that means, but I agree with it. It is just a foot-tapping thing. I am not out to impress anyone. I am just out to get the job done."

Cliff Williams

Clifford Williams was born in Romford (Essex), England, on December 14, 1949. When he was nine years old, his family moved to Liverpool. Cliff's musical influences were the Beatles, the Kinks, and some blues artists. He got his first guitar at the age of ten and by the time he was fourteen, Cliff was playing bass, with his only formal training coming from learning some riffs from a professional bass player. Cliff left school at sixteen to work in a factory.

Following his love of music, Cliff moved from Liverpool to London, and had a short stint with Jason Eddie and his Rock 'n' Roll Show. He also played in some blues bands including Delroy Williams Soul Show. However, life in London was tough and Cliff bounced around from the factory, to a machine shop, a supermarket, to doing demolition work for a contractor, and for a time he was even homeless.

In 1970, he placed an ad in the music paper *Melody Maker* and met guitarist Laurie Wisefield, whose extraordinary guitar playing would later land him a spot in the legendary band Wishbone Ash. Hitting it off immediately, together they played in Sugar and eventually Home, which featured singer Mick Stubbs, keyboard player Clive John, guitarist Laurie Wisefield, and drummer Mick Cook. In 1970, Home signed a recording contract with Epic Records, and released *Pause for a Hoarse Horse.*

While in Home, Cliff supported Led Zeppelin at the Wembley Empire Pool on the second concert date of their *Electric Magic* tour in November of 1971.

By 1972, Jim Anderson replaced Clive John on keyboards, and the band released a self-titled album. That release included their one hit, the song "Dreamer," which made it to #41 on the British charts. Their third and final release was *The Alchemist* in 1973.

Home was asked to support Al Stewart on his first American tour in 1974. Mick Stubbs left the band, and the rest of the group became the Al Stewart Band. Cliff didn't last very long playing Stewart's music. Before the year was out, Cliff left and formed his own band, Bandit. They were immediately signed to Arista Records and released a self-titled debut album in 1977.

After placing an ad in *Sounds* magazine, AC/DC were looking to replace bassist Mark Evans, and had auditioned over fifty bass players. Cliff explained to *Guitar School*, "I auditioned. The band was looking to strengthen up their rhythm section, so they came to London where there was a larger pool of players. They had a few records out at that point, were successful in Australia, and toured Europe once or twice, but hadn't been to the States yet. They were looking to tour the US behind the *Let There Be Rock* album. Anyway, I got a call from a friend of a friend who thought I might be right for the job, and I ended up auditioning a number of times."

AC/DC held the auditions in a tiny room in Victoria, and the first tracks they played with Cliff were "Live Wire," "Problem Child," and an old blues number. Just before his audition, a friend had tipped him off that the band preferred their bassists to play with a pick, rather than with their fingers. Cliff was asked to join the band on May 27, 1977, and Angus was quoted as saying that Cliff was hired due to his good looks being able to attract more girls.

The addition of Cliff Williams delighted Bon, since he was closest to Bon's age by only being three years younger. Cliff also had a lot in common with Bon, liking movies, books, and girls. As soon as he joined the band, they flew back to Australia to work him in. Cliff's contribution to the sound of AC/DC cannot be underestimated.

Cliff is known as the master of the eighth note, attacking each note, as *Guitar School* wrote, "with the vengeance of a teen in heat." Cliff explained, "I never get bored playing eighth notes. In this band I play what's best for the song. I play what needs to be played—and I feel good about it. Know what I mean?"

Cliff's favorite AC/DC songs to play are "Let There Be Rock," "Live Wire," "Gimme a Bullet," "Gone Shootin'," and "Down Payment Blues." When he plays live, he wears a leather brace strapped onto his right arm, which keeps him from wearing away his skin.

Brian Johnson

Fifteen months younger than Bon, Brian Johnson was born on October 5, 1947, in Dunston, Gateshead, in northeast England. He is the son of Alan Johnson, an army sergeant major in the British Army, and his Italian wife, Esther. As a child, Brian sang in the church choir and performed Gang Shows with the Scouts. He also once starred in a television play.

Quitting school, Brian became an apprentice as an industrial fitter in a local turbine factory, and studied engineering at Gateshead Technical College while singing at night in local bands. His first band, the Gobi Desert Canoe Club, was formed with some mates from the factory he was working in. After seeing the Animals at the Club A Go Go in Newcastle, Brian purchased his first record, which was by the Paul Butterfield Blues Band. He also listened to B. B. King, the Yardbirds, and his favorite, John Mayall.

At seventeen, Brian joined the Red Berets Parachute regiment and served for two years in Germany. After returning home, he took work as a draftsman and continued his dreams of singing in a band.

In 1971, at the age of twenty-four, Brian joined the rock 'n' roll band Buffalo, which then became USA. Together with guitarist Vic Malcolm, drummer Brian Gibson, and bassist Tom Hill, they decided to rename the band Geordie, which was more suitable—"Geordie" being an English slang term for a hardworking, hard drinking man, which pretty much covered most of the male population of Newcastle.

Their first single, "Don't Do That," was released at the end of the year by EMI, climbing to #32 on the British charts. A few months later, their second single, "All Because of You," reached #6 on the charts, and their third, "Can You Do It," also made it into the Top Twenty. Riding on the glam rock coattails, Geordie's fourth single, "Electric Lady," only reached #32 in August of 1973.

Over the next three years, Geordie would release three albums, *Hope You Like It*, *Don't Be Fooled by the Name*, and *Save the World*, not including their one compilation album, *Master of Rock*, which was released in 1974. Right after *Save the World* came out, Geordie decided to call it quits. Brian once told *Musician* magazine about following the milkman around at 5 a.m., and stealing half-eaten meals from other people's plates in local restaurants. "I gave it up in about 1975 because it was all wrong. So I left and I didn't think I'd join a professional band again. Ever."

Five years later, right before he got the call from AC/DC, Brian had just convinced his ex-bandmates to reform Geordie and give it another try. After getting back together, Geordie had signed a deal to record a single for Red Bus Records, when Brian got the ultimate job offer. Recruiting Terry Schlesser to take Brian's place, Geordie carried on, freeing Brian to accept the most promising position a working class rock 'n' roller could ever hope for. Five and a half weeks after Bon Scott's death, Brian Johnson became AC/DC's new lead singer.

At the time, Brian was married to Carol, whom he wed in 1968, and together they have two daughters, Joanne and Kala. He was still living in Newcastle, and running his own business called North-East Vinyls, installing vinyl roofs on cars. For the past five years, he had provided for his family, virtually giving up the hope that he would someday make something of himself in the music business. As soon he was hired, the band advanced him some money to square away his debts. AC/DC even compensated Geordie for any lost income they might suffer, and immediately swept Brian off to rehearse for the new album.

As stated in *Pop Rock: AC/DC*, Angus told the British newspaper, the *Guardian* in 2003, "I remember Bon playing me Little Richard and then telling me the story of when he saw Brian singing. And he says about that night, 'There's this guy up there screaming at the top of his lungs and then

This rare gem was one of the first AC/DC postcards released by their record company.

the next thing you know, he hits the deck. He's on the floor, rolling around and screaming. I thought it was great, and then to top it off, you couldn't get a better encore, they came in and wheeled the guy off.'"

After Brian joined AC/DC, the band affectionately nicknamed him "Jonna."

Former/Temporary Members

Throughout AC/DC's history, especially in the very beginning of the band, the lineup changed quite frequently. The core of the band being the Young brothers and original singer Dave Evans (who was replaced by Bon Scott), the rhythm section changed so many times it wasn't easy to keep track. Below is a list of all the musicians who played in AC/DC, including those who only lasted a handful of performances.

Rob Bailey

Bailey played bass in AC/DC from April 1974 until January 1975, and appears in the video clip of the band playing "Can I Sit Next to You Girl" at a gig at The Last Picture Show Theater in Cronulla. Retired from the music business, Rob Bailey went into hotel management.

Colin Burgess

Burgess was AC/DC's first drummer, joining the band at the end of 1973 but only staying until February of 1974. Reportedly fired for being drunk on stage, Burgess filled in for Phil Rudd when he broke his thumb in a bar fight. Burgess now tours with his brother Denny in the Burgess Brothers Band and was inducted into the ARIA Hall of Fame.

Ron Carpenter

Carpenter replaced Burgess on drums, but only lasted for a few weeks in the band. Married, and teaching high school during the day, Carpenter also built a PA prototype, composed, and played at night, and went on to form the six-piece band, Aleph.

Peter Clack

Clack played drums for AC/DC from April 1974 to January 1975. Although he was in the band when their debut album, *High Voltage*, was released, he did not play on the recording.

Russell Coleman

Coleman briefly played drums for AC/DC during the month of February 1974.

Tony Currenti

Currenti played drums for the band before they hired Phil Rudd. A session drummer, Currenti is credited as playing drums on the Australian version of *High Voltage*. He has also played on singles for Stevie Wright and John Paul Young. He now runs Tonino's Penshurst Pizzeria in Penshurst, Sydney. After many years of being out of the music business, Tony has started playing the drums again and enjoys his new popularity among the AC/DC fans.

Dave Evans

Malcolm placed an ad in Sydney's *Sunday Morning Herald* and recruited bassist Larry Van Kriedt and former Masters Apprentices drummer Colin Burgess. Ironically, vocalist Dave Evans had just left the same band Malcolm had been in, when he saw the ad and called the number listed. He was more than surprised to hear Malcolm pick up the phone.

Dave Evans had grown up in a musical household, as well. Born in Carmarthen, Wales, his family had also emigrated to Australia. Dave sang at school concerts, and in the school choir. As a young teenager, he listened to the Rolling Stones, the Kinks, and the Beatles. By the time he started playing in bands, he was into Led Zeppelin, Free, and Deep Purple.

Malcolm's new band started rehearsing in an office complex in Newtown, at the corner of Wilson Street and Erskineville Road. Once Angus's band fell apart, Malcolm asked the rest of the guys if he could audition for them. Even though they were brothers, Dave remembers Malcolm being very considerate to ask first, instead of just telling them Angus was joining.

Evans told me how well they were received: "From the very first gig at Chequers, the crowd just reacted to the energy of the band, which did not let up from the word go and actually intensified as we neared the end of our set. Our attitude was to absolutely *kill* the audience, and that is still AC/DC's attitude today."

Mark Evans

Evans played bass for AC/DC from 1975–1977, appearing on four albums: *T.N.T.*, *High Voltage*, *Dirty Deeds Done Dirt Cheap*, and *Let There Be Rock*. Evans now plays with the former singer of Buffalo in the Dave Tice Band, and with another group called the Party Boys. He is also the only former member who wrote his own book, *Dirty Deeds: My Life Inside/Outside AC/DC*.

Paul Greg

Greg filled in on bass for Cliff Williams on their American 1991 *Razors Edge* tour, when Cliff was stricken with a kidney infection. It is unclear how many dates Greg actually played.

Bruce Howe

Howe filled in on bass in AC/DC for a short time in March of 1975, replacing Paul Matters, and was then replaced himself by Mark Evans. Howe was a good friend of Bon Scott's, having played with him in Fraternity from 1971–73.

Paul Matters

Bassist Matters briefly played with AC/DC during the time of the release of *High Voltage*, only to be replaced by Mark Evans. Matters didn't record with the band, but does appear in some of their promotional band pictures.

John Proud

Proud played drums in the band in November of 1974 and appears on the song "Little Lover."

Chris Slade

Drummer Chris Slade played with AC/DC from 1989 to 1994, and appears on the albums *The Razors Edge* and *Live*. Slade has also played with everyone from Tom Jones to Olivia Newton John to Led Zeppelin's Jimmy Page in the Firm. Slade left when Phil Rudd was asked to rejoin the band in 1995.

Neil Smith

Bassist from the band Jasper, Smith played in AC/DC for a brief time from February to April of 1974. Smith lost his battle with cancer and passed away on April 7, 2013.

Noel Taylor

Taylor, also from the band Jasper, played drums with AC/DC for the same amount of time as Smith before being let go in the spring of 1974.

Larry Van Kriedt

Joining the band as AC/DC's first bass player in November of 1973, he remained in the band until February of 1974. Van Kriedt is the only past member who returned to the band for a short time, before Neil Smith was hired.

B. J. Wilson

Drummer B. J. Wilson was brought in to play on the album *Flick of the Switch* after Phil Rudd left the band, but reportedly none of his tracks were used.

Simon Wright

Drummer Simon Wright answered an ad and was hired to play with AC/DC after Phil Rudd left in 1983. He was in the band from 1983 to 1989, and is featured on the albums *Fly on the Wall*, *Who Made Who*, and *Blow Up Your Video*. Wright left the band to play with Dio in 1990, recording the album *Lock Up the Wolves*. Once Ronnie James Dio left the band to play with Black Sabbath, Wright went on to play with Rhino Bucket and UFO, before returning to Dio.

Alex Young

Young filled in on bass in 1975, as did his brother George whenever the band lacked a bass player. He also played in the band Grapefruit, which was signed to the Beatles' label, Apple. He currently works for Albert Productions and resides in Germany.

Stevie Young

Guitarist and nephew of Angus and Malcolm and son of elder brother Steve, Stevie had a band called Starfighter in the early 1980s, who supported AC/DC on their *Back in Black* tour. He has toured with Ozzy Osbourne and Judas Priest and stood in for Malcolm on the North American leg of their *Blow Up Your Video* tour, and has also played in hard rock band Little Big Horn. In May of 2014, Stevie joined AC/DC in the studio in Vancouver to work on their new album, *Rock or Bust*.

3

Cutting Loose from the Homeland

AC/DC Piss Off the Authorities and Head Overseas

The Early Years

Since New Year's Eve 1973, AC/DC had been traveling back and forth across Australia from Sydney and Melbourne, to Adelaide and Perth. Once they hired Bon, things started to click for the band. Bon felt the band had finally given him the freedom to perform the way he wanted to. He said, "When I sang, I always felt that there was a certain amount of urgency to what I was doing. There was no vocal training in my background, just a lot of good whiskey. But when I met up with [AC/DC], they told me to sound like myself, and I really had a free hand doing what I always wanted to do."

As soon as Michael Browning signed on as their manager, he formed a company called Trans Pacific with his business partner, Bill Joseph. The company was able to pay off the band's debts and set them up in a house in Melbourne. For the first time ever, they were paid a wage and were provided with transportation, money for expenses, and a road crew.

The band relocated to Melbourne and moved into a house at 6 Lansdowne Road in the East St. Kilda district. Everyone was in their twenties except Angus, who was just nineteen. Years later, Malcolm would say that living together in this house was one of the happiest times of their lives. Also one of the craziest.

At the time, the band enjoyed two distinct types of female AC/DC fans, or some would say, groupies. There were friends, like Trudy Worme, whose mom used to drop her off at their house on Sunday afternoons so she could cook dinner for them. Being out of the house for the first time, Angus and Malcolm both missed home cooking. She also baked Angus his favorite chocolate cakes.

Then there were the other girls, who wanted to do more than cook for them. Evidently many lovely creatures of the female persuasion came and went, if you know what I mean. So much so that this is where Bon got the personal inspiration for the song "The Jack." Bon explained:

> The story is, we all had a house together in Melbourne. And we had about twenty chicks who would come around and service the band, the whole thing. So the whole band got the jack [Australian slang for gonorrhea]. And so Malcolm said one day: "Why don't we do a song about it?" So we wrote it that afternoon and played it that night and during the quiet part in the middle I went around and pointed out all the girls, you know . . . "She's got the jack" and "She's got the jack" and so on. And all these chicks are makin' a mad dash for the door. It was quite funny actually.

One time there was a rabid outbreak of crabs, which traveled all the way from the house into the band car. Of course in future interviews, the band blamed all this on the roadies. This medical (or sexual) dilemma, if you will, inspired Bon to write the song "Crabsody in Blue," his take on the classical number "Rhapsody in Blue." The boys were kept so busy keeping their slates clean that some say they once had a group rate at the local clinic.

Once Michael Browning took over, the next plan was to keep AC/DC playing live as much as possible. This constant touring, as anyone in the band would agree, made the band into the powerhouse that it is to this day. No gig was too small or too far away, and the band made constant appearances at pubs, and places that catered to the gay crowd and teenyboppers. The majority of AC/DC's audience were male, hardworking blokes who needed to let off some steam.

Before long, AC/DC's music had become known as "pub rock;" songs to drink by. The new rock magazine *Juke*, which took the place of *Go-Set*, stated, "[AC/DC were] new faces refusing to be restricted by an established music scene . . . brash and tough, unashamed to be working at a music style that many describe as the lowest common denominator or rock music, gut-level rock, punk rock."

The band was now traveling around in an old Clipper bus, which constantly broke down. Julius Grafton, who heads his own companies, CX Magazine and Juliusmedia College in Melbourne, recalls his brief brush with the band. "I did lights for AC/DC at some shows in my home state of

New South Wales. Bon Scott was the new singer, and the band was uncompromising. They had an old Flexible Clipper tour bus that broke down regularly. The band was forced to sit in the front, smoking and drinking Scotch, while the crew loaded the gear in the back. At the time, AC/DC had an edge that no other band could match. Nothing has changed!"

Bon, a prolific letter writer, wrote home to his ex-wife Irene complaining about the bus, being without booze, dope, or women to play with. AC/DC were quickly becoming the hottest band in Australia, and Bon described himself to Irene as a "twenty-nine-year-old, third-time-around has-been."

The constant playing made it very apparent to Malcolm and Angus that their rhythm section wasn't what they wanted it to be. Their search for someone to keep the beat and match their unrelenting passion brought them to the only Australian-born member of the band. His name was Phil Rudd.

At the end of January, AC/DC were scheduled to perform at the Sunbury Festival in Melbourne featuring Deep Purple, which had been booked by Michael Browning. When Deep Purple found out that they had to go on before AC/DC, a fight broke out between the band and the roadies, in front of 20,000 people. AC/DC left the venue without playing a note. Perhaps this is what prompted their hotheaded guitarist Ritchie Blackmore to later accuse the band of "circus tricks." The fact that the roadies sided with Deep Purple, and not the local boys, convinced Browning more than anything that it was time for AC/DC to get out of the country.

Conquering Their Homeland

Their debut album, *High Voltage*, was released in Australia in February 1975, with the first single being "Love Song (Oh Jene)," and "Baby Please Don't Go." The B-side started getting airplay, which pushed the song to #10. It stayed on the Australian national charts for an unprecedented twenty-five weeks.

Local musician Mark Evans had heard they were looking for a new bass player and passed the audition just in time to celebrate the album's release. They played a special performance at the Hard Rock Café, where the admission was only one dollar. Evans moved into the house on Lansdowne Road and happily noted that there were women everywhere! Malcolm soon nicknamed him the "Sand Man," because whenever they climbed into a car to go anywhere, Mark would fall asleep within five minutes.

In March, the band made their first appearance on the ABC television show *Countdown*, which was hosted by Ian "Molly" Meldrum. Molly, known as Australia's "oldest teenager," was a disc jockey and had created *Countdown*. They played "Baby Please Don't Go," with Bon singing live and Angus wearing his Super Ang(us) outfit. *Countdown* became a pivotal outlet for the band, as it was watched by most Australian households every Sunday evening.

By the end of the month they played a concert at the Myer Music Bowl, where over 2,500 people showed up. A local newspaper noted that AC/DC got the best response, and when they were finished, half the audience decided to leave as well. As a reward that night, the band was gifted with super groupie Ruby Lips, whom Bon immortalized in the song, "Go Down," which would be included on their fourth album.

Their second appearance on *Countdown* in April 1975 featured Angus in his schoolboy uniform, and Bon in blond braids and a schoolgirl's dress. He completed his look with makeup, earrings, and fake breasts. At the time, men in drag were not all that popular on television, and his cross-dressing caused a litany of complaints. It has never been determined what was so upsetting: his outfit, smoking a cigarette on air, or exposing his skivvies while rolling around on the floor.

Mark Evans told *Classic Rock* in February 2005 that they never knew what Bon was going to do until it happened.

> Another time was when we performed "Baby Please Don't Go," live on *Countdown*, and Bon got dressed as this schoolgirl. Again he didn't tell us. So here we were, being filmed live on television, and the music starts up and Bon's nowhere to be found and we're all going, "Where the fuck is Bon?" As soon as his vocals are about to begin he comes out from behind the drums dressed as this schoolgirl. And it was like a bomb went off in the joint; it was pandemonium, everybody broke out in laughter. Bon had a wonderful sense of humor. He was the archetypal naughty boy.

Joe Matera, respected Australian rock journalist and renowned guitar player and recording artist for European-based record label W.A.R. Productions, remembers seeing the band for the first time on that infamous *Countdown* appearance where Bon walked out in front of the TV cameras dressed as a schoolgirl. Matera told me, "As a ten year old it blew me away, and Angus' hi-octane guitar playing inspired me to later play guitar too. I can still remember the feelings I felt that first time even today forty years later! I had never seen anything like it and the music just connected. I became a fan there and then."

AC/DC were a phenomenon compared to the other artists regularly appearing on *Countdown*. Their rough and ready rocker following was rivaled by all the screaming teenyboppers. *RAM* wrote, "They were everything the Bay City Rollers didn't stand for. Maybe it was the way Angus Young jumped and rolled around the stage like a demented epileptic while not missing a note of his guitar duties. Maybe it was the way Bon Scott leered and licked his lips while his eyes roamed hungrily up and down little girls' dresses."

The band stayed busy by playing Heavy Metal Nites at the Hard Rock Café, and during the day, a special series of concerts at the Hard Rock called "Schoolkids Week." While not working, AC/DC were known for not hanging out with other bands or musicians. As a matter of policy, they hated other bands, except of course for their idols like Chuck Berry or Little Richard. Their attitude was "if you're not with us, you're against us."

Bassist Mark Evans remembers Bon not always being able to conform to this philosophy. He was known as "Bon the Likeable," after the character Simon the Likable on the television show *Get Smart*, whose secret weapon was that he was impossible not to like. That was obvious, even to Mark's mother, who used to have the band over for dinner, and Bon would always ask to help her with the dishes. Of course she adored Bon, just like every other woman who would cross his path.

Their single "High Voltage," which missed being included on their debut album, was released in June. That same month, they played their first headlining concert at the Melbourne Festival Hall with Stevie Wright and John Paul Young supporting. This performance was shot with four cameras (which was unheard of in those days), with the intent on getting them some interest overseas. A promotional video of "High Voltage" was taken from that footage, and for good measure, they spliced in applause from George Harrison's *Concert for Bangladesh* album.

Melbourne music fan and roadie Raymond Windlow saw AC/DC for the first time when they played the Festival Hall, when he was working for the band Fox. He went on to work with the Dingoes, Skyhooks, and briefly with the Little River Band. Windlow related,

> There were quite a few bands there that day, but being offered a day's work initially with AC/DC was putting money in my pocket. Whilst my musical taste didn't extend to their raunchy, loud, thump, thump, thump music, the appeal of the screaming girls did. It was an amazing concert with the stage being surrounded in a crush of bodies, mostly barely legal females. I almost got my marching orders prior to the guys playing a note.

Being world-wise, I offered to score for them if they wanted something in the dressing room before they went on. The silence was absolutely deafening. The look from their manager had more than daggers in it and when no one spoke up, I assumed I had "dropped a clanger," and left the room mumbling something about checking the sound equipment. One of the management put his arm around my shoulder, and in a gentle fashion said, "No, mate, don't ever mention drugs around the band." And he left the whole conversation at that. I believe that the attention the guys were getting at the time may have opened them up to the possibility of being set up for a narcotics bust.

During their performance the audience was in a frenzy with a mass of bodies pressed hard into the front of the stage. Girls looked pleadingly at the guys on the side of the stage, holding their hands up. Not to grab at Bon or Angus, but for someone to pull them out of the crush. Myself, and a couple of others, did just that much to the annoyance of the management, who admonished us for venturing out onto the stage during their performance. Nonetheless, we survived the night and when the younger members of the band wandered home with their "minders," Bon, myself, and a few guys from other bands wandered off to the local post-gig hotspot, the Hard Rock Café.

Bon and I spent quite a few nights playing eight ball at the Hard Rock during their extended Melbourne visits. Bon was a regular at the Hard Rock after a gig. He loved his drink and whilst we were not bosom buddies, we were pool buddies. I was the roadie who did a few gigs for them and he was the lad who made the girls scream at his stage performance. On occasion some members of the public who paid to get in at the Hard Rock would try to smart arse their way into Bon's bad books. Maybe to get the reputation of having been in a fight with him or what, I don't know.

What I do know is that if ever a fight was in the making, I would have Bon on one side and twenty or thirty roadies right behind us. The music community was tight when it comes to that, and Bon had the look of a classic street scrapper. But the whole time I knew him, not once that I know of did he actually throw a punch. Anyone was welcome to chat, share a smoke or a drink with him and try to beat his ass at eight ball! Not many did. I still reckon we had the longest run on that pool table as unbeaten pair champs.

A mere four months after the release of *High Voltage*, it was certified gold in Australia. Immediately the band left for Sydney to record their second album. Angus and Malcolm moved back into their parents' home in Burwood, while the rest of the band and crew stayed at the Squire Inn at Bondi Junction. Right across the street from the hotel was the hottest nightclub in Sydney, the Lifesaver, and the Bondi Lifesaver was the place to be in 1975. It was a club and restaurant that most fans frequented more than a couple nights a week, so Bon made it his new headquarters.

Albert Studios was located in the old Boomerang House on King Street, which also housed the radio station 2UW. The band recorded in Studio One, which was a small room with bare brick walls. They used the side room, which had two Marshall stacks and a bass rig. The drums were set up in the other room, which was once a kitchen. Most of the songs were recorded live, within the first few takes. The guitar leads and vocals were the only tracks that were overdubbed.

Albert Studios was quickly becoming a hit factory for the Australian music scene. George and Harry had a sixteen-track mixing console shipped over from England, and spent every waking hour writing and recording hits.

Their main clients were John Paul Young, the Ted Mulry Gang, and William Shakespeare, who was a goofy Gary Glitter–type character. It all came together for them when they brought AC/DC into record. Harry Vanda explained, "We tried to capture that energy they had on stage. You had to get them at the right time, when they were really fired up."

Their second album would reveal a more polished approach, opening with "It's a Long Way to the Top (If You Wanna Rock 'n' Roll)," the only rock song to feature bagpipes (that is, until Korn did it almost thirty years later). They rerecorded "Can I Sit Next to You Girl," and added "Rock 'n' Roll Singer," "High Voltage," "Rocker," a cover of Chuck Berry's "School Days," "Live Wire," "T.N.T.," and Bon's ode to venereal disease, "The Jack." I would like to point out that Bon should be credited with originating the phrase "You're the man," since he sings in the song "T.N.T.," "*the man* is back in town, so don't you mess around!"

George Young had a huge influence on his younger brother's writing style. Angus described, "(George) would take our meanest song and try it out on keyboards with arrangements like 10cc or Montovani. If it was passed, the structure was proven, then we took it away and dirtied it up." This formula has stood the test of time. The Young brothers also had the benefit of George and Harry's penchant for picking hits. Angus once said that George didn't work with them because they were family; it was because George thought they were good.

Bon stated that George was more a father figure to the group, rather than a brother. He didn't tell them what to do, but he helped them get more out of what they were doing. Bassist Mark Evans was quoted in *Undercover Media*, saying "George Young fine-tuned things. George is an absolute genius. I have never met a more astute person in the studio than George." Angus and Malcolm were both gifted at coming up with riffs, turning them into songs every time they sat down to jam. Malcolm often came up with a title, and then they would try to write a song around it. Malcolm and George would work it out on the keyboards, leaving Bon to add the lyrics once the backing tracks were done. Bon always had notebooks of lyrics, all neatly printed in capital letters. Although some of his lyrics were quite simple, his phrasing was his strong suit. Bon told *Countdown*, "Things fall into place. Sometimes. You gotta keep your eyes open for lines and words and stuff . . . ideas, just pictures, you know."

Malcolm added, "Back then we went into the studio with anything more than a riff. In fact, we thought a riff was a song. Fortunately, we had the producers there to turn them into songs and it's been pretty much the same ever since. Back then we really didn't know any better."

They spent the rest of the summer of 1975 playing Melbourne and Sydney, becoming regulars at Sydney's Bondi Lifesaver. Their plan to play a series of free concerts at Melbourne's Myer store had to be cancelled when, some say, as many as 5,000 fans stormed the store on the first day, ripping the place apart and ending AC/DC's set after only two songs.

When a fight erupted later at the Matthew Findlers Hotel in Melbourne, Phil broke his thumb, requiring former drummer Colin Burgess to fill in for him. This could be where he got the nickname Phil "Left Hook" Rudd. Reportedly, Phil flew off the drums and hit a guy so hard he knocked him out. To which he explained, "This guy was kicking Angus in the head, so I had to now, didn't I?"

Vince Lovegrove told *No Nonsense* in May 1999, "In Australia in those days it was pretty wild, a bit like cowboy days, the business was still young, and lawless, and the band had a reputation for being wild, mainly due to Bon, really. The rest were wild boys, but Bon was unique. He was from another planet."

In early September, the band played a free show at Sydney's Victoria Park, which was promoted by radio station 2SM. This time Angus would climb up on Bon's shoulders, for their first ever "walkabout." Chris Gilbey used an advertising campaign for AC/DC, which stated "Your mother won't like them." It worked like a charm. To further piss off mothers everywhere, after the Victoria Park concert, Angus was quoted as saying, "That notorious leader of thieves and vagabonds, Bon Scott, to celebrate the success of the show in Sydney, went out and got a new tattoo and pierced his nipples for earrings. The other boys celebrated in other ways."

The Infamous Rosie

Bon had been living in the Freeway Gardens Motel in Melbourne, where he reunited with his friend Pat Pickett, who heard the band was in Melbourne and traveled there to work for the band as one of the road crew. One night during a party at an apartment building, someone offered Bon five dollars to jump off the balcony into the pool. Bon got him to raise it to ten dollars, and in front of everyone (including a terrified Angus), leapt off the second floor balcony and made a perfect dive into the hotel's swimming pool. As he told *Guitar World* magazine, Angus grabbed the guy and said, "Don't ever fucking dare Bon to do something again! Accepting dares was Bon's favorite party trick. He had no fear when it came to things like that." He also had no fear of any woman who might catch his eye.

Freeway Gardens was where Bon met the notorious Rosie. The band, and especially Bon, loved to push each other to do the most disgusting things. When Rosie, a large Tasmanian mountain woman, starting showing up at their shows, an ultimatum was presented to Bon. One morning when Pat Pickett woke up, he looked over and saw a rather substantial lady lying in Bon's bed, with a small tattooed arm sticking out from underneath her. Bon's homage to her is the song "Whole Lotta Rosie."

The band was always amazed at Bon's ability to attract women. One time he managed what Mark Evans recalled as a "trifecta," which was bedding three women a day for four days in a row. Bon definitely loved the ladies, and although he was known to be a street fighter, he usually kept his head about him, and would stand back and watch before he got directly involved in a disagreement.

The only time Bon really lost his temper was when they played on the *TV Week King of Pops* awards show. They played live, and Bon had all kinds of problems on stage. When they were done, they went downstairs and broke a lock off a door to get into a bar. Inside was a stack of *TV Week* magazines with Sherbet's singer, Daryl Braithwaite, on the cover. This enraged Bon, which prompted him to tear up all the magazines. He spent the rest of the night drinking champagne from a frozen turkey.

The "High Voltage" single shot up the charts to #6. The album of the same name had sold more than 70,000 copies, and was catapulted to 125,000 copies once the single was released. Now that they were getting the sales in Australia, it was only a matter of time before they conquered the rest of the world.

Browning signed them to a five-year management deal, and started planning a national tour to promote the release of their new album, *T.N.T.*

The tour started in Melbourne on the way to Perth, and would wind up in Sydney by Christmas. Bon was able to visit his parents, and Chick and Isa were finally able to meet the boys.

While on the road, the local band the Keystone Angels opened for them. Vocalist Rick Brewster recalled the first time he ever saw AC/DC. "We supported AC/DC as the Keystone Angels on their south Australia country tour in 1975. The Port Pirie Hotel was the first gig, and it was the first time I saw them perform live. They were the tightest band I'd ever seen despite the fact that Phil Rudd had broken his wrist [sic] and was not on the tour. We later saw Phil play with the band many times, and he was a machine hammering out one of the hardest of all feels to play well. Malcolm drove the band, called all the shots with minimum effort; Mark Evans played the bass and although he only remained with the band for another few years I always liked his playing."

Brewster continued,

> Bon was right up there with Paul Rodgers as one of the best and most charismatic rock singers I'd ever heard. His tongue-in-cheek delivery was infectious and his ad lib version of "The Jack" . . . well, you had to be there. And then there was Angus. I'd never seen anything remotely like Angus. Superb musicianship complemented his over the top stage antics . . . such an incredible combination. He's still one of the finest guitar players I've ever heard and he reels it off in the same manner as a gifted circus clown who makes a difficult acrobatic feat look easy. And his act was essentially the same as it is today! The Chuck Berry duckwalk, the "Death of a Fly," the schoolboy uniform . . . it was all there in Port Pirie, South Australia, in 1975, and he's spent the next thirty years hammering it home to the rest of the world. I remember Angus telling me in the tour bus on that first tour, "Yeah . . . you know if I was a piano player I'd play with my feet!"

Brewster recalled the funniest thing he ever saw Angus do, when the Keystone Angels and AC/DC played at the Sundowner Hotel in Whyalla. "Angus lost his temper with someone in the crowd who must have been yelling the wrong thing. This guy happened to be a six-foot-four biker. When Angus lost it, he threw his SG down and leapt on him with a full flying tackle from the stage. They went down in a screaming heap and the only reason that Angus is alive today is that Bon followed him into the skirmish and somehow managed to defuse the situation and coax a screaming and kicking Angus back to the stage to finish the show."

After they returned home, Angus, Bon, and Malcolm all told George Young about the Keystone Angels, and Albert Music signed them, changed their name to the Angels, and guided them to becoming one of Australia's most successful bands during the seventies. Eternally grateful, Rick said,

> They saw something in us which I didn't see myself. We weren't very good musically at the time. Maybe they saw "hungry and determined with potential." Whatever it was, we were grateful, having already been turned down by EMI (who ironically, distributed Albert's records). After the boys from AC/DC put in the good word for us, George and his partner Harry Vanda came to see us in Sydney, at Chequers Night Club where we used to play from eight 'til three or four in the morning for $100. We were offered a deal on the spot. One of the best spin-offs from signing with Albert's was working next door to a number of other great acts. Those included Rose Tattoo, Ted Mulry, John Paul Young, Flash and the Pan and, of course, AC/DC. It gave us tremendous insight and inspiration.

AC/DC played another headlining date at the Festival Hall in November, and were back in Sydney to play the State Theatre on the thirtieth. On December 8, 1975, their next single, "It's a Long Way to the Top (If You Wanna Rock 'n' Roll)"/"Can I Sit Next to You Girl" was released, followed by their new album, *T.N.T.*

Landing a Worldwide Record Deal

Michael Browning's sister Coral lived in London and worked for a management company that handled Peter Tosh, Bob Marley, and Gil Scott-Heron. She traveled to Melbourne to see the band and was very excited to be working with them. In December, Michael flew to London armed with the footage that was taken at the Festival Hall, intent on landing the band a record deal. After showing Phil Carson of Atlantic Records a kinescope of the band playing live, Carson offered them a worldwide recording contract. The first deal was a one-album trial, with an option for Atlantic to extend a larger contract in the future.

Atlantic Records was formed in 1947 in New York City, and in the early seventies, after they had signed Yes and Emerson, Lake, and Palmer, two of rock's biggest acts, opened an office in London. The label was crazy for the band, and they in turn were thrilled to be on the same label as Led Zeppelin and the Rolling Stones. Amazingly, Atlantic outsmarted everyone else who had passed on them. AC/DC were now on their way to taking over the rest of the planet, one concert at a time.

AC/DC played the Royal Showgrounds in Sydney on Christmas Eve, and then celebrated New Year's Eve performing in Adelaide. The band had the electricity cut off while they were performing, and Bon incited their fans to storm the stage in protest. Then he triumphantly appeared in the middle of the crowd on someone's shoulders, playing the bagpipes.

By the end of 1975, *High Voltage* was certified triple gold. AC/DC were now the top band in Australia. Considering the nation's birth in 1821 as a dumping ground for the United Kingdom's criminal population, it would be safe to say that they cut their rock 'n' roll teeth on the toughest audiences you could find. The new year would bring yet another member change, and finally, a long-awaited trip overseas.

Before leaving, they attended a gold record reception and farewell party in Melbourne, where they were presented with three plaques, two for *High Voltage* and one for *T.N.T.* After two years of solid touring, *High Voltage* and *T.N.T.* would eventually gain silver, gold, and platinum status in Australia. The night before they flew to England, they also celebrated Angus's twenty-first birthday. Although according to his press kit, he was only seventeen.

Michael Browning had strategically kept their departure to England low-key, having seen too many bands previously fall on their faces and return back to Australia with their tails between their legs. Angus was unaffected by all of this. He was quoted in England's *Record Mirror & Disc* saying, "Success there [in Australia] means nothing. We left on a peak rather than overstay our welcome, and set out to plunder and pillage." They set out to pillage England riding around in a van with Phil behind the wheel. Being a true car fanatic, he was the band's preferred designated driver.

Pillaging England

On arriving in England, the band picked up any club dates they could. The British music scene, as Angus recalled, was a real throwback. He told Jodi Summers Dorland in *Hit Parader*, "When Bon first walked on stage in a little club in London, the audience was made up of your Johnny Rottens and all of those people. Bon, being older, would go out there and really strut his stuff. Then, I remember seeing Rotten and those punks the next week, wearing the same clothes and haircut as Bon."

One of the first things Bon did after arriving in London was to visit the pub in Finchley where he was a bartender during his days in Fraternity. As soon as he walked into the place, Bon claimed someone threw a full pint of beer hitting him square in the face. According to Bon, he had walked into the middle of someone else's fight, which cost him a black eye and a dislocated jaw. That explains the dark sunglasses Bon is wearing in their first photo shoot in England. His injuries forced him to also endure extensive dental work, which he still really needed after his near-fatal motorbike accident.

Upon arriving in England, Atlantic Records' British division issued a combination of *High Voltage* and *T.N.T.*, making this album their first European release. The album was actually the Australian version of *T.N.T.*, plus two songs from the *High Voltage* album. "She's Got Balls" and "Little Lover" were included in place of "Rocker" and Chuck Berry's "School Days."

High Voltage got the attention of BBC Radio One disc jockey John Peel, and in June of 1976, they recorded a four-track session in Maida Vale 4 Studios in London for Peel's radio show. Although Michael Browning's sister Coral wasn't officially on the band's payroll, she was offered an office at London's Atlantic Records to help Michael out with the band. She immediately convinced journalists Caroline Coon and Phil McNeill to come out to see them. McNeill reviewed their performance at London's Nashville Rooms for the *New Musical Express* with the headline "I Wallaby Your Man:" "In the middle of the great British Punk Rock Explosion, a quintet of similarly ruthless Ozzies has just swaggered like a cat among London's surly, self-consciously paranoid pigeons . . . and with a sense of what sells rather than what's cool, they could well clean up . . . We're impressed."

The British rock press at the time consisted of *Melody Maker*, the *New Musical Express*, and *Sounds*, the newest publication, which debuted in 1970. *Sounds* immediately got behind AC/DC, and put them at the top of the list in its "New Order Top 20." Behind them were Eddie and the Hot Rods, the Sex Pistols, the Damned, Iggy Pop and the Stooges, Ted Nugent, Ritchie Blackmore's Rainbow, Motörhead, Judas Priest, and sharing the last position, the Ramones and the Dictators.

Their nine-date tour supporting Back Street Crawler, which had been postponed due to lead singer Paul Kossof's death, opened at the famed Marquee Club in May. This was the place to play in London, featuring acts like Jimi Hendrix; Led Zeppelin; and Emerson, Lake, and Palmer, among many others. Rock journalist Phil Sutcliffe reviewed the show and predicted the band would be huge. He quickly became one of their biggest supporters in print.

On June 4, they played their first headlining gig at the Marquee, launching a nineteen-date club tour sponsored by *Sounds* magazine, aptly titled the

Lock Up Your Daughters Summer Tour. Their set included a live DJ and featured film clips from other bands.

For the last date of their United Kingdom tour at the Lyceum in London, Atlantic Records arranged a "Best Schoolboy/Schoolgirl" competition. Some sources say it was a contest to look for the "Schoolgirl we'd most like to . . ." The winner, Jayne Haynes from Middlesex, England, won a folk guitar and a night out with bassist Mark Evans.

Two nights later the band celebrated Bon's thirtieth birthday, but he never showed up. When he had time off, Bon preferred to go off on his own. This time he was gone for three days hiding out somewhere with his girlfriend, Silver Smith.

In July, they played their first European tour through Holland, Austria, including five dates in Sweden. The Swedish tour was arranged by Tomas Johansen, who represented Abba. He had had trouble getting dates for Abba in Australia, so he struck a deal to bring Abba to Australia and AC/DC to Sweden. Before leaving Sweden, the band filmed a twenty-minute segment for Mike Mansfield's *Superpop* television program, which also featured Malcolm's idol Marc Bolan and his band, T. Rex.

Bon's favorite parts of Sweden were the topless beaches and the swimming pools. According to bassist Mark Evans, the rest of the band couldn't have cared less about these perks. Angus and Malcolm had tunnel vision, and that was to play. They were convinced that someday they were going to make it big, and everything else was secondary. Malcolm's favorite saying was, "We're just waiting around to become filthy rich."

The band managed to fit in some recording time at Vineyard Studios to lay down "Dirty Eyes," "Carry Me Home," "Love at First Feel," and "Cold Hearted Man." The four-song EP was never released, with each of these songs appearing later in various forms on albums, as singles, and in the future box set. That same month, they made their European television debut playing "Jailbreak," on the *So It Goes* show in London.

Their appearance in August at the Orange Festival in Nimes, France, was canceled, but on the twenty-eighth, they filmed a three-track live performance at the Wimbleton Theater in London for the *Rollin' Bolan Show*, which aired on London's weekend television. They followed that by playing the Reading Rock Festival with Brand X, Black Oak Arkansas, and Ted Nugent on the twenty-ninth, in front of 50,000 people.

George Young, Harry Vanda, and Michael and Coral Browning all made the trip to see the band play. There were equipment problems and the band wasn't well received by the audience, and their performance was referred to as a "misfire." This was the performance that incited a blow out between Angus, Malcolm, and George, and eventually led to the dismissal of bassist Mark Evans.

By the end of the summer of 1976, AC/DC had become the house band at the Marquee club in London, breaking attendance records. Every Monday night they would draw over 1,400 people, inspiring the *New Musical Express* to state, "The only sound coming through the wall was chunka-chunka-chunka, while the bar resounded with ribald Aussies telling me to watch for Angus Young to expose himself. When he stripped off to his knickers and leapt on an amp a well-informed source nose said, 'My God, he's been wearing the same underpants for four weeks.'"

Once the United Kingdom's version of *High Voltage* was released, author Mark Putterford's review of this album appeared in *High Vaultage: A Delicious Delve into the AC/DC Album Archives.* Putterford comically reported, "Snotty nostrils a-flarin', crooked teeth a-gnashin', and grubby knees a-tremblin', the crazed Just William exaggeration begins to nod uncontrollably as his pale, boney hands jerk across the live wires in his grasp. The simple infectious riff that marched in 'It's a Long Way to the Top' was the leak that would burst the banks of contemporary rock. It introduced us bewildered Britfolk to the outrageous high voltage antics of Australia's youthful delinquents, AC/DC, who were destined to riff all over the opposition for years to come."

Considering *T.N.T.* was still selling 3–4,000 units per week, Albert Music postponed the release of *Dirty Deeds Done Dirt Cheap* until September 20, 1976, in Australia. AC/DC never stopped long enough to celebrate the album's release, and continued to tour throughout France, Switzerland, Belgium, Denmark, Sweden, and Germany for nineteen dates, supporting Rainbow. Aside from Blackmore's nasty temper, the only downside was a huge replica of a rainbow, which kept falling over during the band's performance. Karma for Blackmore, who once accused AC/DC of "circus tricks."

The *High Voltage* compilation sold 16,000 copies the first week of its release in Germany. Never easy to follow AC/DC, the night Ritchie Blackmore refused to let them do an encore, the fans were so upset, most of them walked out before Rainbow hit the stage. The United States finally got its first taste of AC/DC when *High Voltage* was released on September 28, 1976, but the album barely made it onto the airwaves.

Rolling Stone journalist Billy Altman wrote in October, "Those concerned with the future of hard rock may take solace in knowing that with the release of the first US album by these Australian gross-out champions, the genre has unquestionably hit its all-time low. Lead singer Bon Scott spits out his vocals with a truly annoying aggression, which, I suppose, is the only way to do it when all you seem to care about is being a star so that you can get laid every night. Stupidity bothers me. Calculated stupidity offends me."

Which brings to mind the infamous Frank Zappa quote, "Most rock journalism is people who can't write, interviewing people who can't talk, for people who can't read." I can only hope he was referring to Altman. Fortunately for *Rolling Stone* reviewer Altman, AC/DC had to postpone their first tour of the States that fall, due to visa problems regarding convictions of pot possession for both Michael Browning and Bon Scott. Wherever they played in Australia, the band was followed by vice squads threatening to arrest Angus if he dropped his pants while on stage.

Billboard magazine was much more forgiving than *Rolling Stone*, putting *High Voltage* on the "Recommended LPs" list and stating, "Australia's newest entry is a cross between Led Zeppelin and the Sensational Alex Harvey Band. Lead singer has a very unique sounding voice and the twin guitars are front and center from the first cut. Expect airplay on progressive stations." At their first headlining concert on November 10, 1976, at London's Hammersmith Odeon, half the audience was dressed in schoolboy uniforms, proving that AC/DC were finally catching on.

The bands return to Glasgow, was reviewed by the *East Kilbride News* on November 11, 1976:

> "High Voltage" aroused the audience to greater heights—but the stage reached its climax when the band burst into "Baby Please Don't Go." Angus, having dispensed with the uniform, fell to the floor, wriggling around like a severed worm. Then he climbed to the top of a column of speakers while Bon Scott mounted those on the other side of the stage. Angus reverted to playing his guitar with one hand, Bon screamed out the lyrics before jumping back onto the stage and catching Angus as he leapt down—still clutching his guitar. And the incredible thing about the whole routine was that it was executed to perfection without Angus missing so much as a solitary chord. The audience was left breathless.

What would become a yearly tradition, AC/DC played a Christmas show at the Hammersmith Odeon, and headed back to Australia to launch a twenty-six date tour, called *A Giant Dose of Rock 'n' Roll.* This time they were met at the airport by hundreds of screaming fans, many already sporting tattoos immortalizing their rock 'n' roll heroes.

Enemy Number One on the Vice Squad List

The opening date of their tour was a sold-out show at the Myer Music Bowl. Although they were gaining more and more fans, their saucy lyrics and "lock up your daughter" attitude continually caused problems, and their Australian tour was riddled with them. Many dates were cancelled or threatened in some way. Due to the obscene images of the band that had been generated by the media, Australia's Parliament actually discussed AC/DC, and their possible bad influence on the nation's youth.

When a rich widow started getting phone calls after the fans heard Bon singing, "calling 36-24-36" in the song "Dirty Deeds Done Dirt Cheap," the band got a windfall of free publicity. So much so that their publicist Chris Gilbey had to release a public apology from the band. The Mayor of Tamworth refused to let the band play in his city, and a news crew flew in from Channel Nine's *Current Affair* to report the blasphemy.

A previous supporter of the band, radio station 2SM, which was owned by the Catholic Church, didn't appreciate their tour being called *A Giant Dose of Rock 'n' Roll*. Their complaint was Angus exposing himself on stage. This inspired Bon to state in Australia's *RAM*, "You see his backside in the papers more than you see his face—which is preferential as far as I'm concerned." 2SM's general manager refused them airplay and stated, "Members of the Australian punk rock group AC/DC must decide if they are strippers or musicians. Until they do, the station will not associate with them in any way."

Australian newspapers declared "Rock Band Threatens to Leave Country," which ran a quote from Angus: "It's no good if we drive halfway across the country to stage a concert to find that someone has cancelled it because they consider us obscene. It will only take a couple more hassles from the authorities and we will leave Australia."

Sales of their 1976–77 tour book was pulled from sale at their second date in Albury for its "obscene nature." The straw that broke the Parliament's back was credited to a comment made by bassist Mark Evans, even though it was actually said by Bon. In response to the meaning of his lyrics to "Ain't No Fun (Waiting 'Round to Be a Millionaire)," Bon's priceless quote was, "It means that it takes a long time to make enough money to be able to fuck Britt Ekland." Britt was the Swedish sexpot who married the late Sir Peter Sellers; she also hooked up with Rod Stewart for a while, and somewhere off in the distant future, had her way with one of the Stray Cats.

A small consolation was when an article appeared in Australia's *RAM*, stating, "Loud seems too tame a description for the volume they inflict on

A rare vintage full-color poster promoting their British/European tour supporting their album *Let There Be Rock* in 1977.

an audience. It's more a 'living sound' that actually penetrates the flesh and bones until movement and rhythm come involuntarily and the audience is swept into the same current . . . behind the insistency lies an excellent rock/blues outfit with an amazing singer out front in Bon Scott."

Adding to the shabby treatment of the band in Australia, Michael Browning was alerted to the fact that the American division of Atlantic Records refused to release *Dirty Deeds Done Dirt Cheap* in the US, and the band was suddenly in danger of losing their American record deal. Thankfully Atlantic's Phil Carson in the London office was able to convince the label to stick with the band, although it was also rumored that the American division of Atlantic Records wanted to replace Bon, and that is why they refused to release *Dirty Deeds* over here in the first place. Except for the rare import, the record was unavailable in the States. The record company cashed in on the popularity of the future blockbuster *Back in Black* by releasing *Dirty Deeds Done Dirt Cheap* in 1981.

The band appeared live on *Countdown* on December 5, 1976, playing "Dirty Deeds Done Dirt Cheap," and then took a quick break over Christmas. The six dates in Australia in January of 1977 would be Bon's last official performances in his homeland. Completing a tour between Adelaide, Perth, and Melbourne, bolstered by three years of constant touring, AC/DC would go back into Albert Studios to record their fourth album. Backed by the guidance of Young and Vanda, the new album was divinely christened *Let There Be Rock*.

Only taking a couple of weeks to record the album, AC/DC took off again for the UK, playing Edinburgh on February 18 and launching a twenty-six date tour in support of *Dirty Deeds Done Dirt Cheap*.

The *National RockStar* wrote on February 26, 1977, about the Edinburgh University show,

> The trouble started after the first number "Live Wire," and in the middle of "Eat Dog" [sic]. Some of the audience spilled over onto the stage to sit on the monitor speakers, inches away from their new heroes. Some of the crowd were being held back by the stewards and they didn't like it. Fights broke out all over the front of the hall . . . It was the presence of seventeen-year-old Angus Young in black velvet school blazer and shorts and a little leather satchel which sparked off the bizarre audience reaction . . . AC/DC have it. It's more than just rock—it's provocation. They will be the band of '77.

Let There Be Rock was released in Australia on March 21, 1977. The cover artwork featured their lightning bolt logo for the first time, and whenever Bon was asked if he was AC or DC, he would laughingly reply, "Neither, I'm the lightnin' flash in the middle!"

Their Glasgow University performance was reviewed by Eric Wishart for the *Record Mirror* on February 26: "Angus Young on lead guitar was amazing. Dressed in his standard short pants schoolboy gear he twitched, jerked, and bounded across the stage nonstop, his head whipping back and forth until it looked as if it just had to come flying off . . . Centerplace was an extended 'She's Got the Jack,' [sic] their ode to that dreaded disease which Bob [sic] Scott introduced with a reworking of 'Maria' that would have made the heroes of *West Side Story* think at least twice before approaching Natalie Wood."

Explaining their appeal to the fans, Bon told *New Musical Express*, "The music press is totally out of touch with what their kids actually want to listen to. These kids might be working in a shitty factory all week, or they might be on the dole—come the weekend, they just want to go out and have a good time, get drunk, and go wild. We give them the opportunity to do that." Back in London, Angus and Malcolm moved into an apartment, Phil and

Mark found a place close by, and Bon moved back in with his girlfriend Silver.

On March 5, Ian Flavin wrote in the *National RockStar*, "They sure get down to it. Australia's exiled bad boys came on in strictly 4/4 time and hammered out a mean dose of street corner rock 'n' roll from start to finish . . . Malcolm Young, the rhythm guitarist, seemed to be the driving pivot, churning out slashing bashing power chords with the musical finesse of a caged tiger . . . [Angus] delivered a constant stream of red hot licks in the best guitar hero fashion. He's seventeen. If he's still playing when he reaches twenty-five that might be something truly amazing to dig."

Their single "Dog Eat Dog"/"Carry Me Home" was released in Australia that spring, although the B-side doesn't appear on any of their albums. The single, "Love at First Feel," was the last song to chart in Australia, until they released *Highway to Hell*. On April 3, the band appeared on *Countdown*'s fifth anniversary special, playing "Dog Eat Dog," which had previously been filmed in London.

A twelve-date European tour opening for Black Sabbath ended abruptly when AC/DC kept blowing Black Sabbath off the stage every night. To retaliate, Black Sabbath kept shortening AC/DC's opening set. One night, tensions finally exploded with Sabbath's bass player Geezer Butler pulling a flick knife on Malcolm. Of course Mal started swinging, and AC/DC were fired off the tour. This night would also be bassist Mark Evans' last performance with the band.

Ambushing the United States

At the end of the United Kingdom tour, Mark Evans was dismissed from the band, supposedly over personality clashes with Angus. At first Evans accepted a flat payment of $2,000 against future royalties, but ten years later won a generous settlement from Albert Music.

After placing an ad in *Sounds* magazine, AC/DC auditioned over fifty bass players. The band held the auditions in a tiny room in Victoria, and the first tracks they played with Cliff Williams were "Live Wire," "Problem Child," and an old blues number. Cliff was asked to join the band on May 27, 1977, and once he was hired, they flew back to Australia to rehearse. It was finally time to prepare for the long-awaited tour of the United States. Before they left for America, the band played two undercover dates at the Bondi, first under the name the Seedies, and on the second night, they were called Dirty Deeds.

On July 27, 1977, AC/DC would play their first US date at the Amarillo World Headquarters in Austin, Texas. *Let There Be Rock* hit the American airwaves the previous month, and peaked on the *Billboard* charts at #150.

To handle their arrival in the States, Atlantic Records hired a new promotions team. Perry Cooper's first assignment with Atlantic was to promote AC/DC. He told me,

> I was working with Michael Klenfner of Arista Records, who was vice president of promotions. I was director of special projects, but I had a bunch of titles. We spent two years at Arista during the early days; we worked with Barry Manilow, Melissa Manchester, Outlaws, the Bay City Rollers, it was wonderful. We had a great time. Then when he got offered this opportunity at Atlantic, he took me with him. We were sent over to Atlantic as a package deal.
>
> Right after we went to Atlantic, Jerry Greenberg came to Michael one day, and said, "We've got this band from Australia, they're doing fairly well, and we signed them to a long-term contract. But their lyrics are a little risqué, and we're not getting any radio play. So could you guys look them over and see what you can do?" So he gave us a kinescope, it was really weird, like a film. It had a cartridge that you put into this machine, and we looked at it. No, actually I looked at it. Michael (who will deny this), told me to look at it, because he didn't give a shit. So I looked at it, and saw this guitarist doing a duckwalk. And I thought, well he's a little bit copying Chuck Berry, but we should bring them over here and tour them, because they are terrific live. And that's what we did.

Once Perry Cooper saw the kinescope of AC/DC live, he went back to Greenberg and convinced Atlantic that the band had potential. His theory was to bring AC/DC over to the States. "So they toured their asses off for two years straight. We just said, 'When people see them, they will love them!'"

AC/DC landed in the United States in July 1977. Unlike the Beatles, they were able to sneak into the country without being noticed. Just like the Rolling Stones before them, the band got into a used station wagon, and embarked on their first tour of the United States. The first three American dates AC/DC played were opening for the band Moxy in Austin, San Antonio, and Corpus Christi, Texas. The band went over very well in the Lone Star state, exclaiming Texan people "really know how to party!" On July 30, they played a free concert at the Electric Ballroom in Dallas, Texas, hosted by radio station K2EW.

From Texas, they drove to Florida, starting the long road that would stretch across two years, and later become known as "the highway to hell."

The recording of AC/DC live at Atlantic Studios in New York City was spearheaded by Perry Cooper, who worked for their record company. Originally, copies of the release were only sent to radio stations for promotional purposes. Perry told me that while they were recording, even the cleaning staff that were in the building slipped into the studio to watch.

Roadie Barry Taylor later wrote in his book, *Singing in the Dark*, "In that first tour we covered some 40,000 miles zigzagging the country. One day it was Chicago, a couple of days later Miami. There were times when we could have killed the booking agent, but we certainly got a taste of the diversity of the American lifestyle."

Their first date in Gainesville on August 4 was cancelled. Maybe from not having enough time to drive from Texas to Florida? On August 5 and 6, they co-headlined with REO Speedwagon in West Palm Beach and Jacksonville.

A radio station in Jacksonville, Florida programmed four or five of the band's songs into their playlist. AC/DC had been getting paid $500 a night to play a club, but when they got to Jacksonville, with Pat Travers opening, they played in front of 8,000 people at the Coliseum. This coastal city would become one of AC/DC's strongest American markets. After playing in front of 13,000 people at "A Day for the Kids," a charity date at the Sportatorium in Hollywood, Florida, for radio station WSHE, they made their way into the heartland.

Opening for Foreigner and UFO, AC/DC played at Mississippi Nights in St. Louis, Missouri, on August 9, and at the Memorial Hall in Kansas City, Kansas, on August 10. They appeared at B'Ginnings, a club in Schaumberg, Illinois, and opened for Michael Stanley in Cleveland, Ohio. The next two nights AC/DC opened for the Dictators at the Agora in Columbus, before continuing their drive north toward Wisconsin. Bon wrote home to a friend that he "enjoyed America very much, especially the chicks."

AC/DC were booked to play a campus bar in downtown Madison on Tuesday, August 16, 1977. Technically the fifteenth date of their first American tour, but actually the fourteenth time they played in the States, considering Gainesville had been cancelled.

This monumental occasion would be a life-changing experience for me. AC/DC's appearance at the Stone Hearth in Madison, Wisconsin, fell on the same day The King of Rock 'n' Roll died at the age of forty-two—the end of an era for many, and the beginning of a new one for unsuspecting rock fans around the world. With their gale-force attack using three simple chords, AC/DC were about to change the sound of rock 'n' roll forever.

4

One of the Smallest AC/DC Concerts

The Day Elvis Presley Died

P hil Rudd's candid opinion on their first American tour was stated to *Rock Hard* magazine: "Except in a few cities where we played from the start in large venues, such as Jacksonville, Florida, we played in the worst dive bars this planet has to offer. This has made us strong."

AC/DC had just hit the American shores a couple of weeks earlier, and the fifteenth date on the first leg of their first tour of the United States was at a small campus club in downtown Madison, Wisconsin, called the Stone Hearth. It wasn't anything new for a band to play on a Tuesday night, as in those days, you could see live music somewhere in the city every night of the week. The date was August 16, 1977, the same day that Elvis Presley died.

That hot, sunny afternoon as the radio blared every Presley song ever recorded, I was driving by the local music newspaper that I had just started writing for. I was one of the few female writers, and getting anything bigger than a bar-band review was next to impossible. As I was passing its doors, something told me to pull over and see if I could beg, borrow, or steal another assignment. This was 1977, after all, and most of the women in rock were either on the stage or waiting to catch a rock star behind the stage.

As I walked into the office, my editor, Gary Sohmers, was just hanging up the phone. I eagerly waited for his attention and told him that I was in the neighborhood and thought I would stop and see if there was anything I could do. He replied that he had just gotten off the phone with Stardate, the promotion company based in Milwaukee that booked many of the bands that came through the Midwest. He said that the promoter needed a gofer for the night; someone to fetch drinks and snacks and be of assistance before, during, and after the show. Of course there was no pay involved, but I was told I could get a friend in for free. As they say, beggers can't be choosers, and I jumped at the chance to pick up another assignment, no matter what it entailed. I had time to stop at home, change, and make it to the club by four o'clock, as requested. As I was leaving, I turned around and asked him who the band was. Gary shrugged his shoulders and said, "I don't know, it's some band from Australia called AC/DC." Since I had never heard of them, I didn't think too much about it. Little did I know that after that night, my life would never be the same.

The Stone Hearth was a worn-down rock club in the midst of the university campus. It was a long rectangular-shaped building, with the stage in the middle of the far wall facing the front door. On the right side was a bar, and on the left, seating. Each end had a loft built over it, one with tables and chairs, and the other side closed off for use as a dressing room. As soon as I got there, the promoter sent me out to the liquor store for Blue Nun wine, which was for the lead singer. I only brought back one bottle and was promptly sent out to buy another.

When I got back, I took the bottles up to the dressing area, and helped arrange some deli platters with cheese and crackers, while the band was at a local restaurant eating dinner. Downstairs there was a three-man road crew setting up the show. Not knowing much about the band, or having heard their music, I asked the promoter to see their press materials. He handed me a single sheet of paper with their pictures and a short biography. Their promotion boasted that AC/DC had started brawls from one end of Europe to the other. Backing up that claim to fame were black and white pictures of each band member, none of which looked too happy.

To kill some time, I went back downstairs to watch the road crew set up the gear. I couldn't help overhearing them slagging the U S of A. They had just gotten here, and so far they weren't very impressed. As I listened in, they were laughing about how soft we were in the States, sending our children to school with calculators and the like. As they snickered and bantered about, I slowly walked up to the one with the longest hair and said, "Hey, the airport isn't that far away, can I give you a lift?" Completely shocked but definitely amused, he turned around and asked me who I was. I introduced myself, and as we shook hands, he said his name was Barry Taylor. He was from England, and had just been hired by AC/DC to work the American tour. The other two roadies were Keith Evans and Ian Jeffery, who had just been promoted to tour manager.

Someone said the band was on their way back to the club, so I ran upstairs to make sure all the drinks and snacks were in their proper places. After reading their biography, I certainly didn't want to piss anyone off. Considering their apparent penchant for brawls, I figured the further away

Angus Young wailing at the Stone Hearth in Madison, Wisconsin, on August 16, 1977, the same day Elvis died. Angus' press release stated that he was only nineteen, but he was actually twenty-two years old at the time.   *Photo by Keith Wessel*

from the band I was, the better. So I started to back out of the room, telling this strange group of guys that if they needed anything, to just come downstairs and find me.

Right then a rather intimidating guy with shaggy dark hair and tattoos up and down his arms walked right up next to me, shoulder to shoulder, looked me in the eye, and yelled, "Sit!" I immediately grabbed the first object I could find, which luckily was a chair, and sat down. Then he walked over to the table, and poured two glasses of Blue Nun wine. He walked back over to me, handed me a glass, and said as he extended his hand, "Hi, I'm Bon Scott, you must be Sue." I asked him how he knew who I was. Malcolm, who had walked in and sat down on a couch, laughed and said, "The promoter told us all about you. He said you would give us anything we wanted!" Which got a huge laugh from everyone in the room, except me.

Once I saw them in person, they didn't look all that scary. Bon was about my height, five feet five inches tall with long dark layered hair, lots of tattoos, a twinkle in his eye, and a cute little smile. Even if he wasn't saying anything inappropriate, you could just tell by looking at him that he was thinking it!

Malcolm had long dark hair, parted in the middle, and was no more than five feet four inches tall. His younger brother Angus had long reddish brown hair, blue eyes, and was built just like a little boy. He couldn't have been more than five feet two inches tall. Angus didn't say much, and spent most of his time before the show playing around with his guitars.

Their drummer, Phil Rudd, was five feet six inches or so, and had shorter dark blonde hair, piercing blue eyes, and a mischievous smirk. Cliff, their new bass player, was the tallest in the band, perhaps five feet eight or nine inches tall. He had long dark shaggy hair, fringy bangs, and dark eyes with the thickest eyelashes I have ever seen. As Angus once quipped, they hired Cliff to bring in the women. Seeing Cliff in person, I knew exactly what he was talking about.

After chatting me up with such thick accents that I really couldn't understand half of what they were saying, Cliff asked me to go downstairs with him to get something from the bar. He asked for Smarties, and the bartender thought it was a drink. After several minutes of trying to explain to him what they were, Cliff gave up and went back upstairs. Years later I would learn that Smarties were the English equivalent to our M&Ms. The poor man didn't want a drink; he just wanted some chocolate!

Along one wall of the loft were rectangular windows that ran along the floor. Every time any girls would walk by on the sidewalk outside, Malcolm and Phil would jump up, run over and pound on the glass to get them to look up. Angus, on the other hand, never moved from his position on the couch. After reading in their biography about this little stick of dynamite, I thought to myself, he seems pretty quiet for someone who supposedly blows up on stage. The Hounds, a lackluster band from Chicago, opened the show. The cover was three dollars, and I don't think there were more than seventy-five people in the place, including bartenders.

I spent the Hounds' entire set hanging out in the dressing room with the boys from Down Under. Since I hadn't yet heard any of AC/DC's music, I had no idea what to expect from them as a band. As they started to get ready to play, I went downstairs and found a spot next to the soundboard. Up until this point, I was pleasantly surprised at how nice and engaging they all were. I didn't give it much thought that they would be anything other than your run-of-the-mill rock 'n' roll band. After all, a Led Zeppelin or a Black Sabbath doesn't come along every day. Not until that hot August evening back in 1977.

As the lights went down, the band took the stage. All of a sudden Phil started in with a steady beat on the high hat, accompanied by Cliff's pounding bass. After a few bars, Malcolm joined them, and when Angus came in jamming, the whole band launched into "Live Wire," with their sound taking on an unearthly volume. Bon was standing on the edge of the stage dressed in tight blue jeans, with no shirt on. He looked up into the spotlight, and started to scream . . . *Well, if you're lookin' for trouble, I'm the man to see, Well, if you're lookin' for a satisfaction, satisfaction guaranteed.*

By the time they got to the end of the song, I had backed all the way up against the wall across from the band. The hair on my arms was standing straight up, and I felt like I had just stuck my finger into a light socket. I had listened to a lot of rock 'n' roll in my day, even seeing the Who live, but AC/DC made it sound like they had invented it!

In front of seventy or eighty extremely stunned Midwesterners, the band slid from "Live Wire" into a bluesy, sexy version of "She's Got Balls." Any man who wrote a song about a woman having balls was a man after my own heart. By the end of the first song, I was head over heels in love with them. I was so overwhelmed, I couldn't move from the spot I was standing in. And I couldn't take my eyes off of Bon.

After letting everyone catch their breath, the band rolled into "Problem Child." These lyrics were inspired by Angus, who Bon thought of as "a bit of a juvenile delinquent"—*"what I want I lick, and what I don't I kick, and I don't like you."* The band continued playing at a volume audible in other dimensions, and the sheer energy coming off the stage felt like a freight train rolling right through you.

Within the first three songs, I had decided that Malcolm, Cliff, and Phil were the best rhythm section I had ever heard. In my opinion, they still are today. Angus is an incredible guitar player, able to run all over the stage in a superhuman way without missing a note, but have you ever really noticed what Malcolm, Cliff, and Phil do? Not only are they a relentless powerhouse of swing, but they are a rock 'n' roll rhythm machine.

By now everyone in the bar was standing in front of the band just staring. Just in time for Bon to announce that the next song was called "The Jack." While Angus started the song playing a few notes that fed back, the whole band teased us with a few power chords, before Bon started singing, *"Gonorrhea, I've just had my first dose of gonorrhea . . ."* to the melody of "Maria" from the Broadway hit *West Side Story*.

The band is wailing and Bon is complaining about a chick that gave him the clap. Now Bon's ad-lib lyrics in this song have to take the cake for being the most outrageous of all AC/DC songs— *"She gave me her mind, then she gave me her body, but it seems to me she gave it to anybody, I made her cry, I made her scream, I took her high and curdled her cream. . . ."*

These are the words he sang that night, but are not of course, the same lyrics that are on the recorded version of the song. For the next hour or so, I stood mesmerized by the band. I was riveted by the sound, the beat, the power, the force, and the flash in Bon's eyes. I had been wrong. Once or twice in a lifetime a band like Led Zeppelin or Black Sabbath does come along, and thank God I was lucky enough to be there to witness it.

At the end of their set, Bon dedicated their last song to Elvis, "Who should have played some good hard rock." And that was that. There weren't that many people in the club, but I do believe every single one of them went upstairs into the loft to meet AC/DC. The band was more than cordial, and stood around for quite a while visiting with everyone who wanted to meet them.

I held back, waiting for the room to clear out. I wanted the band, especially Bon's, full attention. As I walked over to him, Bon was sitting on one of the couches relaxing, when he looked up at me, and I said, "God, Bon! You blew my socks off!" He screwed up his face and said, "I did wha?" I explained, "Oh, I'm sorry. Blowing my socks off is a slang term. What I meant is that you were incredible! The band is absolutely amazing!" That he liked, and he smiled and thanked me. I could barely contain my enthusiasm, and I told the whole band that someday they were going to be internationally famous. That statement got a lot of laughs and generated a few smart comments that I couldn't really make out. I continued, "You will be. It will take two to three more years, but you're going to be huge!" Then I blurted out, "Someday you're going to be as big as the Rolling Stones!"

I actually remember the moment I said that, and as it was coming out of my mouth I thought that that wasn't the band I wanted to compare them to. Little did I know that they idolized the Stones, and someday would become the only band in history to ever co-headline a concert with them. When I said that, Angus laughed, pulled off his shoe, and stuck his foot in my face. Looking up at me, he said, "Does that mean then someday I will be able to buy me some new socks?" Yes, Angus, someday you will not only be able to buy yourself some new socks, but your likeness will be embroidered on them, as well.

While I was gushing over the band, their road crew struck the show and loaded the gear into the back of a twelve-foot Ryder van. They were on their way to the next venue. The band was on their way back to the Holiday Inn out on the edge of town. I believe Bon was the one who invited me back to

Another shot of Angus on the move at the Stone Hearth on August 16, 1977, with one of his guitar picks. This night was their fifteenth date on their first tour of the United States, but actually the fourteenth time they played in the U.S. They had to cancel a date on August 4 in Gainesville, Florida, after they realized that didn't have enough time to drive there from their July 30 show in Dallas, Texas.   *Photo by Keith Wessel*

the hotel with them. I politely turned him down, thinking there was no way I was going to get too close to any of the band members. This was one of the best bands that I had ever heard, and I knew they were going to be extremely successful. I wanted to keep them as friends forever, and going back to the hotel would have ruined my image as a serious rock journalist. Now, looking back, I wish I had ruined my image as a serious rock journalist.

As I said goodbye to everyone, Barry Taylor came over and asked me for my name and address, saying that he would keep in touch with me. I found a scrap of paper, and as I wrote my name, number and address out for him, I was silently thinking I would never hear from him again. Barry said they were on their way to Michigan, when they were actually playing in Milwaukee the next night. At least he was headed in the right direction! Before he left, he gave me the only piece of AC/DC merchandise he had, which was a small pin with a picture of two bluebirds hovering over a heart with a lightning bolt through the middle. Not very rock 'n' roll looking, but the image itself actually resembled a tattoo Bon had on his lower stomach.

Brian Schiro, bassist for the local band Punch, and their soundman Richard Kitchen actually went to their hotel to party with them. When Bon and the boys found out that they didn't bring any ladies with them, he wouldn't let them in. Bon screamed over much commotion in the background for Brian and Richard to go away! Unfortunately I have been unable to track down any females who went back to the hotel with them that night. Either they're dead and gone by now, or just not talking.

The next night in Milwaukee, AC/DC played at the Riverside Theater, opening for Head East. From there they drove back through Ohio, and on the night of August 22, their concert at the Agora Ballroom in Cleveland was recorded live by a local radio station and broadcast on the QFM 96 Sunday night special. If you don't already have a copy of this show, you need to find one. It is a rare recording of one of AC/DC's first concerts in the United States. Plus, Bon's ad-lib lyrics in "The Jack" are hilarious.

5

Conquering Two Iconic Venues in One Week

AC/DC Play CBGB and the Whisky

Two days after their show in Cleveland, they made their New York debut as guests of the Dictators at the Palladium, and then opened a midnight show for the Marbles at CBGB on August 24, 1977. The funniest part of this performance is that Bon met the head of Atlantic Records outside the club while he was peeing into a jar. If you have ever used the bathrooms in CBGB, this makes perfect sense.

CBGB's was an extremely small club on Bleecker Street in Greenwich Village, with tons of graffiti all over, no doors on the bathroom stalls, and a small stage for the band to play on. Personally I would love to hear from someone who was in the crowd that night. I can't imagine AC/DC's power being contained within those four walls. It must have been like detonating an atomic bomb in a telephone booth. I bet you could still probably scrape DNA off the plaster from all those who were blasted up against the walls that night!

The New York fanzine, *Punk*, interviewed Bon and Angus, and asked them the very deep question, "What's the meaning of life?" To which Bon replied, "As good a time and as short as possible."

Thanks to an amazing invention by Ken Schaffer, Angus was extremely happy trying out his brand new wireless guitar system. The roadies were even happier. Mr. Schaffer told me, "As I remember Angus's manager at the time was an Australian bloke, and once we got acquainted, I can't remember if this was just before or just after the wireless, he and Angus showed up at my Midtown NYC apartment for the first of a few visits and their intention was to rent the apartment next door. It's a penthouse floor, two apartments . . .

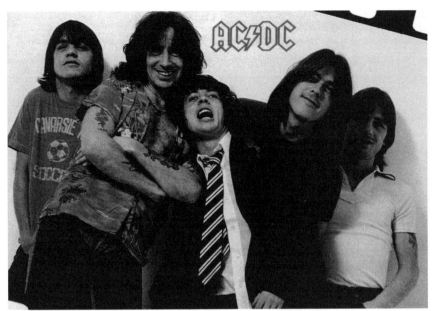

AC/DC color postcard, a rare find in a poster shop long before you could buy AC/DC merchandise. Barry Taylor sent me a light blue shirt just like the tropical-themed shirt that Bon is wearing. I believe they bought them while on the road somewhere in Australia.

I think it would've happened if the apartment hadn't gotten rented out in a flash to someone who outbid the landlord's asking price.

"Another thing I didn't remember at the time but I certainly remember now was on one of my first couple of trips to Glasgow I went to some pub with Angus and Bon and had one single shot of scotch. Next thing I know, I woke up in my bed in the hotel, with no idea how I got there.

"Also, Angus (probably through his roadie) sent a couple of his guitars to my shop requesting that I embed the X-10 SVDS transmitter inside the guitar body itself. And I did . . . I can't remember anybody else ever asking us to do that, though it seems like such a natural thing to do."

After New York, and on their way to California, they played at the Masonic Auditorium in Detroit, Michigan, opening for Johnny Winter and .38 Special. Within two weeks after seeing AC/DC at the Stone Hearth, my first postcard arrived from Barry. The picture was an aerial view of Hollywood, postmarked August 31, 1977. They were booked to play three nights at the Whisky a Go Go in West Hollywood on the twenty-ninth through the thirty-first. This would be their California debut. It is also

A newspaper advertisement for the Whisky A Go Go in Hollywood for August 29–31, 1977. This was the first time they played in Los Angeles, and where they met Gene Simmons, who invited AC/DC to open some shows for Kiss. Notice that Van Halen and the Runaways also played there a couple of weeks before AC/DC showed up.

where Gene Simmons first saw them, and invited them to open for Kiss that following December.

Angus remarked about playing with Kiss to *Guitar World*, saying, "We toured in a station wagon. [Kiss] had everything behind them, the media, a huge show and stuff. And here we were—five migrants, little micro people. It was tough to even get into the show with that station wagon. Many a time they wouldn't let us into the venue 'cause they didn't see a limo!"

While AC/DC were performing with Kiss, my name came up in conversation. It wasn't my name, actually; I think Mr. Simmons's direct quote was, "There's this crazy blonde journalist in Madison, Wisconsin. Sometime you've got to meet her!" Barry said Gene laughed like hell when he heard they already knew me! This prompted Barry to call me from Indiana's Market Square Arena, where they were opening for Kiss. With the band blasting in the background, Barry tried to ask me "What the hell did you do to Gene Simmons?" His question really epitomizes the phrase, "small world."

I told him that it was a long story, but I did reveal that I ran away from Gene, which probably put me in a whole new category with him. In fact, that would be the "crazy category." Not many women ran *away* from Gene Simmons in those days. It was probably the dead tarantula spider encased in plastic as his belt buckle that struck the fear of God into me. That, or the fact that I knew Gene collected pictures of all the women he slept with. And I did not want to be one of those Polaroids that Shannon Tweed-Simmons would burn decades later in a television episode of Gene Simmons' *Family Jewels*.

6

AC/DC's Invasion of America

One of AC/DC's First American Interviews

Everyone loves looking back on the Beatles' first press conference right after they flew into the United States in February of 1964. Their humor, chemistry, and pure magic was evident in how they conducted themselves. They were funny, witty, cute, full of mischief, not at all unlike AC/DC on their first American tour. As a reporter for the *Emerald City Chronicle*, it was my honor to travel to Milwaukee, Wisconsin, on December 4, 1977, to see AC/DC perform at the Electric Ballroom.

It was the second leg of their first American tour, and they were still playing barrooms half filled with people who didn't know what they were in for. The club was actually having electrical problems, and the opening band, Detective, who had just opened for Kiss in Madison the night before, walked out. When AC/DC were asked if they were concerned with starting a fire, Bon replied, "We came here to play, and that's what we're going to fucking do!"

My most cherished memory of that night is Bon looking right at me and my girlfriends while he was singing. Now some of you may own Bentleys, and lots of you might have the bank accounts to match. But standing in front of Bon Scott, with AC/DC soaring around him, and he's looking over at you smiling, with that wicked twinkle in his eye . . . well, as the credit card company says, "that's priceless."

A concert review of this show prefaced the following interview, which included one of my favorite descriptions of Angus: "That mere nineteen [sic]-year-old guitarist of theirs pranced from one side of the stage to the other trailing sweat along the way. He is no flash in the pan axe man. This

Of course, this picture of me with the band remains my all-time favorite. It was taken after they opened for Aerosmith at Alpine Valley in East Troy, Wisconsin, on August 3, 1978. We had taken pictures backstage of the band for the cover of the paper I was writing for. Afterwards, Tom, the photographer, would always tell me to jump into the picture. We got a nice shot of all of us, and Tom said we were done. Right then, Bon leaned his head on my shoulder, looked up and did one of his little squeals. I leaned back on Angus, and I heard the click of the camera. As they say, a picture is worth a thousand words. This one's worth a million.   *Photo by Thomas Giles*

is the boy who's been called a rabid spastic, a caged tiger, a severed worm, cretin-beater, and if that's not enough, is accused of performing with his head wired to the drum kit."

By the end of their set, smoke started pouring out of the air vents above the stage, which caused a short evacuation of the club. Once it was determined it wasn't anything serious, I was lucky enough to sit down with the whole band to do an official interview.

All five band members, my two girlfriends, Bon's girlfriend Silver Smith, and a lady friend of Cliff's crammed ourselves into a small living room that was in the upstairs of the Electric Ballroom. Bon was sitting right next to me on my left. Next to him was his Australian girlfriend, Silver Smith. Next to her were Cliff and a female friend, in a big chair in the corner sat Phil, and on the floor across the table from me were Malcolm and Angus. Most of our conversation I was able to translate, and I think this interview captures their humor and passion, and the sheer craziness of the early days of AC/DC.

Sue: The last time I saw you guys was at the Stone Hearth last August in Madison. How's it been going? How has the reception been since then? You went to Europe, then you came back to the United States, and stuff. Has it gotten better?

Phil: Yes, I suppose. The last tour we did of Britain and Europe, was a few notches above anything we've ever done before.

Angus: This is drummer, Phil Rudd, speaking.

Sue: How do you feel about going on tour with Kiss?

Angus: Well it is, 'cause they're all big guys, they're pretty tall, six foot one. We're all five foot two.

Bon: Yeah, they brought about five dozen hack saws to cut the microphone stands down to our size before we go on. Then mold them back together before they go on.

Angus: Yeah, it should be good.

Phil: We figure we should get some good support.

Sue: Yeah, you will have a lot of good exposure. All the bands that have toured with them so far have really gotten a lot better reception, and things have happened a lot faster because of the exposure that they get.

Angus: And all the young women, too. That is the important part. And I love young women, you know.

Bon: Have you met Angus, Sue?

Sue: I have met him at the Stone Hearth. I met you at the Stone Hearth. Remember, I helped set up the dressing room?

Bon: Well, I'm not quite so audacious as he is.

Sue: He's a little overwhelming.

Bon: High voltage.

Phil: Hey, what's that red light on your tape recorder that keeps going on and off?

Sue: That means that . . . (everyone talking at once), try it out, yeah, try it out.

Sue: What are your plans after this? How long is the tour with Kiss going to be?

Angus: Uh, it's only about five dates.

Malcolm: It's only about five dates. We're not really doing that many, just a few.

Bon: Really, really strategic points, to big crowds. So it doesn't matter, 15,000, 18,000, we're happy, yeah.

Sue: Yeah, definitely! What are your plans after your tour with Kiss?

Bon: We're going back to Australia for about two and a half months. We'll record and play or do about four or five dates there.

Phil: It's just that we've got several birds that we had to leave in some cities in Australia, and we haven't seen them in ages. We haven't toured there; we've got to go around on tour.

Angus: She was a six foot one, eleven-year-old schoolgirl.

Sue: (Laughing) Is that where you got your image from?

Angus: From her, yeah.

Malcolm: She taught him how to be tall.

Bon: She taught him how to stand up.

Angus: Beautiful girl, blonde.

Bon: I love a statue.

Angus: Big six foot one Amazon with two breasts.

Sue: I noticed that you have a cordless guitar now, it looks like it's huh, much easier that way.

Angus: Yeah it is, it's easier, whether it works or not is a little debatable.

Bon: Executions are expensive.

Sue: What are you, with running out into the crowd and stuff, what do you want to achieve the most? What is the best reaction from that? Just getting closer to the people or what?

Bon: Yeah, he smells their armpits!

Cliff: Closer to the chicks.

Sue: You just want them to see what you look like close up?

Angus: Nah, that'd scare them away!

Bon: You've heard of ESP? Well, Angus is ASP. ESP is extra sensory perception, and ASP is ass sensory perception.

Sue: Well, he sweats enough, so. You know.

Bon: He has never been known to smell his own armpits!

Sue: Ah, but the rest of you do! Right?

Bon: Now tell him. (Laughing)

Sue: Well Angus, I'll print it.

Angus: They hate me. They pick on me, all of them.

Bon: Yeah, we'd kill him if he didn't move so fast.

Sue: I noticed it does kind of look like you're chasing him on the stage a little bit.

Angus: That's because he is.

Sue: Every time it looks like you're going to run into each other, you don't, that's what's so funny about it.

Bon: Say that again.

Phil: That's the suspense of it. It's like, "Ahhhhhhhhh!"

Angus: And when we do connect . . .

Phil: Will they, like tune in next week, will they crash together? Will Angus and Bon survive the grueling torment or will it be a fatal collision? And end all!

Angus: Will Angus break a string?

Sue: You've got enough duct tape on that guitar.

Angus: The tape's actually for me.

Sue: Does the tape make it sound better?

Angus: Nah, it's just holding it together. (Laughing)

Sue: I suppose the English and Australian reception is better than the United States, or is it the other way around?

Angus: Ah, it's about the same.

Bon: He who likes you, likes you, who doesn't like us, doesn't come.

Sue: That's a revelation.

Angus: We've got a specific sort of audience, really.

Malcolm: They're very intelligent.

Sue: Really? They're very intelligent?

Angus: Well, you, you came along.

Bon: Yeah, I think you're right.

Malcolm: It fuckin' is. If you fart, you must be intelligent to fart, in front of people that is.

Bon: Only if you fart in key. If we play in C, and I fart in F sharp, it's not on. Some things you just can't perfect. And they all fart, too. (Laughing)

Sue: They get pretty excited.

Angus: Well, you gotta figure for farting.

Bon: Go ahead, because you've been talking for so long, I can't help it.

Angus: Yours aren't the best smelling ones.

Sue: So with all these punk rock bands that are coming out of England, and stuff, how would you categorize your music? You can't be punk.

Angus: A rock band. Just a rock band.

Sue: Just plain rock, huh? I'm not going to get a great description of it, huh?

Malcolm: How would you describe it?

(Bon makes a farting noise, much to everyone's delight.)

Sue: Well, I told him in Madison that it blows your socks off!

Malcolm: It just did!

Bon: Blows your socks off, what do you mean?

Sue: He didn't understand it then, and you don't understand it now. It's just an expression.

Phil: How about blowing your tits off, huh?

Malcolm: What are you talking about?

Sue: If it's really, you know, if it really rocks out, or it really gets you going, it blows your socks off.

Angus: Well, I've got holes in me socks.

Sue: Not too many people do that.

Bon: When I started in this band, that tattoo there, down there, used to be up here.

Angus: A girl in England had sixteen orgasms, one time.

Malcolm: Did she?

Angus: She didn't call me!

Sue: How long have you guys been together?

Cliff: At least seven months.

Angus: He's the newest one.

Sue: You're the newest member.

Angus: As you can see, an ugly cunt, too. Look at him. I'm the good lookin', I'm the sexy one in the band.

Bon: The prick? Oh, you set yourself up for that one, mate. Sorry.

Sue: When you got together, are you doing what you intended to do, musically?

Bon: No. I'm glad you said, musically.

(Everyone cracks up laughing, AGAIN!)

Sue: Come on you guys, you're not giving me nothing here! (Nice grammar.)

Malcolm: Listen, we always wanted to be a Led Zeppelin, but wound up the Monkees!

Phil: We took a wrong "toin" at Albuquerque!

Angus: I always thought we wanted to be the Monkees, and ended up a Led Zeppelin.

Bon: Take that. (He just handed Malcolm the bottle of Jack Daniels he was drinking.)

Sue: What was your main intention when you got together? I mean, don't tell me.

Malcolm: To be filthy rich!

Angus: My main intention was to pay up to the chick down the road. Because she said I was a rotten guitarist when I used to practice at night. And I said, well fuck you! And she still thinks I'm rotten!

Sue: Oh boys, you guys are really helping out, let me tell you. I haven't gotten anything good yet. I want to get some secrets, OK, what are you going to do?

Angus: I'll give you plenty of secrets.

Malcolm: Secrets? Turn the table.

Bon: (Squeals and says something no one understands.)

Sue: No, no. I want to get, ah. All right, are there plans for another album?

Angus: Yes, March, March. Either March or April.

Bon: Or June, or July.

Angus: Nothing very specific.

Bon: Or should we say '76, '77, '78. . . .

Malcolm: Silver, let's do an edition of those snazzy cigarettes.

Silver: For about another week . . . (she hands out cigarettes).

Sue: It's not going to be a live album, is it?

Phil: Can I get one, too?

Bon: We have a live album in the making.

Sue: You do? Ah ha! When is that coming out? You don't want to tell me. You're working on one though.

Bon: Yeah, we're doing it live.

Phil: There's nothing immediate happening. It's just something we're going to do.

Sue: So, after the tour with Kiss . . . you don't know.

Malcolm: It's not only Kiss; there's other things, too, you know.

Phil: We finish on the twenty-second in Philadelphia with Kiss, and we do a few shows in between up until the end of the Kiss gigs.

Malcolm: We're only doing five gigs with that band.

Sue: That should be enough.

Malcolm: And we're doing about thirty, thirty-five gigs in America.

Sue: It should be an experience, though.

Phil: We just finished doing a lot of headlining shows with the band UFO.

Sue: I'm working at it.

Phil: No, no, no what, eight to ten-thousand seaters.

Malcolm: Twenty-eight thousand one night, a hundred the next night.

Phil: Variety's the spice of life.

Sue: Yes, well tonight was definitely not something you'd repeat a whole lot of times, I mean with the power, and Detective walking out.

Bon: Yeah, tonight was pretty quiet. I mean 10,000 people don't make that much noise.

Sue: Did that change your attitude tonight before you went on stage?

Bon: Nah, we hated them before we went on!

Malcolm: Yeah, we'd rather play with ourselves any fucking time!

Angus: Even if there were only ten people there, we'd still go on.

Phil: Your red light is not going on and off.

Sue: Oh yes it is. Yup.

Bon: Thirty bucks. What?

Sue: What?

Malcolm: I've got a hamburger for thirty-five.

Bon: (Laughing) Forty!

Sue: The last time when you were here in August, that was your first United States tour, how did you like it?

Malcolm: Yeah, it was good.

Cliff: It was hot then. We were in Texas to start with.

Angus: And they've got big girls. . . .

Cliff: . . . with big, you know. It was great.

Angus: You should see the size of the ones in Texas! I went out in the mornin' with me lasso, and I brought 'em back. I brought them in.

Cliff: Size forty-twos. . . .

Bon: I got one or two, and this chick had these big tamales on her shoulders, and it burnt, them um . . . tamales . . .

Malcolm: Bon, give me the whiskey.

Angus: Tamales. . . .

Cliff: Tamales. . . .

Sue: I understand you don't appreciate the clubs you've played in in Wisconsin. I don't really blame you. Wisconsin didn't strike you as that great to play in, did it?

Angus: Is this Wisconsin? Isn't this Chicago?

Sue: Yes it is. No, it's a little bit north of that.

Malcolm: This is where *Happy Days*, this is where Fonzie hails from. Imagine the Fonzie sitting downstairs, what a thrill!

Sue: I have a message from the Dingoes. They said to say hello. Karen Tolhurst said to say hello to you, specifically.

Bon: Well, tell them a big hello, uh, miss boomerang.

Sue: Oh, OK. . . .

Phil: Fuckin' hell!

Bon: Is that good, or what? Give me a break!

Sue: Give me a break, oh no, yeah give me a break, why don't you tell me something so I don't have to ask you any more questions.

Angus: What are you doing tonight?

Bon: What are you up to?

Cliff: What do you want to know?

Bon: You ought to know!

Angus: We're at 313.

Cliff: Yeah, 313, we're both at 313.

Angus: You're a bit short for me.

Sue: Do you . . .

Malcolm: Yes!

Sue: Angus, do you do anything, anything specific to get that much energy on stage?

Angus: Yeah. . . .

Sue: I know you kind of, I know you're pretty quiet before the show, but is there any routine?

Sue: You what?

Phil: It starts when he gets out of bed in the morning.

Angus: That's a big event. It starts in the morning, and get out of bed, and you figure, "Why did I get out?"

Phil: See, he loves bed, and by the time it gets to be the time that we get on stage, he's been out of bed for so long, that he's like really, he's really upset and he's thinking about getting back to bed. He reckons he's been out of bed all day, so that's why he's jumps up and down on the stage because he's really pissed off.

Angus: If I can get a woman, we both might get pissed off together.

Sue: How do you like the image that you have of being, well, I'm sure that it was intended, but how do you like the image of being, really you know, I don't know what you'd call it—mean brawlers, you know. Just tearing the stage apart. (Malcolm is grunting and growling at me. Everyone starts laughing.)

Angus: We're not mean!

Phil: If you move that fuckin' truck down, I'll wring your neck! (What?) (Malcolm continues to growl and crawl across the coffee table towards me.)

Sue: Really! I was told that you guys have been in fights, and you're really dangerous!

Cliff: We've never been in a fight. Not one fight.

Sue: It's all promo, huh?

Bon: You're so passive!

Phil: It's all bullshit.

Cliff: We're all into Hare Krishnas.

Angus: I'm a divine ??

Cliff: He's got the third eye, you know. He's amazing.

Bon: Occasionally.

Sue: So do you have any other motive . . . that you would like to . . .

Malcolm: Uh huh.

Sue: All right, let me change that.

Phil: We're also craving sex fiends.

Sue: You know this article is going to be hilarious. It's going to go right along with your promo, you're a bunch of rowdies.

Angus: Yeah, they are, but I'm a nice boy.

Phil: We're all virgins.

Angus: I am. I'm a virgin.

Bon: If you say one thing wrong about us, we'll fuck ya silly!

Sue: Now you're giving me stuff I can't print!

Angus: These are all nasty, these are all nasty people.

Sue: Well that's the image, so . . .

Angus: Yeah, they are. But I'm nice. You could say that Angus is nice, Angus is a nice boy who likes sweet girls, so I can ravage them.

Malcolm: Is that what you call it? (Bon does his best Tarzan yell.)

Cliff: That's the end of the tape, by the way.

Sue: Oh yeah? Nope, it's still flashing. Do you have any other intentions than what you're doing now?

Bon: Many.

Malcolm: Yes.

Sue: Do you have any plans career-wise, except for getting a lot more famous?

Bon: We'd like a lot more money.

Angus: Money? I can do that.

Phil: We were going to buy a couple of countries each, and get our armies out and have war games.

Bon: I'll do your country, and you do mine.

Phil: I've already negotiated with Russia.

Sue: So, what's your impression, do you guys like the punk rock that's around now?

Malcolm: Yeah, great. It's magic stuff.

Bon: We need it!

Sue: You do? Why?

Malcolm: Makes us angry. It makes us play better! In fact, it sucks!

Sue: Now that's the kind of answers I want!

Angus: I, me personally, hate everything.

Bon: I can see the headline now, "They Suck!"

Sue: Oh. No.

Malcolm: I'm the headline sucker.

Sue: No, actually I like your music.

Malcolm: Thank you.

Phil: We're glad.

Cliff: Stupid girl.

Phil: Poor misled child.

Sue: So what have you been doing about promo? I haven't seen that much, but maybe Wisconsin is too isolated.

Malcolm: Well, we put up about 200 photos last night around here. We've been using super glue so people can't take them off.

Sue: I saw that fantastic picture of you and Bon in *Circus*, I think it was, or *Creem*, you were standing on the table.

Bon: I haven't the courage to stand on a table.

Sue: What? Maybe I'm sitting too close, I can't understand.

Malcolm: Hey Bon, let us have the whiskey before you get drunk!

Bon: I think he might of. Now wait a minute. There. On the window ledge, about seven people. I can't, can you? . . . (growls).

Malcolm: Yes, in Wisconsin, we do drink whiskey.

Cliff: Whiskey in Wisconsin.

Sue: I hope this thing is working right . . . Yeah, it is. Every once in a while. There is no grand message you want to get across to the people?

Phil: Yes. Buy more fuckin' records!

Angus: Would you like to marry me?

Sue: (Laughing) It's your turn Malcolm.

Malcolm: Tell her, you can't even find your room key! Actually it's room three. . . .

Sue: Are you getting the kind of coverage that you want?

Phil: Nah, we want front page.

Sue: Why not?

Phil: We'll have front page.

Angus: Well, for a start, I would like long pants.

Malcolm: I'd like something for my ears.

Sue: Something for your ears . . . I can . . . No really, I haven't seen that much written about you, but you know, I keep in touch with the tour and everything.

Phil: They don't like to write about us.

Sue: Well I'm going to write about you!

Malcolm: We'll write about you, too.

Angus: If you come back to my room, I'll write home to Mother!

Cliff: The last thing they fuckin' wrote about us was that we were born in a cesspool!

Sue: They did?

Malcolm: Suspect?

Cliff: Well, whatever. They're wrong! Because I was born. . . .

Malcolm: Hey Cliff, what is a cesspool anyway?

Cliff: I don't know mate, I just read it.

Sue: Do you have any more plans to commercialize at all? Like a lot of people are doing T-shirts.

Malcolm: Yeah! AC/DC makeup.

Cliff: AC/DC knickers.

Malcolm: AC/DC fingernail polish, AC/DC skid marks on your own underpants.

Cliff: Make a fortune!

Malcolm: Fuckin'. . . . AC/DC toilet paper. Once or twice. . . .

Cliff: PTL one side.

Malcolm: Yeah, please turn over.

AC/DC
"Powerage"

There are few groups whose name alone is such a fitting suggestion of the nature and effect of their music as is the case with AC/DC—for this is a band for whom *electricity* has become the by-word. Released in the spring of 1978, the appropriately-titled "POWERAGE" is this Scottish/English/Australian combine's third album release in the U.S. Recorded at their home base of Albert Studios in Sydney, Australia during February and March—with their famed producing team of Vanda and Young at the controls, the LP captures better than ever the fresh aggressive style, the compelling high voltage rock that has already put AD/DC at the top of the charts across Europe, Britain and Australia.

In the beginning, there were the Young brothers—Angus and Malcolm, who formed AC/DC in Australia just over four years ago. With a sound that was raucous and rocky, they built up a strong initial following on the rough pub circuit throughout 1974 and into early '75. As the word spread, it wasn't long before the club crowds were swollen well beyond normal proportions. Following not too far behind were platinum, gold and silver disc awards for their first two Australian LPs, "HIGH VOLTAGE" and "T.N.T." (later combined into one album for their debut worldwide release)—with the records hitting the #1 spot on charts across the country.

After touring steadily for two years throughout Australia, AC/DC (with a worldwide Atlantic recording contract in their collective pocket) arrived in the United Kingdom in the spring of '76. A virtually unknown quantity, it was like starting all over again—as their first show was in a small London pub called the Red Cow (by the second set, the place was packed, as patrons from the early set lit up the switchboard with calls to their friends). It wasn't long before the group had won over the English rock'n'roll constituency with their high-powered stage act. During a highly successful residency at the Marquee Club, they kept breaking their own attendance record week after week. Dates all over Europe followed, with equally ecstatic reaction. By the end of '76 (just as "HIGH VOLTAGE" was hitting U.S. streets) AC/DC found themselves playing at a venue just "down the road" from the Red Cow—for an *sro* crowd at the famed Hammersmith Odeon. Having literally torn up the countryside with their no-holds-barred style, the group was making front page news across Europe.

In December '76, AC/DC triumphantly returned to Australia for an extensive tour, undeniable rock'n'roll heroes. Then it was back into the studio for the recording of "LET THERE BE ROCK," released in the States last spring. As the LP topped European/U.K. charts, AC/DC rocked the Continent again with a massive concert itinerary. Then, at last, AC/DC hit the U.S.A. in the hot summer of '77, introducing themselves to American rockers with a blistering show that made all sit up and take notice. They visited the colonies again in the fall, as "LET THERE BE ROCK" hit the national charts and FM airwaves to great response. As a result of these two initial tours, AC/DC received offers to return and headline in cities across the country, from New York to San Francisco.

As "POWERAGE" makes its presence known, AC/DC begins their 1978 world tour, starting in the U.K. and hitting the U.S. for a three-month series of shows that promise to rival the summer sun for amount of energy released. As Angus describes it, "We like to work up our audiences and leave them to go home with something to remember." Whether it's on vinyl or on stage, AC/DC is one band that you're not likely to forget.

Page one of the official press release sent out with the debut of their album *Powerage*.

Angus: Angus Young snot.

Sue: What is the difference between, like, the English crowds that come to see you and the American ones?

Cliff: Well, they're English and one's American.

AC/DC is:

Angus "has to be seen to be believed" Young Born March 31. 1959 in Glasgow. Scotland. Angus co-founded AC/DC with his brother Malcolm. Apparently, he literally stepped out of the classroom onto the stage, as he still wears his schoolboy uniform in performance (although somehow we doubt that he's particularly inspired by old school ties). Angus, a superb *electric* guitarist, is also known for his highly energetic (might we say compulsive?) on-stage mannerisms—never missing a note while roaming, falling, kicking, running, writhing and sweating...a total showman all the way. Angus co-writes all of AC/DC's music with Malcolm and Bon.

Malcolm "riffmaker" Young Born January 6. 1953 in Glasgow. Malcolm has been called the innovator and "brains" behind AC/DC. He plays airtight. powerchord rhythm guitar, and the others in the band have dubbed him the "riffmaker," as his writing talent has been largely credited with giving AC/DC its unmistakable, intense sound. Malcolm played with a few Sydney boogie bands (the Young family having emigrated to Australia) while literally waiting for Angus to get out of school so they could start AC/DC.

Bon "over the top" Scott Born Ronald Belford Scott on July 9, 1946 in Kirrimuir, Scotland. we have been assured that Bon was once a child, although it's hard to imagine in light of his leering aggressiveness as AC/DC's lead singer. The prolific lyric writer of the band. Bon had been with various rock and R&B groups (as singer/drummer) before linking up with AC/DC. Besides playing, he also worked as a chauffeur for other groups. It was in the latter capacity that he found AC/DC, who decided he was a better singer than driver. Bon has touched our hearts with such tributes as "THE JACK" and "WHOLE LOTTA ROSIE" (the insatiable lady that she is), while also developing into one of rock's great frontmen.

Phil "can I take you for a ride" Rudd Born May 19, 1954 in Melbourne, Australia. the story goes that Phil was nearly born in the back of a delivery van—and he later decided to take his aggressions out on life via the drums. Several local Melbourne groups provided the training ground for his entry into the intensity of AC/DC. Phil's also a car-maniac, and he even holds certificates from England's Brand Hatch race track. Whenever possible, he drives the group when they're on tour, and his hobby has inspired him to go so far as to carry a portable electric model road-racing set with him (which has been set up in Holiday Inns throughout the world). Fortunately, Phil's "driving" skills apply to his music as well, and his expert stick-work provides the rhythmic backbone of AC/DC.

Cliff "I was good looking 'til I joined AC/DC" Williams Born December 14, 1949 in Romford, England, Cliff is the newest addition to AC/DC. He was chosen from over 50 bass players at auditions held in London last year. and his considerable playing experience over the past few years included stints with the English groups Home and Bandit. Besides, as the always sensible (!?) Angus proclaims, his good looks would be sure to bring in the women—a pasttime enthusiastically shared by the entire entourage.

Page two of the *Powerage* press release. Notice that the record company is still claiming that Angus was four years younger than he really was.

Sue: Boy, you guys are easy to interview, let me tell ya. I haven't gotten one question answered.

Bon: That means you have to go tomorrow night, too.

Malcolm: You mean you were like the only person who's ever interviewed us!

Sue: Oh no! Come on!

Cliff: You don't want a straight one, do ya? Like what foods you like.

Sue: No, no, no, I'm not like a *Sixteen* (magazine).

Phil: I use Crest toothpaste.

Angus: I don't use any toothpaste!

Sue: Is that it? You've never been interviewed before and that's the thing? I've never read an interview of you guys.

Angus: That's because . . .

Malcolm: Listen Angus, you're drunk.

Angus: I'm trying to, man. I'm so, I'm incoherent.

Sue: Why don't you interview each other and maybe I'll get more information out of you? Is there anything you wanted to ask Bon, all these years, what is he doing up there, I want to know, I want to know!

Cliff: What are you doing on stage? Why do you continually . . . Why have you got tattoos?

Bon: Cliff, Cliff! (Screams) On stage I am filling a space, and you say . . .

Cliff: No, no, I didn't say that.

Bon: Why do you have a space? Cliff?

Cliff: What?

Bon: Why do you have a space?

Angus: I wear no underwear. I wear thermal underwear.

Bon: Angus Young wears thermal underwear. . . .

Angus: BVDs, BVDs. . . .

Sue: What were you doing before you joined AC/DC?

Angus: Wearing BVDs!

Cliff: Who? Who are you talking to, me? I was a painter, a painter and decorator. I was, actually. I was a painter and decorator.

Sue: You weren't in a band before AC/DC?

Cliff: No, I've never been in a band before in my life. This is my first band.

Angus: I was a homosexual.

Malcolm: No one ever asks me what I do, no one ever asks me what I did before.

Sue: All right. I know you dropped out of school. Right? Did he really do that? Do you have plans on going back and finishing up? Do you think they'd accept ya?

Angus: I'm repenting. I'm repenting. You come sit in my lap and it'll make a great interview.

Bon: I'm going fuckin' home, fuck it. Because this is giving me the shits!

Malcolm: You're being interviewed for the first time in your life, and it's givin' you the shits?

Bon: It's a pain in the ass!

Cliff: Bon come on, don't fuckin' desert us now, come on.

Angus: You're the life of the party.

Malcolm: Come on, Bon! We've been waiting on you all fuckin', we've been waiting for you to put your shoes on! Now you're taking them off!

Angus: If you're not coming back . . .

Sue: Well, I think I got about as much information as I'm going to get.

Bon: We've been waitin' for fifteen years to bring the fuckin' money out, yeah! Bring a little cash, and we'll talk.

Sue: Money? I have to pay for an interview, huh?

Angus: Especially if you have two cents American.

Malcolm: Now that interview's gotta be censored now.

Sue: Oh it will be, believe me.

Malcolm: FYI

Cliff: Is it totally fucked? Is it totally fucked?

Sue: Well, I didn't get a whole lot of real info, but I did get a good insight on how much fun you guys are off stage. You were like that in Madison.

Angus: I'm good to you.

Sue: Real fun loving, and nice, real nice guys. You know, I'm sure I . . .

Cliff: You're really talented guys. You're fucking joking!

While Cliff is talking to me, Angus picks up the tape recorder and before turning it off, says "Hello, hello, hello, hello. . . ." It's not your typical rock 'n' roll interview, or is it? The more I listen to it, the more it just sounds like I was partying with all five band members of AC/DC back on their first American tour, and it was miraculously caught on tape.

If the interview wasn't funny enough, the band's hijinks didn't stop there. We all walked outside to our respective modes of transportation, my 1974 lime green Pontiac LeMans, and their faded yellow Milwaukee taxi. Right after they climbed in, Angus, Malcolm, and Bon jumped out and grabbed my girlfriend Terry. They threw her into the cab, and shoved Malcolm out at me. Laughing, Bon and Angus hopped back into their car and took off. Katy, Malcolm, and I got into mine, and followed them back to the hotel. Katy rode shotgun, and Malcolm sat in the backseat directly behind me, with his arms around my neck. He was supposed to be directing me to the hotel, but had lots of fun trying to cover my eyes and grab the steering wheel. Fortunately the hotel wasn't that far away!

As we were walking up to Malcolm and Angus's room, we passed Bon's along the way. He was leaning in the open doorway, with a great big smile on his face, wishing everyone sweet dreams. Directly behind him was Silver getting ready for bed, completely naked. Which explained Bon's cat-who-ate-the-canary grin. We wished them both good night, and ended up on Malcolm's bed chatting. By this time of night, I don't remember much of what we talked about. I do remember we stayed for a while, as Angus visited across the room with a couple of attractive Amazons he had somehow picked up along the way. After about an hour, we said our goodbyes and left, secure in the fact that Malcolm and Angus would be sufficiently tucked in.

7

With All That Money, Why Does He Play the Same Guitar?

AC/DC and Their Equipment

From the beginning of his musical career, Angus Young has always played a Gibson SG. His first SG was a late 1960s Gibson SG Standard model (exactly dated between 1970 and 1971). It was once retired from the live scene in the late 1970s, and he still plays this original model to this day. On each tour, the selection of guitars varies slightly.

His vast collection includes hundreds of Gibson SGs spanning from every era of early production, including early 1960s (1961/1962 Les Paul SG), 1964 SG Standards, and a variety of late 1960s (1967, 1968, 1969) and early 1970s (1970/1971). Additionally, he can be seen with the mid-1980s with later SG models (various types of 1980s designs). Aside from the original Gibson production, Angus at least on one occasion had a custom SG built for him, by Luthier Jaydee of Great Britain. Other guitar models that he tried and collected over the years include Gibson Les Pauls, Gibson 335s, and Gibson Firebirds, the latter being the guitar of choice by one of Angus' guitar heroes, Johnny Winter.

While backstage on the *Razors Edge* tour, Angus and I compared hands, proving that his pinkie finger is the same size as mine, which is about two inches in length. Angus told me that night that his decision to play a Gibson SG was because it was the only guitar neck he could comfortably fit his hand around.

Angus later explained, "For some unknown reason, whenever I'm playing it's like, being a little guy, where most people bend a note on a guitar, my whole body bends. Then when I hit a chord down at the bottom end of the guitar, I just follow it. Other guys let their fingers do the walking. With me, my body does the walking."

For guitar picks, Angus uses Fender extra heavies, and through his endorsement with Ernie Ball, he has also used custom picks in extra heavy. On the *Black Ice* tour, Angus' picks were extra heavies with the AC/DC logo in black lettering on white on one side and on the other, a color picture of Angus.

Regarding amplification, Angus mainly uses Marshall amps, having used live and in-the-studio models that include, among others, the classic Marshall models 1959, 1987, 2203, JTM50, and JTM45. In recent years, both Angus and Malcolm have also added Wizard Amplifiers to their already vast range of amplifiers. During some of his tour performances, Angus has also had at least one Marshall head running through an isolation speaker box that is stationed under the stage and is fed directly into the PA system, mainly for his solos. Angus preferred to use the JTM50 with EL34 tubes on most of his recordings, only using the JTM45 with 6L6 tubes on the *Ballbreaker* album.

When looking for a thicker lead sound, Angus uses a 100-watt Marshall, as in the earliest days of AC/DC's recording and live performances. Over the years, his solos were often coming through 50-watt guitar amplifiers because it added a tonal warmth to his sound. The amps stacked behind him on stage are usually Marshall 1959 reissue 100-watt heads. Each head connects to two $4' \times 12'$ custom made cabinets. Most of the amps are wisely doctored by amplifier guru Rick St. Pierre.

Describing his fondness for SGs, Angus told *Guitar World* in 1984, "It had a really thin neck, almost like a custom neck. I liked the SGs because they were light. I tried Fenders but they were too heavy and they just didn't have the balls. And I didn't want to put on DiMarzios because then everyone sounds the same. It's like you're listening to the guy down the street. And I liked the hard sound of the Gibson."

Another important part of Angus' performance style, and even guitar tone, has been the use of several wireless systems along the years, starting with the first—probably the most famous one—a Schaffer-Vega Diversity System, developed by inventor Ken Schaffer. The Schaffer-Vega Diversity System, or SVDS, was admittedly the only "effect" Angus has ever used; the unit sports a compressor and clean boost internally (i.e., a device to drive the amplifier even farther allowing notes to sound fatter and sustain longer). Since the use of the SVDS, Angus started using wireless systems systematically live and in the studio, to drive his amplifiers to a richer distortion.

Angus was recently gifted with a replica of the first wireless system he used—called The Schaffer Replica—brought to him personally by Ken Schaffer, the original inventor, and Solo Dallas, a fan of the band for many years. Allegedly, Angus has used the new unit (giving him back his old

Angus Young and Ken Schaffer, who invented the Schaffer Vega wireless guitar system. Angus first started using it in the early winter of 1977, and this picture was taken when Angus visited Ken's apartment in New York City.   *Ken Schaffer Collection*

sound) on the new album the band recorded in Vancouver in the summer of 2014.

As a rock 'n' roll band that started right at the time when rock was popular music and was played through authentic instruments and amplifiers (as opposed to reissues, replicas, clones), it's not surprising that AC/DC started with equipment that is now considered very much sought after. "Vintage" is the term that many of us would use when addressing that type of gear today. At that time, in the early 1970s, that was the most available type of gear. Plugging a late 1960s to early 1970s Gibson SG with humbucker pickups into a Marshall amplifier would achieve very similar guitar sounds to those that are featured on some of AC/DC's earliest albums.

The two main guitars that have been extensively used by the Young brothers are now extremely well-known and recognizable icons: the Gretsch Jet Firebirds and Gretsch Duo Jets for Malcolm and a selection of different Gibson SG Standards for Angus. Although it is hard to say exactly which ones were used inside the studio for any given part, it is entirely possible

Another publicity shot of Angus armed with his trusty Gibson SG, sent out at the time of the release of their *Powerage* album. It's a great example of how his personality changes once he puts on the schoolboy uniform and takes the stage. He once told me, "He's not the God of Rock, he's the Monster!"

that during recent years the Young brothers have been using pretty much the same guitars for recording in the studio as they use for performing live.

Malcolm's favorite guitar is the 1963 Gretsch Firebird, which was a gift from Harry Vanda that he has played since the early 1970s. That guitar is routed for a middle pickup and then left with only the bridge pickup in.

As for Angus, his two "lightning bolt" Gibson SG Standards are a rebuild (using some original parts) of one of his very early guitars that had been rotting because of sweat and stage abuse, and the other one a copy made by Gibson itself. As for his 1969/1970 or 1971 Gibson SG Custom, the black color is either a custom color directly from Gibson or a refinish. The two generally available colors of Gibson SG Customs of that era were in fact, white or walnut. The middle pickup was removed and a white pick guard was installed.

It is also a generally accepted fact that the black 1964 Gibson SG Standard had its original Lyre Vibrola removed (a common destiny of several of Angus' Gibson SGs from the 1960s), and it had been refinished (black) somewhere in the past. Gibson SG Standards from 1964 are well known for being light and easy to play, with a slightly wider fretboard (as opposed to the typical narrower one of the later 1960s that has been Angus' favorite for decades).

As for their amplifiers, similarly to what seems to be true for their guitars, AC/DC likes to achieve a similar sound on stage and in the studio. The microphones used live may differ from the ones used in the studio, though. For instance, on stage the amps might be miked with Audio Technica AT4047s (a type of microphone inspired by the great vintage Neumann U47 FET). In the studio, amp mics include the classic rock combo Shure SM57 and Sennheiser MD421, one of each per Young brother, exactly the same combination of microphones used to track the album *Highway to Hell.*

Throughout his career, Malcolm has used a couple of his old vintage Marshall JTM 45/100 and Marshall Superbass amplifiers that have been his main amps, live and in the studio (with a transition during the late 1970s through other types of Marshall amps, including combos, Marshall Lead Master 2203s, and Super Leads).

Angus has instead brought over a larger number of amplifier types, most likely to mimic what had been used in the studio. They have ranged from Marshall JMP Superleads (1970s-style model 1959 Super Leads), Marshall Plexis, several Marshall JTM45s, and JTM50s (in reissue, Marshall head-boxes) that have on several occasions in the past been used for leads (an Angus Young trademark since about the year 1980), and Wizard amps. It is also known that Wizard amps have been used for the studio album sound both in 100 and 50 watts formats, as well.

A special mention must be made to the fact that the whole range of Malcolm's and Angus' amplifiers have been modified to various extents by the very knowledgeable AC/DC resident amplifier and guitar technician Rick St. Pierre, founder of Wizard Inc.

The only song Malcolm ever recorded playing something other than his Gretsch Jet Firebird is "High Voltage." Because his guitar was broken,

Malcolm had to use a Gibson L-5 on that song, which still bothers him every time he hears it. Angus had to do the same on "Live Wire," playing a Les Paul. But you won't hear it, because as soon as his Gibson SG was fixed, he rerecorded the song!

Bassist Cliff Williams has used Music Man StingRays through Ampeg SVT amplifiers and cabinets. Williams claims he always goes back to the Music Man instrument, which he described as "a tremendous work horse of a bass."

Drummer Phil Rudd has used, live and in the studio, a Sonor drum kit for over thirty years. In 2009, Phil and Sonor teamed up to release a Special Edition drum kit. His drum shells include: Maple Light (ML) shell, Solid Black (Colour Code B), chrome-plated fittings, single lugs, Maple Light tom tom and floor toms with nine plies (6.3 mm, three layers of three plies each), and Maple Light bass drum with twelve plies (8.4 mm, four layers of three plies each). Phil's drum sizes include: 22″ × 18″ bass drum (no mount, designer-style spurs), DB 2218 ML B 13″ × 13″ tom tom (H-Bar mount), DT 1313 ML B 16″ × 18″ and 18″ × 18″ floor toms (designer-style brackets), and DF 1616 ML B.

Equipment Used at Albert Studios: Early Production and *Powerage*

In the early years, when the band recorded their first four albums at Albert Studios in Sydney, there were two studios (recording room/control room combinations): Studio One, with a Neve console, and the other with an MCI J500 (installed later in the late 1970s). Early AC/DC production saw George Young and Harry Vanda directly involved with microphone placement and sound design in Studio One, using the Neve console.

Toward the end of the 1970s and precisely for the production of *Powerage*, the guitar amps were in a third separate room for sound separation (but still allowing for some spillover between each other), where engineer Mark Opitz used a Neumann U47 FET microphone with a 10DB pad on the mic for each Young brother. He would then experiment to find where to place the mikes for the best sound. The band laid down their rhythm tracks as a band, with usually only Angus' solos being overdubbed.

Phil's Sonor drums were miked with a Neumann KM64 pencil mike on the snare drum, which was switched to a Sennheiser MD441 miked from above. Underneath, Opitz used a Electro-Voice RE20 on the toms and a Neumann U87 for the overheads.

Bon Scott used a Neumann U47 FET running through the Neve 1073 mic pre, a mic pre/equalizer module that has been AC/DC's favorite sound module in the studio since their very first years of recording. (They also utilize another widely renowned Neve, the 31106, which is used by the band's production unit to this day.) The signal then went into a big Fairchild compressor (an old AC/DC favorite) that sat on the desk, and then straight onto the tape.

8

Don't You Start No Fight!

The AC/DC Member That Packs the Biggest Punch

L et's face it, AC/DC includes five guys that all have an attitude. I don't think messing with any of them would be a good idea. However, it seems Malcolm Young has always been at the center of most of the major skirmishes. Which makes sense, because Malcolm is the leader of the band, and most likely, the most protective.

Mötley Crüe first met AC/DC when they played on the *Monsters of Rock* tour in 1984. For some reason, Tommy Lee and Nikki Sixx were in a "drunken, biting-people rage tour," as told to author Anthony Bozza, in *Why AC/DC Matters*. Tommy claims that they were roaming the backstage area looking for people to bite, and Nikki chose Eddie Van Halen, who was not at all happy with being accosted by a drunken Sixx. After sinking his teeth into Van Halen, Sixx set his sights on Malcolm, who happens to be about half as tall as Sixx. All Malcolm did was look at him and say, "You fucking bite me, mate, and I will fucking *kill* you." Needless to say, there was no biting of any AC/DC member on that day, or any other.

At the end of January 1975, AC/DC were scheduled to perform at the Sunbury Festival in Melbourne featuring Deep Purple, which had been booked by Michael Browning. When Deep Purple found out that they had to go on before AC/DC, they tried to pull all their equipment off the stage, which would have delayed AC/DC's appearance. One thing led to another and a fight broke out between the band and the roadies, in front of 20,000 people. AC/DC left the venue without ever playing a note.

Michael Browning told the authors of *AC/DC Maximum Rock & Roll*:

> I had the band [AC/DC] at the side of the stage when Deep Purple finished and all of a sudden the riggers arrived and they started

WELCOME TO THE **A C / D C** RAZORS EDGE TOUR 1990-91

    To continue to make this a successful tour, please adhere to the following guidelines:

    1) You should now have one ticket and one **A C / D C** PHOTO pass.
    2) Have your pass highly visible at all times.

    3) Meet at Stage Left during the intermission between the opening acts set and **A C / D C** set. **A C / D C** 's Security Director Bob Wein will coordinate your activities.

    4) Shoot the FIRST THREE SONGS ONLY, unless your pass indicates differently.

    5) Absolutely, **N O F L A S H !!!**

    6) If you are staying for the remainder of the show you will be required to remove your camera from the building. You will be allowed to take you camera to your vehicle and return for the show.

THANKS IN ADVANCE FOR YOUR COOPERATION.

             Mike Andy
             A C / D C Tour Manager

A fun piece of AC/DC memorabilia stating the rules for photographers on the *Razors Edge* tour.

pulling down all the lights. Deep Purple's production manager decided that they were going to take everything that came with them down and the other bands had to wait until something like four o'clock in the morning before they could go on. I just said, basically, bullshit! And I gave my instruction to the road crew to set up and the instruction to the band to start playing. What happened then was, I had AC/DC, my road crew, George Young, and myself in a major brawl in the middle of the stage.

AC/DC promptly left.

David Coverdale told *Blabbermouth* in January 2007, "After a 'less-than-satisfactory performance' by Deep Purple, to a dwindling, rain-sodden crowd, the band left only to hear more music coming from the stage." He said, "Apparently, a young Aussie band had jumped on stage, plugged into our gear and started playing! Well, all hell broke loose, from what I was

Angus Young and Ozzy Osbourne on the night that Angus inducted Ozzy into the UK Music Hall of Fame, November 15, 2005.   *Photo by Brian Rasic*

told. Our roadies (big buggers to a man) wrestled with the young band to get them off our equipment and off the stage. Chaos and frolics ensued."

Of course, the band was a very young AC/DC. "I cracked up when I heard," Coverdale continued, "I thought it was great! And that is how I remember that episode. I worked with and got to know the lads many years later and we recalled that time over a pint or two. Very funny memory!"

On their European tour in Sweden with Black Sabbath, tensions mounted after AC/DC kept blowing Sabbath off the stage. To retaliate, Sabbath kept shortening AC/DC's opening set. One night the sparks finally flew when Sabbath's Geezer Butler pulled a flick knife on Malcolm. As the folklore goes, Malcolm came out swinging and AC/DC were fired off the tour.

Although in *Q* magazine in the "Cash for Questions" fan feature "In Blackened Sabbath: The Official Account of Events," it stated, "AC/DC has come clean about a knife-pulling incident during the group's 1977 tour opening for Black Sabbath in Europe." Malcolm's version of the story: "We were staying in the same hotel, and Geezer was in the bar, crying in his beer, 'Ten years I've been in this band—ten years—wait 'til you guys have been around for ten years, you'll feel like us.' I said, 'I don't think so.' I was giving him no sympathy. He's had many, too many (drinks), and he pulled out this silly flick knife." As luck would have it, Ozzy walked in. He yelled at Butler to go to bed and Malcolm and Ozzy sat up all night talking.

There might not have been fisticuffs with Butler, but Malcolm has also been known to having thrown a punch to a promoter who tried to cheat the band over money, and things got physical between Malcolm and Phil Rudd when Phil was let go from the band.

Bon and Brian have been known not to be afraid to defend themselves, and Phil Rudd gained the nickname Phil "Left Hook" Rudd when he knocked out a guy who was kicking Angus in the head one night at the Matthew Findlers Hotel in a Melbourne. This encounter cost Phil a broken thumb, and although he finished the gig that night, former drummer Colin Burgess had to take Phil's place for a couple of weeks until Phil recovered. His injury eventually required surgery to correct the problem.

After a performance at Reading, England, where the band was not received that well by the audience, afterward AC/DC retreated to the house they were renting on Lonsdale Road in Barnes, outside London. Once inside, George Young lit into Mark Evans over his attitude during the show. According to Evans, the atmosphere got even more negative, resulting in a punch up between George Young (who had flown in from Australia to see them perform) and his two younger brothers Malcolm and Angus. The Reading debacle was the only time AC/DC failed to win over their crowd, not counting various drunk Aussies who frequented their shows back in the early days of playing the Australian pubs.

During their first tour of England, after playing the Lyceum, the band went back to the Russell Hotel and got into a discussion, with Angus declaring that he saw the Beatles live when he was a kid. The story didn't jive with bassist Mark Evans and unfortunately he challenged Angus on the legitimacy of his facts. Angus and Mark didn't get on that well in the first place, so this was probably not the smartest thing for Mark to be doing. The end result was Angus punching Mark in the face, with Michael Browning pulling Mark off of Angus. To no one's surprise, except unfortunately for Mark, he was sacked from the band shortly thereafter.

Former manager Michael Browning told Mark Evans in his book *Dirty Deeds*,

> Malcolm was the thinker, the internal organizer; no two ways about it, he's the boss. It was just Malcolm's grasp of what was going on around him on a business level. As a manager you soon find out who there is in the band that you can have a rapport with, and I sussed things pretty early in the day and I found out it was Malcolm. He, from the

band's perspective, ran the show. If I had something I wanted to sell them, I'd talk to Malcolm first, and from there we'd go and sell it to the rest of the band.

Malcolm once declared, "We were all quite fiery guys in those days and we'd all have our share of getting one too many drops down our necks and things, but generally I don't think I punched Bon because Bon would have fucking punched me back and I would remember that. I mean, I've punched other people. Bon's punched other people."

Former bassist Mark Evans attested to Malcolm's clout by saying, Malcolm is the "the planner, the schemer, the 'behind the scenes guy,' ruthless and astute."

That being said, Malcolm still holds the title for being the member of AC/DC you don't want to mess with.

9

AC/DC's Ladies

The Women Who Influenced AC/DC

Ruby: The First to Be Immortalized in AC/DC's Lyrics

The first lady to be mentioned in any of the band's lyrics was Ruby, whose real name was Wendy. The band met her at a performance at the Moomba Festival in Melbourne in 1976, although other reports claim Bon was "gifted" with Ruby after their performance on the television show *Countdown*, in March of 1975. Either way, "Ruby Lips" left enough of an impression on Bon to be immortalized in the song "Go Down" on their *Let There Be Rock* album.

Rosie from Tasmania

While living at Freeway Gardens, Bon hooked up with the infamous Rosie. Bon's homage to her, in the song "Whole Lotta Rosie," is proof that he had more fun with her than he expected.

The title of "Rosie" is Bon's nod to Led Zeppelin's "Whole Lotta Love." This song is the epitome of how Bon's female conquests inspired his song-writing. If perhaps she wasn't the most memorable encounter while on the road, she was at least the largest. Later, a trimmer Rosie visited with the band while on tour, much to Bon's disappointment, after seeing that her measurements no longer fit the song. Rosie will forever be remembered in the song and in the larger-than-life balloon that inflates every time the band plays "Whole Lotta Rosie."

In *The Story of AC/DC: Let There Be Rock*, "Pyro" Pete, who has worked with the band since 1983, had lots to say about Rosie.

> They love their toys, and everyone loves Rosie! Every now and then there wouldn't be enough room. Venues would vary in size, and I've seen Rosie knock over cymbals and stuff. Then roll over on top of the

drummer. We would inflate her, and then we would have to pull her back while we were deflating her. If we didn't get her pulled back in time, she would land on the drum kit and pull cymbals over, knocking the drummer off the chair. One time I could still hear the bass drum, but all the cymbals were knocked over, and that's all he could play. Drummers are stuck, they can't run away. If you're the guitar player, and you see Rosie deflating on you, you can run! Rosie has definitely caused a fair bit of trouble!

Rosie riding the Rock 'n' Roll Train the *Black Ice* tour.   *Photo by Jim Johnson*

My vintage *Highway to Hell* T-shirt with my press pass from the *Emerald City Chronicle*. If I had known how valuable that T-shirt would become, I would never have worn it, but had it hermetically sealed.   *Photo by Teal Kozel*

Jene and Suzy: Women to the Left of Me and Women to the Right

The only other ladies to be mentioned in their songs are Jean (misspelled "Jene") in "Love Song" ("Oh Jene") on their first album, *High Voltage*, and Suzy, who is mentioned twice in the song "Down Payment Blues," on *Powerage*.

I certainly can't prove it, but while the band was recording *Powerage*, I was in constant contact with their roadie, Barry Taylor, who claimed more than once that he "helped" Bon with some of his lyrics. It is extremely flattering to think that Bon was referring to me, but knowing Bon, I'm sure he had plenty of Suzys in his life.

Barry used to call me from all over the world between the years 1977–80. One day the band stopped at a roadside telephone somewhere in Scotland, I believe in the spring of 1978. Bon followed Barry to the telephone and made kissing noises and other inappropriate remarks into the phone. The more we laughed, the more he would continue, to the point of finally giving up and agreeing to talk again at another time. He did enjoy teasing Barry in regard to me, so it is possible he was referring to me in the song. Unless someone can prove otherwise, I'm claiming it.

The Real Life AC/DC Ladies

The men of AC/DC are very devoted to their wives, children, and grandchildren. During the recording of *The Razors Edge*, Brian Johnson went through a divorce from his first wife, Carol. They have two daughters, Joanne and Kala. Brian is now married to Brenda, a former journalist from Chicago, who shares his love of cars and does some racing on her own. Brian became a grandfather when one of his daughters had a baby boy in 2011.

Angus has been married to Ellen, a model he met in Holland, since 1980, and they have no children. When asked if they have children, Angus has said that Ellen claims she only has one.

Malcolm is still married to his first wife Linda, and together they have a son, Ross, and a daughter, Cara. Malcolm became a grandfather in late 2012 when Cara gave birth to a daughter, Myla.

Cliff Williams married a flight attendant named Georganne, and they had a son, Luke, and a daughter, Erin, who models and acts under the name Erin Lucas. Cliff is now remarried to a lady named Trish (Patricia).

Drummer Phil Rudd has been married at least once, to Lisa O'Brien, and is the father of sons Tommy, Steven, and Jack and daughters Milla, Tuesday, Lucia, and Kora. Phil became a grandfather in 2011 when his eldest son had a baby girl.

10

AC/DC's Largest Concert

Rockin' the Soviet Union

A C/DC performed their largest concert ever when they appeared at the Tushino Airfield outside of Moscow on September 28, 1991, along with Metallica, the Black Crowes, and Pantera. AC/DC were invited to play a free show for the youth of the Soviet Union. The event was staged as a gift to the younger generation for their resistance against a recent failed military coup. It was called a "Celebration of Democracy and Freedom."

Brian Johnson explained in his book that the band got a call just three days prior, asking them to come to Russia to perform. "Boris Yeltsin had just outcouped a coup and was standing on a tank promising the young people who had stood by him anything they wanted. 'AC/DC!' they screamed." So within three days, they managed to get six buses, twelve trucks, and the band from Barcelona, Spain, to Moscow to play for their Russian fans. Half a million people were expected, but an estimated 1.2 million showed up.

AC/DC were invited due to the high demand for their music, which up until then could only be purchased on the Russian black market. Their concert was also filmed by Wayne Isham, for a projected live album.

Although it was a bright sunny day, the promoters were concerned for the weather. With one million people gathered in one place, the last thing they wanted was to be rained out. That's when the Russian government used the latest in weather control technology. Tour manager Mike Andy, told me for *The Story of AC/DC: Let There Be Rock* that he remembered the intense security provided for the event. Andy was told by the government that they would make certain there would be no rain. He explained, "Moscow has weather similar to the northwest of the US, very rainy, like Seattle. Well, thank God we don't have hundreds of troops marching around Seattle like they do in Red Square. After telling us it wouldn't rain, the Russian government promptly ordered fighter jets to 'seed' the clouds above Tushino Airfield, guaranteeing no rain for at least six to eight hours, something they commonly did, so their troops wouldn't get rained on. That night it didn't pour until less than an hour after the show was over." Or as Brian confirmed, they used a "Russian secret vepon."

A collector's edition of the *Ballbreaker* tour book.

With one million Russian rockers let loose to party, things went along peacefully until the band pulled out the cannons in "For Those About to Rock." Angus said, "When the military heard the cannons, they really freaked. You saw their mouths drop. You almost heard them say, 'We've been tricked! It's a dirty imperialist trick!'"

While on stage, Brian declared, "Opera and ballet did not cut the ice in the Cold War years. They used to exchange opera and ballet companies and circuses, but it takes rock 'n' roll to make no more Cold War." Afterwards he stated, "Boy, were we nervous. There weren't any change rooms. There were just army tents with duck boards on the bottom of them. We were pacing up and down and taking a quick leak round the back of the tent. Every time I went out to take a leak, there'd be CNN or the BBC saying, 'What do you

One of the many advantages of getting backstage at an AC/DC concert: being able to save the *Razors Edge* poster from the band's dressing room door once the show was over.

think of this?' 'What do I think?' I said. 'You've got to be kidding. I'm not thinking anything at the minute. I just want to get on (stage).'"

Back in the States, *Newsweek* wrote, "Just what are the East Germans who flock across the crumbled Berlin Wall spending their money on? While champagne and fresh fruit were once hot items, recorded music is becoming the purchase of choice. Business in West Berlin record shops went up 300 percent. The top sellers: AC/DC and the *Dirty Dancing* soundtrack."

AC/DC's Wealth of Material

Albums, DVDs, and Songs

Starting their recording career in Albert Studios in Sydney, Australia, in early 1974, AC/DC were produced and guided by Angus and Malcolm's older brother George Young and his recording partner, Harry Vanda. Their first four albums were recorded there, and under the wing of George Young, Angus and Malcolm were taught to stick to their guns, play the way they wanted to play, and never forget that they were a rock 'n' roll band.

And that is the point. AC/DC has been and always will be a band who writes and plays rock 'n' roll because they love it. They are the masters of keeping it simple, and not taking themselves too seriously. No matter what they have endured over the past four decades, they kept going, never looking back, and never letting their critics get to them.

Commenting on the endurance of AC/DC's music, Joe Matera stated, "It is because the music connects with the everyday person, the working class, the underdog, and those of all walks of life, as it provides a means of not only entertainment but something to identify with. We all have an innate desire to belong, and I think AC/DC tap into this at the basic level of each one of us."

And so it goes. AC/DC's music can always be depended upon. When you hear their music, you are always going to feel better, you're going to remember what it is like to be young, and you're going to be dancing or at least tapping your foot—exactly what rock 'n' roll is all about. If there is any band out there that is the personification of that, it would have to be AC/DC. If you're not sure about that, just have a listen.

High Voltage

Members: Angus and Malcolm Young, Bon Scott, Mark Evans, Phil Rudd

Produced by: George Young and Harry Vanda at Albert Studios

Released in: Australia and New Zealand by Albert Productions/EMI Records on February 17, 1975

Cover art: A cartoon of an electrical box behind barbed wire, with the words "AC/DC High Voltage" on it, featuring the lightning bolt between "AC" and "DC" for the first time.

High Voltage (Australian Version): Their very first album, and the record company didn't like the cover, especially the dog lifting his leg for a leak. Reportedly Bon went into the company and charmed them into accepting it. He was a pretty persuasive guy when he put his mind to it.   *Jim Johnson Collection*

Next to the electrical box are beer cans strewn on the ground and a dog lifting his leg to take a leak. Supposedly the record company was none too happy about the cover art, but Bon Scott went in and charmed the record executives into accepting it.

Albert Studios was located in the old Boomerang House on King Street, which also housed the radio station 2UW. The band recorded in Studio One, which was a small room with bare brick walls. They used the side room, where they set up two Marshall stacks and a bass rig. The drums were located in the other room, which was once a kitchen. Most of the songs were recorded live, within the first few takes. On their very first album, which was recorded in ten days, Angus and Malcolm traded off playing lead.

Malcolm playing lead guitar on four songs was explained by Angus. He said, "Mal played solos on four tracks from our first album, when the two of us had traded off. Mal is a good soloist. He can probably do what I do quite well. He plays lead like he would play rhythm, and that doesn't sound like anyone else. When we used to trade licks, it was always the same way. He's a very good performer, the heart of the band. I sit and watch him play rhythm, and I go, 'Ah, I'll play that now.' I'll try to copy what he's doing."

Albert Production's A&R manager Chris Gilbey commented on the first version of the album *High Voltage* in Heather Miller's book, "The album went on to become an even bigger hit without the song 'High Voltage' on it! And by the time we had sold a load of albums we were ready to release the next full-length, which did have the song on it, but of course had a different name and that second album was an instant hit. Amazing hit!"

Their first four albums were recorded at Albert Studios in Sydney, where the control room walls and ceilings were painted black. Mirror tiles were installed on the walls around the drum kit for a bright sound. One whole wall was covered in graffiti from all the musicians that recorded there, and in a smaller room stood a Yamaha grand piano.

Harry Vanda once said, "There was always that sort of immediate, spontaneous thing. They all used to be together in one room anyway, all the amps lumped in one room with the drums! I suppose it was a recording nightmare, but it worked."

High Voltage Tracks

"Baby, Please Don't Go"

"She's Got Balls": When Bon's ex-wife Irene complained to him that he never wrote a song for her, he wrote this song for her, and when she

High Voltage (International Version): Although this album contained more songs from *T.N.T.* than it did *High Voltage*, they called it *High Voltage* and started utilizing the lightning bolt that would become part of their trademark.   *Jim Johnson Collection*

asked him to choose between her or the band, well, you know how that turned out.

"Little Lover": Came from a song that Malcolm originally composed at the age of fourteen.

"Stick Around"

"Soul Stripper": Malcolm plays lead.

"You Ain't Got a Hold on Me": Malcolm plays lead.

"Love Song (Oh Jene)": Within this song title, the name should have been spelled "Jean," instead of "Jene."

"Show Business": Malcolm plays lead.

T.N.T.

Members: Angus and Malcolm Young, Bon Scott, Mark Evans, Phil Rudd

Produced by: George Young and Harry Vanda at Albert Studios

Released in: Australia by Albert Productions/EMI Records on December 1, 1975

Cover art: Features a picture of two railroad ties with the letters "T.N.T." branded on them.

Producer Harry Vanda recalled, "I suppose there might have been one or two tracks on the first album, a few things that they were experimenting with, which probably later on they wouldn't have done any more. So I suppose you could say that *T.N.T.* was the one that really pulled the identity—like, 'This is AC/DC, there's no doubt about it, that's who it's going to be and that's how it's going to stay.' Once you know an identity, then you know what not to do."

When *T.N.T.* was released, it became an instant hit, played on all the radio stations across Australia. AC/DC were still living in the band house on Lansdowne Road in Melbourne, Malcolm recalled, "Everything was taken care of: there'd be a knock on the door at three in the morning and a bunch of waitresses just off work would be there with bottles of booze, a bag of dope, and everything else. Never a dull moment. The cops used to come around because of the noise and the smell of the dope, but they let us alone. They'd just go, 'Oh, can I have a go on the drums?' You name it, it happened in that house. We were poor but living like kings!"

To promote AC/DC's sophomore album, *Countdown* shot a video of the band playing "It's a Long Way to the Top (If You Wanna Rock 'n' Roll)." The song was #5 on the Australian charts, and the band lip-synched their way through Melbourne on the back of a flatbed truck, accompanied by three professional bagpipers, lots of fans, and a camera crew.

Later, they were filmed in a rock quarry in the western suburbs of Melbourne playing "Jailbreak." Paul Drane directed the videos for "Jailbreak" and "It's a Long Way to the Top," using a budget of only $5,000. Drane was quoted in Peter Wilmoth's book, *Glad All Over: The Countdown Years, 1974–1987,* "We had a set in a quarry where we could use explosives. Our special effects guy was thrilled because in those days there wasn't a lot of opportunity for that sort of stuff. Part of the set blew up and you can see me in the clip running away. Bon Scott was in the foreground, just before the bit where he got shot. A makeup artist had put some pellets in his back.

Nobody got hurt, but Angus, who was standing on a rock playing guitar, got a bit of a fright during one of those bangs."

In the August 2001 issue of *No Nonsense*, Australian fan Rob Tognoni remembered seeing AC/DC right after *T.N.T.* was released: "Well, the shock that you could have seen on my face and the faces of everyone in the place when the first glimpse of Angus, silhouetted by an intense strobe behind him, launched into 'High Voltage' would have been a sight. We had never heard such incredible volume before. I made my way to the front row and stood in stunned disbelief of what I was witnessing. All I could think was 'Fark!!!!' Bon leered from stage left clutching the microphone in one hand and stretching the cable looped in the other."

T.N.T. sold 11,000 copies in the first week of its release, reaching #2 on the national charts. Within weeks, *T.N.T.* was certified triple gold, with the release of their next two singles, "T.N.T." and "Rocker."

T.N.T. Tracks

"It's a Long Way to the Top (If You Wanna Rock 'n' Roll)": This song title was spotted by George Young in Bon Scott's folder of lyrics, which was always filled with Bon's own life experiences. He was very keen to his surroundings and was constantly capturing phrases and titles for future songs. The song has now been added to the National Registry of Recorded Sound of Australia.

"Rock 'n' Roll Singer"

"The Jack": This song was written by Bon lamenting the band's sexual adventures, which included contracting an all-too-common STD once known as the clap, or for those in Australia, the jack.

"Live Wire"

"T.N.T.": The band was stuck on writing the chorus to this song when George Young heard Angus chanting the title in the background, and suggested they keep doing it. You can also clearly hear Malcolm singing along to the chorus, with his unique voice making it sound all the more menacing. Bon lifted the line "I'm dirty, mean, mighty unclean" from an Aussie television ad for a mosquito spray.

"Rocker"

"Can I Sit Next to You Girl": Malcolm plays lead.

"High Voltage": This song made it to #6 on the Australian charts. The album of the same name had sold more than 70,000 copies, but once the single was released, the album sales shot up to 125,000 copies.

"School Days"

T.N.T. (Australian Version): This album was only released in Australia and New Zealand, and the cover shot was a nod to the explosiveness of their music. That and the artwork must have been extremely economical.   *Jim Johnson Collection*

High Voltage (US/British Version)

Members: Angus and Malcolm Young, Bon Scott, Mark Evans, Phil Rudd

Produced by: George Young and Harry Vanda at Albert Studios

Cover art: A picture of Angus in his schoolboy uniform, guitar in hand and a lightning bolt striking his foot.

Combining their first two albums, this version of *High Voltage* was released by Atlantic in the UK and Europe on May 14, 1976, and by Atlantic Records on September 28, 1976. The first album deal with Atlantic Records was for a mere $25,000 advance with a twelve percent royalty rate. It was a one-album deal with an option for two more albums each year, with four more options.

Years later, *Billboard* magazine would declare, "*High Voltage* as 'the blueprint' for a rock subgenre the band would pioneer and shape over the next three decades," adding that the record possessed "every single one of AC/DC's archetypes." By the end of the year, *High Voltage* was certified triple gold in their homeland of Australia.

High Voltage Tracks

"It's a Long Way to the Top (If You Wanna Rock 'n' Roll)"
"Rock 'n' Roll Singer"
"The Jack"
"Live Wire"
"T.N.T."
"Can I Sit Next to You Girl"
"Little Lover"
"She's Got Balls"
"High Voltage": The chord progression in the chorus of this song is actually
     A, C, D, C, which was suggested by big brother/producer George Young.

Dirty Deeds Done Dirt Cheap

Members: Angus and Malcolm Young, Bon Scott, Mark Evans, Phil Rudd

Produced by: George Young and Harry Vanda at Albert Studios

Released by: Albert Productions/EMI Records in Australia and the UK in September 2, 1976

Cover art: The album cover was a caricature of Bon swinging his tattooed arm, and Angus flipping the bird.

Angus came up with the album's title, which was taken from the cartoon *Beanie and Cecil.* The villain, Dishonest John, used to carry a business card that said, "Dirty Deeds Done Dirt Cheap. Holidays, Sundays, and Special Rates."

Dirty Deeds Done Dirt Cheap Tracks

"Dirty Deeds Done Dirt Cheap"

"Ain't No Fun (Waiting 'Round to Be a Millionaire)"

"There's Gonna Be Some Rockin'"

"Problem Child": Another song Bon claimed was inspired by Angus.

"Squealer"

"Big Balls"

"R.I.P. (Rock in Peace)"

"Ride On": The AC/DC song that could be the closest they've ever played to a ballad.

"Jailbreak": During the recording of "Jailbreak," Bon worked so hard in the vocal booth to get the song down that he kept guzzling Green Ginger

Dirty Deeds Done Dirt Cheap (Australian Version): A caricature of Angus flipping the bird, and Bon throwing a punch. A perfect portrayal of their "love us or we'll hate you" attitude.

Jim Johnson Collection

wine. Each time he tried to record the line, "With a bullet in his *back!*" they would ask him to redo it. After so much singing, with guzzling wine in between, when you hear that space right after the word "back," there was silence in the vocal booth. Bon had passed out. He recorded the rest of the song the next day.

Let There Be Rock

Members: Angus and Malcolm Young, Bon Scott, Mark Evans, Phil Rudd

Produced by: George Young and Harry Vanda at Albert Studios

Released in: Australia by Albert Productions/EMI Records on March 21, 1977. Atlantic Records released it in the United States on June 23, 1977, and the UK on October 14, 1977.

Cover art: Features the band live on stage, and for the first time includes their official logo.

Let There Be Rock was recorded over several weeks during January and February of 1977. The album cover depicted the band's logo, which was designed by Gerard Huerta, who had been commissioned by Atlantic Records' art director Bob Defrin.

Malcolm told *Metal CD*, "I suppose we were a bit more serious and we wanted a rawer sound and cut out the commercial choruses like 'T.N.T.' We knew exactly what we wanted, which was to have three really strong live tracks to flesh out the set. 'Whole Lotta Rosie,' we knew would be a surefire winner, and 'Bad Boy Boogie' and 'Let There Be Rock' were the other two we felt would really go the distance on stage. Those three have really overshadowed most of the other songs on the album and ended up in the live set for years after."

Malcolm elaborated to journalist Murray Engleheart,

> We could go in the old days, set up the kit and the amps, be in there two hours, we're knocking out tracks. We used to come in from the gigs, we'd work five or six gigs a week, finishing at about two in the morning, then drive down to the studio . . . we'd have a party and rip it up, get the fast tracks, stuff like "Whole Lotta Rosie" and "Let There Be Rock," done right so it was the same loose feeling like we were still on stage. The studio was just like an extension of the gig back then.

Producer Harry Vanda added,

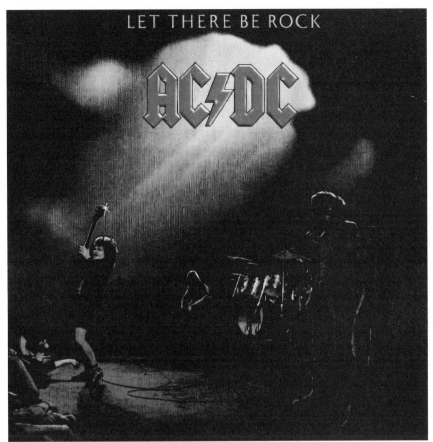

Let There Be Rock: The first album to actually show the band on stage, featuring the band logo that they still use today. Commissioned by Atlantic Records' art director Bob Defrin, it was designed by graphic artist Gerard Huerta. *Jim Johnson Collection*

Spontaneous is basically the word. I suppose we were talking at the time about no-bullshit rock 'n' roll, we meant it! Balls everywhere! Not like the Americans' no-bullshit rock 'n' roll, which takes two years to record. [The band] had very, very, different ideas what it is they wanted to be. And so did we. In that field, you're always looking for bigger and better bass drums, bigger and better snare drums, and as a result everything comes up with it.

We never worried that much about whether things were that correct as sounds. To us, it was always more important whether it had the balls and the atmosphere, you know, whether it had the heart. So if we had to choose between a take which had all the heart and it was farting and buzzing and all that, we'd go for that, because we'd prefer that to the sterile version, which might have been correct but it was boring. On *Let There Be Rock*, we managed to marry a few of those things where the sound was good as well, plus the performances were all there. We tried to capture that energy they had on stage. You had to get them at the right time, when they were really fired up.

Angus concurred, "We got in there and did 'Let There Be Rock,' 'Whole Lotta Rosie,' most of them. We used to go in with a few ideas, and then really do the big percent of it in the studio, arrange it and everything. In the early days, we didn't even rehearse. Nowadays we try to save time. We don't like spending too much time in the studio. We get the band together in rehearsals, try and get as many songs as possible, and then take them into the studio."

On Bon's writing style, ex-tour manager Ian Jeffery told author Murray Engleheart,

> The lyrics were sketchy but that's the way Bon did it. It was like a little notebook that he'd flip over and make a few notes, scribble one or two lines, cross them out, add one thing, sometimes one word would change, or he'd write two words on one page. Bon was quite organized. He had a folder with all [his potential lyrics] inside. Believe it or not, Bon used to come to work with a folder and he'd leave with it. That was his life. That was Bon. And he'd have postcards in there that he was writing to people. He was the best communicator in the world.

Let There Be Rock went gold immediately, and had sold over two million copies by the end of the seventies. *Billboard* magazine stated, "Shaved down to the bone, there are only eight tracks, giving [*Let There Be Rock*] a lethal efficiency . . . It has a bit of a bluesier edge then other AC/DC records, but this is truly the sound of the band reaching its peak."

Let There Be Rock Tracks

"Go Down"

"Dog Eat Dog"

"Let There Be Rock": Phil Rudd nailed his drum parts for this song on the second take. This is also the same song during which Angus' amp started spewing smoke, but George waved him on to keep playing.

"Bad Boy Boogie": This song became the anthem for Angus' infamous mooning the audience during their live performances. Angus dropped his pants for the first time at the Bondi Lifesaver in Melbourne on March 27, 1976, right before they left Australia for the first time on a tour of England.

"Problem Child"

"Overdose"

"Hell Ain't a Bad Place to Be"

"Whole Lotta Rosie": The song lyrics, written by Bon, were in tribute to a Tasmanian lady who sported the measurements 42-39-56. Angus recalled, "We'd been in Tasmania and after the show Bon said he was going to check out a few clubs. He said he'd got about 100 yards down the street when he heard this yell: 'Hey! Bon!' He looked around and saw this leg and thought: 'Oh well!' From what he said, there was this Rosie woman and a friend of hers. They were plying him with drinks and Rosie said to him: 'This month I've slept with twenty-eight famous people,' and Bon went: 'Oh yeah?!' Anyway, in the morning he said he woke up pinned against the wall, he said he opened one eye and saw her lean over to her friend and whisper: 'Twenty-nine!' There's very few people who'll go out and write a song about a big fat lady, but Bon said it was worthy."

In 1981, the June issue of *Kerrang!* voted "Whole Lotta Rosie," as the top heavy metal song. Regarding this song, Malcolm said, "We were always big fans of early rock 'n' roll , like Elvis and 'Heartbreak Hotel,' things like that, the stop and start things, the dynamics. If anything, for 'Whole Lotta Rosie' we were looking for a feel like Little Richard, a good old steamin' rock feel, and see what we could lay on top with the guitars. It evolved into that, but you're just looking for the vibe, what's exciting and that's what we were listening to. Simple to put together, but still around like a classic."

Powerage

Members: Angus and Malcolm Young, Bon Scott, Cliff Williams, Phil Rudd

Produced by: George Young and Harry Vanda at Albert Productions

Released by: Atlantic Records in the UK on May 5, 1978, in the US on May 25, 1978, and in Australia on June 19, 1978

Cover art: A picture of Angus with exploding wires coming out of his jacket sleeves in place of hands, and on the back a great, if slightly menacing, group picture. You may notice that Phil is showing off his southern solidarity by sporting a lone star state T-shirt. And I don't have to remind you how much they liked their Texan tamales. Their love affair with Texas continued into the Brian Johnson era when Brian mentions Texas in the lyrics of "Thunderstruck," on their *Razors Edge* album.

Powerage: Many cite this record as their favorite AC/DC album, including Malcolm Young and Keith Richards. The cover features Angus electrified, complete with wires coming out of his sleeves instead of hands. Notice that on his coat is the old logo that used to be on all of his school-boy jackets.   *Jim Johnson Collection*

This album happens to be Malcolm's favorite, and it's also a favorite of Keith Richards. Malcolm stated, "I know a lot of people respect it [*Powerage*]. A lot of real rock 'n' roll AC/DC fans, the pure rock 'n' roll guys. I think that's the most underrated album of them all."

Angus stated to author Paul Stenning, that he "always thought that album set us apart from a lot of other bands." Malcolm also told *Metal CD*, "That album was more of the same, except our original bass guitarist Mark Evans had quit and Cliff Williams had joined. We were happy to stay in the same area as *Let There Be Rock*, because all that stuff was going down so well on stage. 'Sin City' was the big one on *Powerage*, and we're still getting some mileage out of it when we play it live even now."

This album marked the premiere of new bassist Cliff Williams, who was delayed making it to the studio due to visa problems. Roadie Barry Taylor waited to leave England until Cliff got his paperwork straightened out, so they could fly to Australia together. Barry called me from London on February 15, 1978. He and Cliff were hoping to leave for Australia at any time.

A week later, the band and road crew finally checked into the Corban Hotel on Coogee Bay Road in Sydney to ready themselves for recording their fifth album. They spent most nights recording and then went out fishing as the sun came up, before catching any sleep. Barry wrote about rearranging their rooms to make things more comfortable, including adding plants, Phil's rather large stereo, and a cooler to keep them in fresh cheese sandwiches and fruit.

He was quite excited about the new album, stating in a letter to me, "The stuff they've been putting down in the studio has been excellent. They've got some very good, strong songs together. I think the album will go down very well. I'm pretty sure that you'll love it, the whole thing is a lot more powerful and much classier, not just crash, bang, wallop!"

I also received a letter at the *Chronicle* (the newspaper where I was working at the time) from Coral Browning, on the progress of *Powerage*, dated February 24, 1978. "From all reports in Sydney the boys are putting down the best rock ever. They'll be in Albert Studios for another month, then go to England in April and hopefully the US tour will start in May. Will advise as confirmed dates come in."

I received another letter from Coral, dated March 10, 1978. It was a relief to discover that she actually liked my article. Of course for a writer, it was the ultimate compliment coming from someone so close to the band. "Dear Sue, Well today I at last received the right issue with the article on AC/DC—thanks a lot—it's great—most amusing—you wrote it well. I hope when they return sometime in May, you can do another piece. I'm sure they'll be doing Milwaukee again. They should be in the US for the whole summer—so it's going to be hot! I just got a postcard from Barry and Cliff, they are thoroughly enjoying Sydney and they say the album is sounding fantastic—I can't wait to hear it."

New engineer Mark Opitz explained to author Jake Brown how he set up the equipment for that album. "I went through every Marshall amplifier and speaker box, and tested each amp against not only each box, but each speaker. I did that every day until I came up with what I thought was the right amp top and right speaker box for Malcolm, and the right amp top and right speaker box for Angus. They were J&P Marshalls with Celestion speakers. I remember I had a notebook where I cross-referenced everything I liked until I matched everything up. That's how we did the whole record, and we had great amps and speaker matches."

Angus was very happy with *Powerage*, stating, "I like the album. I think because it has got a good mix for me. You've got rock tunes, but you've got a few things in there that are different."

Circus magazine declared that "*Powerage* shows AC/DC to have evolved . . . to full-blown competence," and gave the credit to "mainly Angus and his brother Malcolm, who maintain a deliciously fat and nasty two-guitar sound throughout the album." Upon its release, Angus was sent to Australia to promote *Powerage*, and their new single. He quipped, "We drew straws to see who would come and I lost."

By the end of 1978, *Powerage* had sold 150,000 copies, making it AC/DC's first gold album here in the States. The record reached #13 in Britain, and for the first time, made it into the Top Fifty on the American charts.

Powerage Tracks

"Rock 'n' Roll Damnation": This song was recorded after the album was finished to satisfy the record company, who felt there wasn't a hit single on the album, much to the band's dismay. That is why some of the first pressings of *Powerage* released in the UK don't include this track. When it was included on the UK release, the song made it up the charts to #24, making it their first hit single in the United Kingdom.

"Down Payment Blues": This is the song that mentions the name "Suzy," supposedly a nod to Barry from Bon, in regard to his fondness for me.

"Gimme a Bullet"

"Riff Raff"

"Sin City": Although the record company didn't believe that there was a hit single on the album until the band added "Rock 'n' Roll Damnation," this song became a huge hit for the band. It was the song they played when they debuted on the American television show *The Midnight Special*, and Malcolm later said, "It was the big one on *Powerage*, and we're still getting some mileage out of it when we play it live."

"What's Next to the Moon"

"Gone Shootin'": Some believe this song was written about Bon's girlfriend Silver Smith, who was known to use heroin. In the very early days, Bon did try heroin once and overdosed on it. After that scare, he was more than happy to stick with Jack Daniels.

"Up to My Neck in You"

"Kicked in the Teeth"

"Cold Hearted Man": This song only appears on the European version of *Powerage*.

If You Want Blood (You've Got It)

Members: Angus and Malcolm Young, Bon Scott, Cliff Williams, Phil Rudd

Produced by: George Young and Harry Vanda and recorded live on April 30, 1978, at the Glasgow Apollo Theatre in Scotland

If You Want Blood (You've Got It): Yet another AC/DC album cover that caused controversy, because of its graphic impaling of Angus with his own guitar. At this point in their career, they had been on the road for so long, the album title made perfect sense.   *Jim Johnson Collection*

Released by: Atlantic Records in the UK on October 13, 1978, the US on November 21, 1978, and in Australia on November 28, 1978

Cover art: A surreal picture of Angus being impaled by his own guitar. Considering the grueling schedule they had endured since early 1974, giving blood was the least of it.

Malcolm told *Metal CD* that the live LP reflected "exactly where we were at that stage of our career. That record summed up the band perfectly and it was recorded at one of the last gigs from that tour, at the Glasgow Apollo."

Engineer Colin Abrahams recalled mixing the album to *No Nonsense*: "I do remember the arrival of the master tapes for the *If You Want Blood* album.

I had to do twenty-four-track safety copies before they were mixed down. The tapes came in on massive fifteen-inch spools. While the tapes were being copied I turned up the faders on the desk to have a listen and check things . . . I remember the sound was awesome! There was an unbelievable sense of excitement in those raw recordings. Vanda and Young mixed them down to four-track (two sets of stereo pairs) to allow overlapping of the applause between songs before mixing it down to two-track."

Classic Rock magazine would declare *If You Want Blood (You've Got It)* among the top fifty live albums of all time.

If You Want Blood (You've Got It) Tracks

"Riff Raff"
"Hell Ain't a Bad Place to Be"
"Bad Boy Boogie"
"The Jack"
"Problem Child"
"Whole Lotta Rosie"
"Rock 'n' Roll Damnation"
"High Voltage"
"Let There Be Rock"
"Rocker"

Highway to Hell

Members: Angus and Malcolm Young, Bon Scott, Cliff Williams, Phil Rudd

Produced by: Robert John "Mutt" Lange at Roundhouse Studios in London

Released by: Atlantic Records on July 27, in the UK and the US on August 3, 1979

Cover art: At the last minute, the record company took an already released black and white glossy of the band and for the first time ever, superimposed a tail and horns on Angus, making him into a "little Devil."

David Fricke from *Circus* magazine wrote *AC/DC: Wired for Success* in January of 1979, for which he interviewed Bon, who stated, "There's been an audience waiting for an honest rock 'n' roll band to come along and lay it on 'em. There's a lot of people coming out of the woodwork to see our kind of rock. And they're not the same people who would go to see James Taylor or

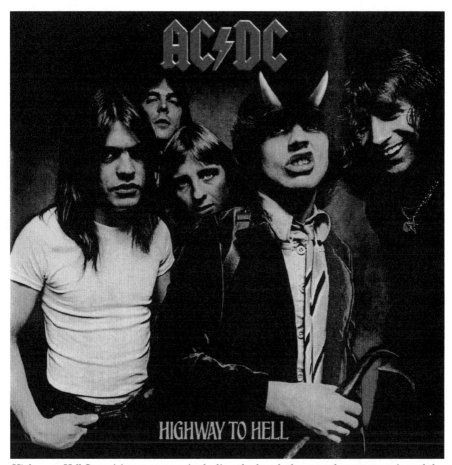

Highway to Hell: Surprising everyone, including the band, the record company rejected the original pictures for the album cover and used a publicity shot of the band that had been previously released. They superimposed horns and a tail on Angus and this was his official debut as the "Little Devil." Further fueling demonic rumors regarding the band, Bon is wearing a pentacle around his neck, but one that is pointed upwards, which is supposed to protect the wearer from evil.   *Jim Johnson Collection*

a punk band." When asked how he was withstanding the constant touring, Bon replied, "It keeps you fit—the alcohol, nasty women, sweat on stage, bad food—it's all very good for you!" When Fricke asked what he would do if his voice ever gave out, Bon shot back, "Then I'd become a roadie."

As the band recorded rough tracks at Albert Studios, Atlantic Records was hatching a new plan. They felt that George and Harry weren't producing radio-friendly records, so they put pressure on the band to work with legendary producer Eddie Kramer, who had previously worked with Jimi Hendrix, Led Zeppelin, and Kiss. This change was not met with much

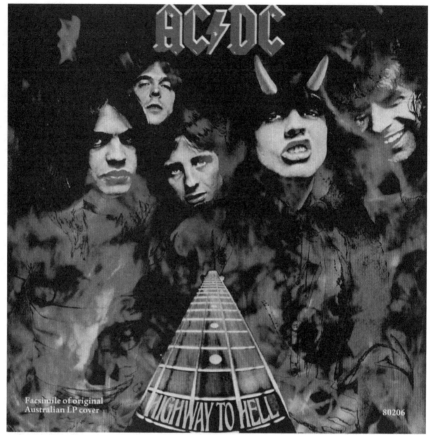

Facsimile of original
Australian LP cover

80206

Highway to Hell: The Australian version of the cover of *Highway to Hell.* They also didn't
get to use the picture with the Devil driving the car, but at least they got some flames.
Jim Johnson Collection

enthusiasm from the band, especially since they were not used to recording
anywhere else but Albert Studios. It also must have been a hard pill to swal-
low being told to fire your own brother, the one person who had stuck by
the band from the very beginning, and had produced their first six albums.

It would turn out to be a good move for the band, but in a roundabout
way, considering more than one person would lose their jobs over it.
Although George and Harry weren't at all happy, Angus claimed George
gave them the go-ahead, but told them, "Don't let them mess with what you
are. Always remember you're a rock 'n' roll band."

The original plan was business as usual, record an album in three weeks,
then tour Japan in February of 1979. A farewell party was organized for
the band at the Strata Inn in Cremorne, where Bon, Angus, and Malcolm

jammed with George on bass and Ray Arnott on drums. This would be Bon's last live performance in Australia.

Right before the band was to leave on their first tour of Japan, work visas were denied, and the tour was called off at the last minute. I received a postcard from Barry Taylor sent from Japan—unfortunately, the crew wasn't informed of the cancellation until they got there. Instead, AC/DC flew to Miami to meet their new producer and record the new album at Criteria Studios.

The seriousness of the situation didn't stop them from blowing off some steam during their off hours. Tommy Redd from Nantucket recalls running into Bon and Malcolm while at a club in Hollywood, Florida, called the Tight Squeeze. Ironically, they would see a local band that night also called Tight Squeeze. When Bon ripped his off his shirt and got up on stage to sing with the band, Malcolm looked over at Tommy and said, "Oh, now he's showing off again."

While trying to record with Kramer, who kept urging the band to add keyboards, Malcolm made many frustrated calls to Browning. Hearing things weren't going well, Atlantic sent Michael Klenfner and Perry Cooper down to Florida to hear the rough tracks. Perry Cooper told me,

> Michael and I loved the band, and after I got them to come over and tour, he decided that Eddie Kramer would produce their next album. So they came to Florida to rehearse, and get ready to record with Eddie. Michael and I got a call to come to Florida.
>
> We fly down there, and Michael's listening to it. I go into the bathroom, and Angus, Malcolm, and Bon follow me in there. They say, "What do you really think of it?" And I say, "It sucks." I really did. I said it sucks, and something ain't right. I can tell you're not having a good time and they said, "Ah, thank God!" But I was not a major player then. And we walked out of the bathroom, and later on we went back to New York and Eddie Kramer was fired. It just wasn't working; the vibe wasn't working. Michael got fired right after that. He had been adamant about Kramer producing their next album. Up until this point, their brother had produced everything for them. And you don't want to go up against your brother. They were forced into using Eddie, and they don't like being forced to do anything.

Michael Browning just happened to be visiting Clive Calder, who represented a producer born in Rhodesia (now Zimbabwe), named Robert John "Mutt" Lange. Coincidentally, Lange was staying with Calder when Malcolm's call to Browning came in. After hearing a demo of the new album, Lange agreed to take on the project. Lange had previously worked with City Boy, the Boomtown Rats, Graham Parker, and the Motors. AC/DC would be his first heavy rock band.

Bon was quoted in *RAM* as saying, "Three weeks in Miami and we hadn't written a thing with Kramer. So one day we told him we were going to have the day off and not to bother coming in. We snuck into the studio and on that one day we put down six songs, sent the tape to Lange and said, 'Will you work with us?'"

Lange was impressed with the recording, which had Bon singing and filling in on drums. Although Lange had never worked with such a heavy band before, this ended up being a great decision for all of them. Previously the band had never spent more than three weeks on recording an album. This time AC/DC spent nearly three months at London's Roundhouse Studios. *Highway to Hell* would wind up being a groundbreaking record for them. Lange added new sounds to their recording, such as harmonies and double tracking. Mutt pushed Bon to sing more, instead of scream. Angus told *Musician* magazine, "I think the thing about *Highway to Hell* was that Mutt knew what FM stereo sounded like and we didn't. I know Bon was very happy with him. Mutt taught Bon to breathe, bring in from your stomach. After we'd done the album, Bon said to Mutt, 'I like what you've done. Do you think it would be worth it for me to go off and learn with somebody?' Mutt said, 'No, I don't. This is you.' I think he was impressed that we could play and knew what a song was, as opposed to just a riff."

Regarding his vocals, Bon later stated, "The bottom line is still very much hard rock, but we've used more melody and backing vocals to enhance the sound. It's possible there is more commercial structure to the music, without going the whole way. In the past, it's just been a total scream, so I worked on it a lot more this time."

Malcolm summed up *Highway to Hell* in *Metal CD*: "That was a definite change for AC/DC. Atlantic Records in America were unhappy because they couldn't get the band on the radio, and they were desperate for us to come up with something more accessible. Mutt [Lange] seemed to know music, and he looked after the commercial side while we took care of the riffs and somehow we managed to meet in the middle without feeling as though we compromised ourselves. In fact, there was no way we'd back down on anything. We were a pretty tough band for any producer to work with."

Always going for the most live sound, Phil Rudd explained what really guides the band in the studio is "a lot of human element in our music. It isn't perfect and it isn't meant to be. That can be a little frustrating when machines can nail everything. You can give people the wrong impression about your music when it is not in machine time. But the excitement is natural. There is a pregnant pause involved. When you play an accent, if you play it in a hurry it doesn't have any weight. You write the beat on the line in the music, but there is a lot of room around that line as to where it can actually go. The boys like that I don't play on top of things. They like it laid back, not on top. It is how you get excited about it. If you get in front of the beat, then all the weight is gone out of it. It gets light. You gotta maintain the weight . . . I have never been a drummer's drummer. I am not a technical drummer. I don't make any claims to anything else."

Engineer Mark Dearnley told author Jake Brown what he thought made AC/DC's sound so unique. "Most bands rotate around the feel of the drummer, whereas AC/DC rotates around Malcolm's feel, in my opinion. He's the one who absolutely sets it rock solid, and everyone sits down around him, and that's very unusual."

As soon as the album was completed, AC/DC were back out on tour supporting UFO at the Dane County Coliseum here in Madison, Wisconsin, on Tuesday, May 8, 1979. Afterwards I hung out with the band backstage for a while. Their spirits were high, and it was obvious they were happy to be back on stage again. Later on, I ended up sitting in Phil Rudd's hotel room across the highway from the venue. Phil was very excited about the new album, and told me they were convinced that this was going to be the record that would put them over the top. He eagerly popped a cassette into his boom box, and we sat and listened to *Highway to Hell,* from front to back. Talk about rare rock 'n' roll privileges! I was stunned by the new songs and the polished sound of the new record. Lange had amazingly brought out the best in them, surprising everyone.

Atlantic Record exec Perry Cooper spent so much time with them on tour that they used to have a spot on the stage marked "PC," so he always had a place to stand and watch them. He fondly recalled how much fun they were. "If I remember exactly, they were not the best of boys in the early days. They were the best guys in the world, you just wanted to be around them. They were funny, but they were never malicious, they would never hurt anybody."

Reportedly, their constant touring put a strain on Albert's finances, which put pressure on Michael Browning. The band had started being courted by bigger management companies, and when Leber and Krebs expressed interest in the band, Michael accepted a settlement for the last year of his contract.

Steve Leber and David Krebs formed a high-profile New York management company in 1972 after leaving the mighty talent agency William Morris. By then their main clients, Aerosmith and Ted Nugent, were both experiencing less drawing power, so snapping AC/DC up was a major score for them. The company hired Peter Mensch as the band's personal manager. Browning went on to establish Deluxe Records, who enjoyed success after signing nineties rock sensation INXS.

Right in the middle of their American tour, they flew over to Holland to appear on the *Veronika* TV concert in Arnhem, Holland, at the Rijnhallen on July 13. This could possibly be where Angus met his future wife, Ellen. Their performance was filmed for the television show *Countdown*. Immediately, resuming their relentless tour, the band flew back to the States and played in front of 60,000 people at the *Day on the Green* festival in Oakland Stadium along with Ted Nugent and Aerosmith.

A week after that, they played the *World Series of Rock* for another 80,000 people at Browns Stadium in Cleveland, Ohio, supporting Aerosmith, Ted Nugent, the Scorpions, Thin Lizzy, and Journey. AC/DC spent the rest of July and the first part of August touring through Indiana, Ohio, and Pennsylvania. On August 4 they opened for Ted Nugent at Madison Square Garden in New York City. This was their first appearance in the Holy Grail of venues in the Big Apple. Their popularity started to explode when *Highway to Hell* was released in the States on July 30. Songs like the title track, "If You Want Blood (You've Got It)," and "Shot Down in Flames" are still audience favorites today.

If You Want Blood (You've Got It) had hit the quarter million mark, and this new album would skyrocket them even further. There had definitely been hell to pay for this particular release, considering it cost George, Harry, Michael Browning, Eddie Kramer, and Michael Klenfner their jobs. With Lange's more lush production, and the band's radio-friendly choruses, *Highway to Hell* was quickly certified platinum.

The album was released in the United Kingdom at the end of July and made its way into Britain's Top Ten, stopping at #8, while taking off like wildfire in Germany, Holland, and Scandinavia. Eventually selling seven million copies worldwide, the album finally made it into *Billboard*'s Top Twenty, peaking at #17. After the *Festival De Bilzen*, AC/DC played five dates in Ireland and France before appearing live on the German television show *Rock Pop*, playing "Highway to Hell." While in Munich, the band also filmed five promotional clips for their brand new, about-to-breakthrough album.

Blender magazine reported, "Mutt Lange sanded off a few of AC/DC's rougher edges and bolted the steam-hammer riffs and Scott's foul wit to pop-friendly choruses." *Kerrang!* magazine stated that the band "sounds impossibly ALIVE!"

Highway to Hell Tracks

"Highway to Hell": So much has been said regarding the choice of this title. If you realize how much driving AC/DC actually did in the first seven years of touring, it's not surprising that the term "highway to hell" was coined when Angus was asked by a reporter what it was like to travel so much. Angus quipped that waking up with your singer's stinky socks in your face was as close to being on a "highway to hell" as he could think of. This song is also a favorite addition to numerous movie and television soundtracks, including *House, the Simpsons, Little Nicky,* and *School of Rock.*

"Girl's Got Rhythm"

"Walk All Over You"

"Touch Too Much"

"Beating Around the Bush": This song was inspired by Bon's suspicions regarding an unfaithful girlfriend.

"Shot Down in Flames"

"Get It Hot"

"If You Want Blood (You've Got It)"

"Love Hungry Man"

"Night Prowler": This song was unfortunately linked to the infamous serial killer Richard Ramirez, due to his leaving behind an AC/DC baseball cap at one of the murder scenes. Angus once stated that the song was about slipping into your girlfriend's bedroom window in the middle of the night.

Back in Black

Members: Angus and Malcolm Young, Brian Johnson, Cliff Williams, Phil Rudd

Produced by: Robert John "Mutt" Lange at Compass Point Studios on the island of Nassau in the Bahamas

Released by: Atco Records on July 21, 1980, by Atlantic Records in the UK on July 31, 1980, and in Australia on August 11, 1980

Back in Black: According to Angus, the all-black cover was a sign of mourning for Bon, but the record company insisted on the gray outline around the band's logo. It has since gone on to become the second biggest album in music history, selling over 49 million copies, as well as the best-selling album by a band (tied with *The Dark Side of the Moon* by Pink Floyd), the best-selling album ever released by an Australian musical group, and the best-selling hard rock album of all time.   *Jim Johnson Collection*

Cover art: Solid black in memoriam to Bon. Producer Mutt Lange thought it was too bleak. Angus explained, "No, because it's for Bon, it's our tribute to him, and that's the way it's going to be."

For thirty-three years, Compass Point had been known as the "Home Studio to the Stars." Owned by producer Chris Blackwell, founder of Island Records, some of the illustrious clients at Compass Point are Talking Heads; U2; Judas Priest; Joe Cocker; Emerson, Lake, & Palmer; The B-52s; Mick Jagger; Status Quo; Bob Marley; Eric Clapton; David Bowie; Dire Straits; the Cure; the Rolling Stones; Robert Palmer; Iron Maiden; ELO; Whitesnake; Roxy Music; Eurythmics; Power Station; and Bad Company. Compass Studios was built in 1977, housing a MCI 500 series mixing desk along with state-of-the-art equipment, all installed in one room. By 1979, a second room was built to accommodate the bands wanting to record there.

During the recording of *Back in Black*, engineer Tony Platt placed a couple of room microphones around the studio so that when you heard the album, you would feel like you were in the same space as the band when they played it. Tony Platt told author Jake Brown, "After *Highway to Hell* there were certain things I wanted to achieve when I was asked to go and do *Back in Black*. I wanted to start out with more ambience on the drums, and wanted there to be more leakage between the guitars and the drums. We recorded *Back in Black* much more live I think than *Highway to Hell* was recorded, and I wanted to employ those techniques of allowing controlled leakage between the instruments."

The guitar sounds were very straightforward, without any double tracking. Platt felt that the heart of AC/DC's sound comes from the brothers' intuitive musical ties; where Angus isn't the best rhythm guitar player, Malcolm is the best rhythm guitar player on the planet. What makes their sound so unique is that they play in unison but using different positions, using different inversions of the same chords. Angus prefers not to use double tracking; the natural sound of what they end up with is, "The hard rhythm is how Malcolm plays, and between him, Phil, and Cliff, they hold down that back line rhythm, and it allows Brian and I to be the color."

Realizing what they had actually accomplished didn't happen until they left the Bahamas and went to New York City to mix the album. *Back in Black* was mixed in Studio A at Electric Lady, the studio founded by Jimi Hendrix. Malcolm stated, "Until we got out of the Bahamas and into the mixing room in New York. After about a week of not hearing any of it we thought, 'Fucking hell, this is a monster!' And sure enough it was."

Back in Black hit the *Billboard* charts at #4 and remained on the charts for the next year and a half. To this day, sound engineers around the world use *Back in Black* during their sound checks to find the perfect sound levels for their bands. Engineer Tony Platt was once witness to this at a Van Halen concert at Madison Square Garden.

Back in Black Tracks

"Hell's Bells": Opening with the infamous church bell that starts the song, this would be the first song fans around the world would hear Brian Johnson sing in place of Bon.

"Shoot to Thrill"

"What Do You Do for Money Honey"

"Given the Dog a Bone"

"Let Me Put My Love Into You": This song was one of two tracks that Bon jammed on (playing the drums) in the studio just days before his death.

"Back in Black": The opening riff to this song was played for Angus by Malcolm while on the road, who had it on a cassette tape that he was going to erase. Angus described, "It's three in the morning, and I'm trying to sleep, and he's saying, 'What do you think of this?' I said, 'It sounds fine to me.' He was going to wipe it off and reuse the tape,

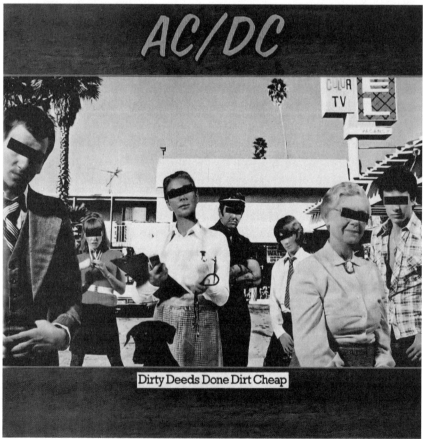

Dirty Deeds Done Dirt Cheap (International Version): Up until this point, this album had only been released in Australia, and the record company at the time questioned keeping Bon as the singer. After his death, to cash in on the enormous success of *Back in Black*, the company put a new cover on it and released it worldwide. The concept behind a group of people standing in the parking lot of a motel with their eyes blacked out is beyond me. Apparently everyone is capable of dirty deeds, and they all want to stay anonymous, except of course for the dog.   *Jim Johnson Collection*

because cassettes were a hard item for us to come by sometimes! In fact, I was never able to do it exactly the way he had it on tape. To my ears, I still don't play the thing right!"

"You Shook Me All Night Long": This song has the distinction of being one of the most popular songs to be played at strip clubs. To direct a video for "You Shook Me All Night Long," AC/DC called upon David Mallet. The filming took place in Jacob Street Studios, with the outdoor scenes being shot in northern England. Any MTV junkie can recall the comical content of the video, with one particular scene showing Brian coming home to find a scantily clad cowgirl riding a mechanical bull in the middle of his living room. Typical teenage fantasy! One of the band's crew met and fell in love with the girl in the video, eventually marrying her. AC/DC's wedding gift to the couple was naturally a mechanical bull.

"Have a Drink On Me": This is the second song Bon jammed on the last day he dropped in on Angus and Malcolm in the studio right before he died.

"Shake a Leg"

"Rock 'n' Roll Ain't Noise Pollution": This title was said to come from something Bon yelled back at his landlord, who was complaining about the volume of his music.

Dirty Deeds Done Dirt Cheap (US Version)

Members: Angus and Malcolm Young, Bon Scott, Mark Evans, Phil Rudd

Produced by: George Young and Harry Vanda at Albert Studios

Released by: Atlantic Records on April 2, 1981

Cover art: Seven people and a dog standing in the parking lot of a motel. Everyone eyes are covered by black boxes, except the dog's, who was apparently unconcerned with hiding his identity.

Billboard magazine reviewed the album after its 1981 release: "More than most of their songs to date, it captured the seething malevolence of Bon Scott, the sense that he reveled in doing bad things, encouraged by the maniacal riffs of Angus and Malcolm Young, who provided him their most brutish rock 'n' roll yet."

Dirty Deeds Done Dirt Cheap went platinum within ten weeks, and peaked at #3 on the *Billboard* charts, staying there for three consecutive weeks. The rerelease also sent the title track to the top of the charts, as well. Thanks to massive airplay, some of their more enterprising fans started dialing

"36-24-36," causing a telephone nightmare for an Illinois couple who filed a lawsuit against the band. Their attorney stated to the *Chicago Tribune* that his clients were hearing an "8" after Bon sings "36-24-36," thus creating the couple's phone number.

Dirty Deeds Done Dirt Cheap Tracks

"Dirty Deeds Done Dirt Cheap"
"Love at First Feel"
"Big Balls"
"Rocker"
"Problem Child"
"There's Gonna Be Some Rockin'"
"Ain't No Fun (Waiting 'Round to Be a Millionaire)"
"Ride On"
"Squealer"

For Those About to Rock (We Salute You)

Members: Angus and Malcolm Young, Brian Johnson, Cliff Williams, Phil Rudd

Produced by: Robert John "Mutt" Lange

Released by: Atlantic Records worldwide on November 23, 1981, and in Australia on December 7, 1981.

Cover art: A picture of a cannon and the words "For Those About to Rock" in black, against a gold background. The Spanish edition features a gold cannon and lettering on a black background.

Selling one million copies in the first week of its release, *For Those About to Rock* was the very first hard rock/heavy metal album to reach #1 on the *Billboard* charts, where it stayed for three weeks. This album was originally to be recorded at the EMI Pathe Marconi Studios in Paris, but they just couldn't get the sound they were looking for. So the band opted to record in a warehouse on the outskirts of Paris using the Mobile One studio, with vocals recorded later at Family Sound Studios, with overdubs done at HIS Studios.

The first concept of a Mobile One Studio was used by the Rolling Stones in 1968 when the band decided to record at Mick Jagger's house

FOR THOSE ABOUT TO ROCK

For Those About to Rock (We Salute You): Inspired by hearing cannons being fired on television at the end of Prince Charles and Princess Diana's wedding, the band went with cannons, and they have become part of their set design ever since. A live AC/DC concert is not complete without the salute of a blaze of the cannons, to properly send you on your way.   *Jim Johnson Collection*

in Stargroves, and all the equipment had to be brought to the house. A number of top producers and engineers were brought in for ideas and the actual studio creation was done by Helios Electronics, a company owned by Dick Swettenham. Helios Electronics produced the first working version of the Mobile One Studio. Specifically designed just for the Stones, its popularity caught on and some of the biggest bands in rock used it, including the Faces, the Who, and Led Zeppelin.

The original unit supported up to twenty microphones and the recording format was eight channels. Recording bands live quickly made it necessary to upgrade to a sixteen-track console. Angus later told *Guitar Player,*

"We had lots of equipment there for *For Those About to Rock*. We brought in a mobile, and recorded in a big rehearsal room to see what we could get away with." During the recording of the album, the band heard cannons being blown off at the end of the television broadcast of Prince Charles and Princess Diana's wedding, and that's where the idea of using cannons on the new tour came from.

Brian Johnson declared that their ultimate goal was to keep pushing themselves to do their best, even though *Back in Black* was a huge success. "It sold twelve million albums and I'm chuffed to bits! But with the new one, you can never be complacent. You can't sit back and say, 'Hey, the last one worked.' It's still up to the kids whether they buy it or tell you to piss off and try again—'Don't try to bullshit us.'" Following a monster hit like *Back in Black* was a formidable task, but *For Those About to Rock* was an undeniable success, to which a critic for New York's *Village Voice* claimed, "I recommend you go get it."

For Those About to Rock Tracks

"For Those About to Rock (We Salute You)": The title song was inspired by a book about Roman gladiators called *For Those About to Die We Salute You*. Angus said, "So we thought 'for those about to rock' . . . I mean it sounds better than 'for those about to die.' Actually, that song's got a lot of meaning to it. It's a very inspiring song. It makes you feel a bit powerful and I think that's what rock 'n' roll is all about."

"Put The Finger On You"

"Let's Get It Up": In homage to their female fans, Brian Johnson joked, "Pure filth. We're a filthy band."

"Inject the Venom"

"Snowballed"

"Evil Walks": Another song title inspired by the sound of the opening chords, which to Angus sounded evil.

"C.O.D.": Many have thought that "C.O.D." stood for "Cash on Delivery" or "Cash on Demand," but Angus came up with "Care of the Devil," although he insisted it did not have anything to do with black magic or Satanists. He claimed, "I don't drink blood. I may wear black underwear now and then but that's about it."

"Breaking the Rules"

"Night of the Long Knives"

"Spellbound": Another song about being naughty. According to Angus, "like peeking through the keyhole at somebody changing their knickers or something. Nothing bad. We're just pranksters more than anything. You're having fun and that's all there is."

Flick of the Switch

Members: Angus and Malcolm Young, Brian Johnson, Cliff Williams, Phil Rudd

Produced by: Malcolm and Angus Young with Tony Platt engineering and mixing. The brothers also gave credit to George Young and Harry Vanda,

Flick of the Switch: This production was where things went off the rails. The band hadn't taken a break since Bon's death, punches were thrown, and Phil left the band. The cover shows a tiny Angus pulling down a big switch, which is an innocent image for such an implosive album. *Jim Johnson Collection*

listing them as the "Dutch Damager" and the "Gorgeous Glaswegian." Recorded at Compass Point Studios in Nassau in the Bahamas.

Released by: Atlantic Records on August 15, 1983

Cover art: A pencil drawing of a tiny Angus pulling down on a huge switch.

Tired and frustrated by waiting for Mutt Lange to find the perfect sound for the new album, Malcolm and the band made the decision to go ahead and produce this album themselves. Although engineer Tony Platt wasn't available when they recorded *For Those About to Rock*, luckily he was free to help the band record the new album.

Angus revealed his writing process: "Usually I start a few weeks after we've gotten off the road. I'll tell everyone not to bother me because I don't want to know anything about rock 'n' roll for a while. But after about two weeks, I find myself drawn to the same old battered SG that I've been playing for years, and I start to play certain chords. Before I know it, a great deal of a song is written. That's when Malcolm or Brian will come in and help me finish off. It's really a very simple process. I guess you could say I write most of the songs out of boredom."

Relying on keeping it simple, Angus said, "Because it's simple and direct, you don't have to think about it. It makes you dance and tap your feet. I've never been impressed with someone who can zoom up and down [the guitar neck]. I can do that myself, but I call it practicing." Angus prefers to track his solos when his mind is clear. Describing his method of madness to *Guitar Player*: "When your mind is totally blank on what you're doing, then you just go and do it."

Paying tribute to his brother Malcolm's judgment when a second take is needed: "[If] he thinks they're not happening, if he thinks they're not rock enough or don't suit the song. It's mainly the songs we worry about. I won't sit there and spend twelve hours on a guitar solo. I couldn't. That's pointless. I like to go in and just go, bang away at it."

Engineer Tony Platt felt the album missed the mark for a number of reasons. AC/DC went back to Compass Studios in the Bahamas and set up the equipment the same way as they had when they recorded *Back in Black*. Once they started listening back to the recordings, first on Cliff Williams' portable stereo system and then at the board of Electric Lady Studios, the consensus was that it sounded too much like *Back in Black*, and that was when the decision was made to change the sound of the album. One that Platt eventually realized was a mistake.

Regardless, the band was happy with the final results and Brian Johnson stated, "The album is a really good rock album, that's all it is. We weren't trying to do anything else, just different this time, because we didn't have a producer, but that turned out to be an advantage. It was like, we had our own thoughts and there was no outside influence to stop us. It was a struggle at times to produce ourselves but that was half the fun of it."

Critics were happy with it as well, stating the band had forgone the eighties hair band approach, and returned to their blues influence from their earlier recordings. *Kerrang!* declared the album a beauty, claiming that no album since *Flick of the Switch* has ever quite matched the excitement and energy of their live shows.

Mark Putterford's review in *High Vaultage* stated, "Listen to the start of 'Guns For Hire,' and you'll hear that pale bony hand jerk across the live wires. You'll visualize that screwed-up brat face and the ever-present schoolboy uniform that accompanies it. You'll be able to feel the rising power as the legs twitch and the head nods faster and faster. . . ."

Flick of the Switch eventually reached #4 on the UK charts, but only made it to #15 here in the States. Malcolm defended the album in *Double Decade of Dirty Deeds*: "We did that one so quickly and I guess it was a reaction to *For Those About to Rock*. We just thought, 'Bugger it! We've had enough of this crap!' Nobody was in the mood to spend another year making a record, so we decided to produce ourselves and make sure it was as raw as AC/DC could be."

Unfortunately, during the recording of this album was when Phil Rudd left the band. Angus revealed, "The biggest change I saw in him was when Bon died. He couldn't take it so well because, as a band, things had been that tight between us, it was pretty thick. We had done a lot together, lived in a house together, set up all the equipment together, slept with the same women—at the same time! When Bon died, it hit him harder than anyone. He really thought that I in particular wouldn't be doing it anymore. So, when we carried on, he thought that the early thing—the tightness—had gone, which wasn't the case." Years later, Phil Rudd stated, "We had been together for too long. After a while, you kind of lose the plot. It wasn't the music."

Flick of the Switch Tracks

"Rising Power"
"This House Is on Fire"
"Flick of the Switch"

"Nervous Shakedown"

"Landslide"

"Guns for Hire"

"Deep in the Hole"

"Bedlam in Belgium": The band played the Thierbrau Sportshall in Kontich, Belgium, and the police stormed the stage, one with a machine gun, trying to stop the show. This lack of respect for rock 'n' roll incited a riot, and the best part is that it also inspired this song.

"Badlands"

"Brain Shake"

(Thirteen tracks were originally recorded, but only ten of them made it onto the album.)

'74 Jailbreak

Members: Angus and Malcolm Young, Bon Scott, Mark Evans, Phil Rudd

'74 Jailbreak: Possibly giving the band time to find a new drummer, the record company decided to release this collection of five songs from the Bon Scott era.

Jim Johnson Collection

Released by: Atlantic Records on October 15, 1984

Produced by: George Young and Harry Vanda at Albert Studios

'74 Jailbreak Tracks

"Jailbreak"
"You Ain't Got a Hold On Me"
"Show Business"
"Soul Stripper"
"Baby, Please Don't Go"

Fly on the Wall

Members: Angus and Malcolm Young, Brian Johnson, Cliff Williams, Simon Wright

Produced by: Angus Young and Malcolm Young, recorded at Mountain Studios in Montreux, Switzerland, in October, 1984

Released by: Atlantic Records on June 28, 1985, and voted the best album of the year by *People* magazine.

Cover art: A rendering of a wooden wall with the album title scrawled across it. There is a hole with an eye staring back at you, and of course, a fly perched (you guessed it) on the wall.

This was the first album recorded with new drummer Simon Wright, formerly of Dio. Malcolm stated, "He knew what he was doing and we just had to guide him in the right direction and leave him to get on with the job. It's a simple thing, playing drums for AC/DC, but sometimes it can be hard to keep it simple."

Mountain Studios was a large round room sectioned off where the amps were isolated. To enter the control room you have to climb a ladder. The band again tracked live off the floor through a Neve console. Mountain Studios was originally owned by Queen's Freddie Mercury. Established in 1975, the studio was enclosed within a modern casino building and was equipped with a sound system designed by Westlake Audio Inc. of Los Angeles.

Angus and Malcolm decided to produce the album, Angus citing, "We wanted to pick it up a bit more for this album, so we tried our hands at

Fly on the Wall: Now with Simon Wright behind the drum kit, this album was promoted with a twenty-eight-minute video featuring six songs from the album. The storyline featured a small New York City club filled with questionable characters, and a drunken fly sailing through their lives while the band plays on stage.   *Jim Johnson Collection*

producing it ourselves again, but putting some more time and thought into what we were doing instead of just taping ourselves."

Engineer Mark Dearnley felt comfortable with this arrangement, confirming that everyone knew what their jobs were, especially the Young brothers. Angus told *Guitar Player*, "I just think as brothers you can sort of shout each other down. You can go, 'Hey, cut that out!' So you've just got a good rapport. Malcolm does inspire me. He has very high standards in his way of playing and everything. He's very musical-minded, but he can go to the extremes. Like if we are in the studio and I have to do these things like solos, he'll say, 'I want this to rock like thunder,' and you've got to make it rock. He just says something like that and you know exactly what he means."

Once the album was released, unfortunately, the music press wasn't as enthusiastic. The *Village Voice* stated, "an unremarkable but hardly terrible AC/DC album," and *Billboard* magazine gave a bit better review by stating, "As with nearly every AC/DC album, there are a few good songs. . . ."

Dearnley added that following the incredible success of both *Highway to Hell* and *Back in Black* would be hard for any band. Brian Johnson told *Kerrang!* that Angus and Malcolm both warned him about taking a hit by the critics. Brian's reply was, "Well, I'm going to take stick anyway, taking this lad's place. But luckily these guys are so much like a fucking family that you never get the chance to feel alone."

Acknowledging MTV's grip on the eighties, the band took up residence in the World's End Club in New York's Alphabet City to shoot promotional videos for the new album—not exactly Park Avenue, if you know what I mean, at least not back then. The video, which was released in July, ran twenty-eight minutes and featured six songs from the album. The concept was based on the band playing a gig in a small New York club filled with shifty characters. A drunken cartoon fly sails through their lives while the band is on stage. Angus quipped that he loved the neighborhood, and "was planning on taking his next vacation there."

Fly on the Wall Tracks

"Fly on the Wall"
"Shake Your Foundations"
"First Blood"
"Danger"
"Sink the Pink"
"Playing with Girls"
"Stand Up"
"Hell or High Water"
"Back in Business"
"Send for the Man"

Who Made Who

Members: Angus and Malcolm Young, Brian Johnson, Cliff Williams, Simon Wright

Produced by: George Young and Harry Vanda, Robert John "Mutt" Lange, Angus Young and Malcolm Young

Released by: Atlantic Records on May 24, 1986

Cover art: Angus standing between tall stone columns, guitar in hand, head down, with a spotlight shining up from behind him.

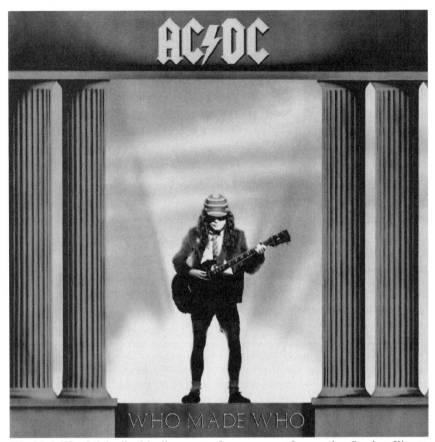

Who Made Who: Originally, this album came from a request from author Stephen King to use some of their songs for the soundtrack to his movie *Maximum Overdrive*. The band wrote "Who Made Who" to add a new original song to the collection King had selected. This prompted a whole concept of Angus look-alikes that appear in the video and also appeared on stage while promoting the album on tour.   *Jim Johnson Collection*

This release came from a request by author Stephen King to use some of their songs for the soundtrack to the movie *Maximum Overdrive*. King, a musician himself, was also a huge AC/DC fan, stating, "I like rhythm 'n' blues, I like rock 'n' roll. AC/DC I like a lot—very loud!"

"D.T." and "Chase the Ace" were two new instrumentals, but AC/DC insisted on writing a single to add to the soundtrack, which ended up being "Who Made Who." Going back to the dream team of Young and Vanda to produce the new single, Malcolm stated, "I think [it] was what we needed. 'Who Made Who' was a return to form for the band."

Billboard agreed, stating, the new album "put the band right back on track commercially." Selling over five million copies, *Who Made Who* became one of the biggest selling albums for the band since *For Those About to Rock*.

On February 27 and 28, 1986, the band took over Brixton Academy in South London to film the video for "Who Made Who," with David Mallet directing. Hundreds of AC/DC fans had been summoned from all over the United Kingdom to act as Angus clones, wearing specially made Angus school uniforms. The concept centered around Angus, and his look-alike minions.

Who Made Who Tracks

"Who Made Who": This song also sparked a nationwide radio contest for fans to dress up just like Angus and appear on stage standing all around him at the opening of each concert. "Pyro" Pete tells a humorous story about how the crew handled these Angus clones in Chapter 15.
"You Shook Me All Night Long"
"D.T."
"Sink the Pink"
"Ride On"
"Hell's Bells"
"Shake Your Foundations"
"Chase the Ace"
"For Those About to Rock (We Salute You)"

Blow Up Your Video

Members: Angus and Malcolm Young, Brian Johnson, Cliff Williams, Simon Wright

Produced by: George Young and Harry Vanda, recorded at Miraval Studio in Provence, France

Released by: Atlantic Records on January 18, 1988. The band's thirteenth album made it to #2 in the United Kingdom, the highest to chart there since *Back in Black*.

Cover art: Sticking it to the reign of music videos that dominated the eighties, the cover of this album is a picture of Angus busting through your television screen.

Happy to be back recording with both his brothers, Angus told *Guitar World*, "[Malcolm] can always tell me if I'm playing good or bad. He's a tough critic. I know if I can please Malcolm I can please the world. A lot of people say, 'AC/DC—that's the band with the little guy who runs around in shorts.' But I wouldn't be able to do it without Malcolm and the other guys pumping out the rhythm. That makes me good."

Brian also said, "The album is smashing, and we just knew it was going to be good. George has this father-figure approach and he knows more about rock 'n' roll than any fucker! Then you've got Malcolm and Angus there, so happy to work with their own brother, and Harry [Vanda] too!"

Blow Up Your Video: This album cover hints at the band's rebellion against band videos and how much they had become a promotional tool. Forever old school, touring was the method to their madness. During the North American leg of this tour, Malcolm took a break to quit drinking and their nephew Stevie Young filled in for him.

Jim Johnson Collection

Blow Up Your Video quickly became double platinum in the States, making it into Billboard's Top 200. Blender magazine hailed the single "Heatseeker" as the best song in years.

Malcolm stated, "We just try hard to please ourselves really. You gotta do what you do best. You get lots of people saying, 'Oh, when are you gonna change?' and plenty say, 'Don't change.' We couldn't change 'cause we only know the stuff we like—straight-ahead rock 'n' roll, no frills, and good performances. The music really is the important thing—that's the bottom line. Personally, that's all I'm interested in. I'm not even much up for the rest of the thrills of it."

Blow Up Your Video Tracks

"Heatseeker"
"That's the Way I Wanna Rock 'n' Roll"
"Meanstreak"
"Go Zone"
"Kissin' Dynamite"
"Nick of Time"
"Some Sin for Nothin'"
"Ruff Stuff"
"Two's Up"
"This Means War"

The Razors Edge

Members: Angus and Malcolm Young, Brian Johnson, Cliff Williams, Chris Slade

Produced by: Bruce Fairbairn. Recorded at Little Mountain Studios in Vancouver, B.C. Canada.

Released by: Atco Records on September 24, 1990.

Cover art: A gash ripped through the middle of a silver sheath, revealing the album's title on a red background.

The band and Fairbairn, whose credits included Aerosmith's Permanent Vacation and Pump, and Bon Jovi's Slippery When Wet, which went on to sell 28 million copies, hit it off immediately when the producer told the band, "I want you to sound like AC/DC when you were seventeen." Angus told

Razors Edge: Definitely suffering a loss of direction in the mid-eighties, the band were still mourning the loss of Bon. Malcolm got well, they switched Simon Wright out for drummer Chris Slade, and they came back to take over the nineties. The cover depicts a ripping of metal to show the band's logo and album title, and this album did just that. By the end of the *Razors Edge* tour, AC/DC were back on top, the album spawning two major hit singles, "Thunderstruck" and "Moneytalks." Ten years after the death of Bon Scott, AC/DC were bigger than ever.   *Jim Johnson Collection*

journalist Paul Stenning, "Bruce told Malcolm that he didn't want us to change AC/DC. And he didn't want us to do anything that we'd be uncomfortable with. These days it's hard to find people who are rock producers. A lot of people say they are, but as soon as you start working with them, they'll push their ballads at you. The material was all ready to go when we got to Vancouver. Fairbairn just brought out the dynamics a bit. Bruce was a great fan of our older albums; he said he liked the excitement, rawness, and lack of production on them. He wanted to capture that in-your-face sound again and he did a good job doing it. There were very few overdubs."

Fairbairn later explained the success of Little Mountain Studios to *Billboard*: "Little Mountain isn't a first-flight studio compared to some others. It hasn't got the best gear and it's certainly not a fancy place. But it does have a unique sound to it only four or five people in the world can capture . . . There's a certain, unpretentious feeling there, a certain something you can't define, that is conducive to making great rock records."

Due to Brian Johnson's divorce, Angus and Malcolm took over the lyric writing. Angus explained, "Mal and I thought it would ease the pressure on him if we wrote the words. We've always contributed in the past anyway. We'd sit down, the three of us—me, Mal, and Bon—sometimes four of us with my brother George, and we'd have this big shoot-around. We always gave Bon a helping hand in the past; same with Brian, because if you have a lyrical idea while you're writing it can save you a lot of heartache and trouble at the end of the day."

During the North American leg of the *Blow Up Your Video* tour, Malcolm took time off to quit drinking, and his nephew Stevie Young filled in for him. Once he was feeling better, for the first time in his career he got to see the band from the audience's perspective. That was when he made the decision to change drummers, and Chris Slade, who had previously played with Gary Moore, Manfred Mann, and Jimmy Page (in the Firm), was hired.

Angus was asked how AC/DC had maintained their musical consistency over the years, and he explained, "The only change that really had a major effect on us is when Bon died. That almost put an end to the group. But when Brian came in, he brought us new vitality and energy that kept everything rolling in the right direction. But my brother Malcolm and Cliff have been here all along, so the core of the band really hasn't changed that much. We do have Chris Slade in the band on this tour, and he's worked out very well. He's just as old and ugly as the rest of us!"

"Thunderstruck," the first single from the album, was released on September 29 and reached #13 on the UK charts. *Razors Edge* went all the way to #4 in Britain, and #2 in the States. On October 4, the RIAA (Record Industry Association of America) certified platinum sales for *If You Want Blood (You've Got It)*, *Let There Be Rock*, and *Powerage*. *Dirty Deeds Done Dirt Cheap* had been certified triple platinum, and by October of 1990, *Back in Black* had sold ten million copies, pushing AC/DC's total album sales to over sixty million.

Hitting the *Billboard* charts at #2, the magazine claimed, "Aussie headbangers shoot our first release for new label Atco, and it's a doozy. With one of the more distinctive voices on the rock 'n' roll planet, Brian Johnson growls, rasps, screams, and generally peels the paint off the walls through twelve scorchers by the brothers Young . . . Fairbairn wisely lets the band's true grit shine through and doesn't try to polish the rough edges that make AC/DC one of the most imitated but never duplicated bands in the world."

Mark Putterford wrote in the United Kingdom publication, *Select*, "Malcolm Young's rhythm guitar still chugs along faithfully, sticking like glue to the relentless thud of the drums; Cliff Williams' bass still rumbles like clockwork thunder; and Angus Young, his lead guitar as mischievous as his spiteful schoolboy stage persona, still buzzes around in the mix like an irate mosquito. And Brian Johnson, the band's singer, still hasn't taken his tonsils back to the parrot house at Whitley Bay Zoo."

The Razors Edge Tracks

"Thunderstruck": This song title was inspired by Angus who was flying over East Germany during a thunderstorm. When a loud crack of lightning scared everyone on the plane, a flight attendant remarked to Angus that they had been struck by lightning, and he exclaimed, "No, we were struck by thunder, because it boomed." It was also reported in *Classic Rock* in August 2014 that this song cost the producers of the movie *Varsity Blues* $500,000 to use it in the film, making "Thunderstruck" one of the most expensive songs in cinema history.

"Fire Your Guns"

"Moneytalks": The band had fake dollars made up with Angus' face on them, and literally dropped approximately one million Angus dollars onto the audience per week while on tour. They were fined 2,000 pounds in England for depicting Angus's likeness on money, in lieu of the Queen, on the cover of the single. Describing the lyrics, Angus said that money is the big divider. "In Europe, they think you've got to be born with class. In the US, they think you buy it, it comes with the tux. So it's just our little dig at the lifestyle of the rich and the faceless."

"The Razors Edge"

"Mistress for Christmas"

"Rock Your Heart Out"

"Are You Ready"

"Got You by the Balls"

"Shot of Love"

"Let's Make It"

"Goodbye & Good Riddance to Bad Luck"

"If You Dare"

AC/DC Live

Members: Angus and Malcolm Young, Brian Johnson, Cliff Williams, Chris Slade

Produced by: Bruce Fairbairn in Little Mountain Studios in Vancouver, this was the first live album since the band released *If You Want Blood (You've Got It)*.

Released by: Atco Records in October 27, 1992

AC/DC Live. The band had never before relied on a greatest hits album. Their first live release since *If You Want Blood (You've Got It)*, this album used songs from 153 shows performed in 21 countries, successfully showcasing their onstage energy. As Ian Fletcher wrote in *Classic Rock Special 2005*, "The critical and commercial pull of AC/DC's studio albums may fluctuate these days, but live they've always been unstoppable. And on *Live*, they prove that once again."   *Jim Johnson Collection*

AC/DC Live was issued in four different formats: a fourteen song single CD, a twenty-three song single cassette, a specially packaged twenty-three song double CD, and an eighteen song laser disc. At the end of the year, the live footage shot on high quality 35-millimeter film at *Monsters of Rock* was released as *AC/DC Live at Donington*, although when they played Donington on August 22, 1981, the bass end of the PA system was blown out before the band went on.

Live included the tracks "Thunderstruck," "Shoot to Thrill," "Back in Black," "Sin City," "Who Made Who," "Heatseeker," "Fire Your Guns," "Jailbreak," "The Jack," "The Razors Edge," "Dirty Deeds Done Dirt Cheap," "Moneytalks," "Hell's Bells," "Are You Ready," "That's The Way I Wanna Rock 'n' Roll," "High Voltage," "You Shook Me All Night Long," "Whole Lotta Rosie," "Let There Be Rock," "Bonny," "Highway to Hell," "T.N.T.," and "For Those About to Rock (We Salute You)."

Commenting on the *Live* album, Angus said, "We wanted to capture it before the hair and teeth drop down. We didn't want to be on life support systems . . . The album really is more for the AC/DC collector. When you're talking to them at the shows, it's always the first thing—'When are you guys going to do another live album?' Probably the most asked question of anyone in the band is, 'When are we going to get another live dose?' But we wanted to wait until Brian had a lot of studio albums under his belt, so he's got a fair shake."

Angus also told *Rolling Stone*, "Live is like ordering whiskey. It's gonna go right down the gullet. We're just a good-time rock 'n' roll band—nothing more, nothing less."

Malcolm also told *Metal CD* in 1992, "Everyone said right from the start that AC/DC are a live band and that the studio records never matched us live. After *If You Want Blood (You've Got It)*, and Bon's death, the question was always there about when we would do another live album. We wanted to wait until we had enough live material with Brian to give him a fair shot, so he wasn't just up there singing old Bon songs. The album has all the best AC/DC songs on it from both eras of the band, and some of the old stuff, like "Whole Lotta Rosie," still has a real kick to it."

The *Live* album, using songs chosen from 153 shows performed across twenty-one countries, successfully brought their onstage energy home to their fans. As Ian Fletcher wrote in *Classic Rock Special 2005*, "The critical and commercial pull of AC/DC's studio albums may fluctuate these days, but live they've always been unstoppable. And on *Live*, they prove that once again."

AC/DC Live (Collector's Edition): This version included two CDs which were slipcased into a book, and also contained an AC/DC dollar. The album was rereleased as part of the AC/DC Remasters series in 2003.   *Jim Johnson Collection*

AC/DC Live (Collector's Edition)

Members: Angus and Malcolm Young, Brian Johnson, Cliff Williams, Chris Slade

Produced by: Bruce Fairbairn

Released by: Atco Records on October 27, 1992

AC/DC Live Tracks

"Thunderstruck"
"Shoot to Thrill"
"Back in Black"
"Sin City"
"Who Made Who"

"Heatseeker"
"Fire Your Guns"
"Jailbreak"
"The Jack"
"The Razors Edge"
"Dirty Deeds Done Dirt Cheap"
"Moneytalks"
"Hell's Bells"
"Are You Ready"
"That's the Way I Wanna Rock 'n' Roll"
"High Voltage"
"You Shook Me All Night Long"
"Whole Lotta Rosie"
"Let There Be Rock"
"Bonny"
"Highway to Hell"
"T.N.T."
"For Those About to Rock (We Salute You)"

Ballbreaker

Members: Angus and Malcolm Young, Brian Johnson, Cliff Williams, Phil Rudd

Produced by: Rick Rubin

Released by: EastWest Records on September 26, 1995

Cover art: A picture of Angus standing on top of the world with the title wrapped around it carved in stone. He is surrounded by stone columns and lightning bolts.

AC/DC met in New York City in October of 1994 and started recording at Sony Studios, with Rick Rubin producing. Rubin had petitioned the band's management many times to work with them, and in light of the success of their single "Big Gun," they chose to go with Rubin and his coproducer Mike Fraser. Rubin was a longtime fan of the band, and told *Rolling Stone*, "'DC were kicking with that great huge guitar. I remember being impressed by all the things they tell you are wrong—volume, power, the simple riffs. And Bon Scott was just brilliant . . . I'll go on record as saying they're the greatest rock 'n' roll band of all time. They didn't write emotional lyrics.

They didn't play emotional songs. The emotion is all in that groove. And that groove is timeless."

Fraser was happy to be back behind the board again, and told author Jake Brown, "Right from the get-go, from when we'd done *Razors Edge*, the band had really liked the guitar sounds I helped get. And because I've been a fan right from the beginning, I also sort of 'got' their sound, and as a fan appreciated it, and could help them get it and retain it. I understand that sound, unlike other engineers who go in and start putting reverb on their drums and making Angus play through a delay pedal or something—that's not who they are."

After ten weeks in New York City even after trying different studios, including the Power Station, they were unable to get the sound they were looking for, especially the drum sounds, where they went to great lengths to get what they wanted, including bringing in a "drum doctor" from Europe and erecting a tent over the drum kit, and putting carpeting on the walls, all to no avail. Once they switched to Ocean Studios in Los Angeles, the band was able to complete the album.

Ocean Way Studios had become the place to record in LA by the early 1990s, attracting producers like Don Was, who worked with Bob Dylan, the Rolling Stones, Iggy Pop, Willie Nelson, and the Black Crowes. Senior staff producer Rob Cavallo, who worked for Warner Brothers, stated that the new owner, Allen Sides, carried on the tradition of keeping an eye on the big picture with great-sounding monitors, functioning boards, and the best in equipment maintenance.

Despite having had five years pass since their last studio recording, Angus said, "When we get together and go to work, something special always happens. It doesn't matter how long we may have been apart—once we're all in the same place at the same time, we become AC/DC."

Malcolm explained that they had put close to a year into this new album, so by the time they reached LA, "Things got really tight, the sort of thing you usually get on tour. So that gave us a great vibe in the studio. We want our albums to sound like our best live gigs, and normally you have to shut your eyes and imagine you're back on stage again. But this time we were already in the stage mode."

Striving for their original feel, Malcolm and the band went to great lengths to bring back their no-frills sound. This included firing up all the old Marshall amplifiers, complete with vintage tubes. Malcolm even had his guitar tech locate the original Gibson Sonomatics guitar strings that he used to use twenty years earlier. He described the recording of *Ballbreaker* to

Ballbreaker. For the first time in twelve years, Phil Rudd was back on drums, and the title track inspired an ingenious stage setup. It involved a whole wall of "bricks" with a row of garage doors running underneath them. As they opened, a very large wrecking ball with a screeching crane shot sparks while knocking down the wall. The doors then opened, revealing the band members, including Phil at his drum set that slid out onto the stage.
Jim Johnson Collection

Guitar World in 1995, "We just wanted to get back to the old feel of the rhythm. The feel dominated this time. And really the best feels are the simplest, I guess."

Brian added, "We did all the vocals right in the control room, just sitting around like we're sitting here now. Malcolm was sitting on one side of me with [engineer] Mike Fraser on the other. 'Cause I don't like going into the vocal booth to sing. I like it to be more like when I'm on stage with the others. To have them around me like that." The band was so happy with the album's outcome that Fraser was given a producing credit.

Phil Rudd had seen the band on the *Razors Edge* tour, and thought new drummer Chris Slade was doing a great job. After being gone for twelve years, he never dreamed of being asked to rejoin AC/DC. He hadn't seen the band in eight years when he and Malcolm sat down for a drink. Phil joked with him and said, "Any time, Mal." He later told *Musician* magazine, "I was absolutely gobsmacked. I had seen them with another drummer who was doing a good job, so I never expected that they would have the need to call me again. I hadn't seen him in eight years when they phoned me up and wanted me to come to the show. There were no hard feelings . . . It is just a groove thing. I didn't really think about it too much. We have a good thing—there is a natural interplay between us that we are very conscious of and we enjoy, but without thinking about it. It is just what it is."

Once they started recording, Angus and Malcolm agreed to ask Phil to come and jam with the band to see how it would go, and once Phil was back behind the kit, it felt like the old days. Having the Rudd backbeat guaranteed AC/DC's ability to capture their original swing. Cliff was quoted in *Guitar School* in March, 1995: "Yeah, Phil's back! He was the band's original drummer, but needed to step out for a number of years for various reasons. Now he's back with a vengeance, and we're working very well with him. It's great to have him back—he's always been the right man for the job."

Rubin agreed, stating, "The thing that separates AC/DC as a hard rock band is that you can dance to their music. They didn't play funk, but everything they played was funky. And that beat could really get a crowd going . . . You can hear it in how he drags behind the beat. It's that same rhythm that first drew me to them in junior high."

Unfortunately for Chris Slade, Phil's return to the band wasn't as celebratory. Slade was so upset by being replaced he didn't touch his drum kit for three years.

The band ended up being very proud of the final outcome. Angus stated, "I can honestly say I love every one of the songs—and that's saying something, coming from a band that started just before the crucifixion!"

Malcolm eloquently explained their popularity to *Guitar World* in November of 1995, saying, "People can go out and hear R.E.M. if they want deep lyrics. But at the end of the night, they want to go home and get fucked. And that's where AC/DC comes into it. I think that's what's kept us around so long. Because people want more fuckin'."

Ballbreaker debuted on *Billboard*'s Top 200 albums chart at #4, and went on to sell two million copies.

Ballbreaker Tracks

"Hard as a Rock": To accompany the first single, "Hard as a Rock," the band
    shot another video, their seventh collaboration with David Mallet. Four
    hundred London-area AC/DC fans were bussed to a soundstage at Bray
    Studios in Windsor, England, on August 22, 1995. During the shoot,
    Angus spent most of his time hanging in mid-air on a giant demolition
    ball, which he eventually used to crash through a window amidst explod-
    ing fireworks and flying shards of sugar glass.

Andrew "Don" Williams was one of the lucky fans to be included in
    the filming. "I heard about it from the AC/DC fan club, which I don't
    think is around anymore. The day was boiling hot and inside it was well
    over one hundred degrees. I've even seen the video interviewing Angus
    and Brian, who said how hot it was in there. They had to keep spraying
    them with water, but Brian was his usual joking self, and all of them were
    smoking like troopers. I got to meet all the band, and Phil got great
    applause from the crowd. It was his first time back, and it was great to
    see him pounding away on the kit. We were told by the director not to
    ask the boys for their autographs when they come on stage, because they
    wouldn't get any work done. They were happy to sign autographs later,
    and I had to laugh when a guy gave Brian a Led Zeppelin CD to sign,
    which was all he had with him. Brian said, 'No bloody way!' and pre-
    tended to throw it away, but came back with it signed by the whole band."

"Cover You in Oil": Despite the sexual connation of the title, Angus claimed
    it came from his passion for oil painting. Hence, "cover you in oil."

"The Furor"

"Boogie Man"

"The Honey Roll"

"Burnin' Alive": This song was written about the stand-off with cult leader
    David Koresh in Waco, Texas in 1993.

"Hail Caesar"

"Love Bomb"

"Caught with Your Pants Down"

"Whiskey on the Rocks"

"Ballbreaker"

Bonfire Boxset

Released by EastWest in the US on November 18, 1997. *Bonfire* was released in the UK on the EMI label after AC/DC signed a deal with EMI covering the United Kingdom exclusively.

When the band started gathering materials for the *Bonfire* box set, there were no unreleased tracks with Bon. All they had to work with were demos, which were the recordings right before the final cut was made. Beginning in March of 1997, Angus and Malcolm spent hours in the studio listening to tapes, choosing the ones where Bon sounded his best. With George's help, they remixed songs from the master tapes, and had the whole package finished by that summer.

The five-CD box set included Disc One, "Live From The Atlantic Studios," recorded live in December 1977 at Atlantic Studios in New York. This recording had only previously been available as a promotional CD. The tracks included were "Live Wire," "Problem Child," "High Voltage," "Hell Ain't a Bad Place to Be," "Dog Eat Dog," "The Jack," "Whole Lotta Rosie," and "Rocker."

Discs Two and Three, "*Let There Be Rock* The Movie, Live In Paris," was the soundtrack recorded on December 9, 1979. The tracks included were "Live Wire," "Shot Down in Flames," "Hell Ain't a Bad Place to Be," "Sin City," "Walk All Over You," "Bad Boy Boogie," "The Jack," "Highway to Hell," "Girl's Got Rhythm," "High Voltage," "Whole Lotta Rosie," "Rocker," "T.N.T.," and "Let There Be Rock." Some of the special features were the full version of the song "Walk All Over You," and the missing track "T.N.T.," which had been dropped from the movie.

Disc Four, "Volts," featured working and alternative versions of some of their classics: "Dirty Eyes" (which became "Whole Lotta Rosie"), "Touch Too Much," "If You Want Blood (You've Got It)," "Backseat Confidential" (which became "Beating Around the Bush"), "Get It Hot," "Sin City" (live on *The Midnight Special* in September, 1978), "She's Got Balls" (live from a Bondi Lifesaver concert in 1977), "School Days," "It's a Long Way to the Top (If You Wanna Rock 'n' Roll)," "Ride On," and a spoken-word montage from Bon. This CD even includes a guitar solo by Angus that was played at a sound check in Metz, France, on December 6, 1979.

Disc Five was a version of *Back in Black*, released in a double carton sleeve with all the original components of the vinyl release. This edition of *Back in Black* is exclusive to *Bonfire*. Angus explained why it was part of the package: "It was our tribute to Bon, so we felt it should be included. The whole album

Bonfire box set: After waiting seventeen years after Bon's death, the band finally went through all the recordings with Bon and put together a *Bonfire* box set, named after the solo album Bon always said he would record someday. The cover of the box set shows Bon with Angus on his shoulders, and the package includes five CDs: *Live from the Atlantic Studios;* two CDs from the *Let There Be Rock* movie; *Volts,* which featured alternative titles to some of their most popular songs; and a copy of *Back in Black.*   *Jim Johnson Collection*

was our dedication to him. And also to show how AC/DC carried on afterwards."

 Bonfire included a forty-eight-page booklet, a two-sided poster, an AC/DC sticker, a removable tattoo, a guitar pick, and a keychain/bottle opener. The booklet, with a brief history of the band, also featured some of Bon's handwritten lyrics, and rare black and white and color photos of the band. The cover of *Bonfire* has a picture of Angus riding on Bon's shoulders, and right inside the cover is the best picture of all. It's a black and white shot of Bon as a young boy, in his kilt, beaming with pride, holding up an award.

As their promotion materials said, *Bonfire* was a whole box of goodies "that Bon would have wanted you to have."

In October, the single "Dirty Eyes" was released, but not made available for sale. On Halloween, the Album Network aired the world premiere of *Bonfire*. To help promote the new release, AC/DC went cyber. For the first time, Angus and Brian sat down at the computer and hosted a chat with their fans on America Online (AOL). Aside from squeezing in a quick hello to me before the chat officially began, the most comical part of their discussion was when someone asked Angus, who was now in his forties, if he felt too old to rock 'n' roll. Within seconds Angus shot back, "The name's Young, always has been, always will be."

Right before *Bonfire* was unveiled, Bon's friend Bernie from the French band Trust appeared on the radio show *Zig Mag* on November 13. That night he premiered "Ride On," which was recorded in London just six days before Bon died. This would be the first time it was heard by the public.

Bonfire was released on November 18, 1997 in Europe and Australia and in the US the following day. Less than a month later the box set would be certified gold by the RIAA. As for waiting seventeen years before compiling material for *Bonfire*, Angus told Mick Wall for *Record Collector*,

> For us as a band, it's something that we've wanted to do for a long time, but we just didn't know when. There was no way we were gonna do something like this at the time of Bon's death, 'cos it would have been seen as a grave-robbing exercise. And we were very conscious of not letting anything like that happen. For Brian's sake, we had to get space and time between what had happened and allow Brian to give it his best shot. Also, there was too much emotion to handle at the time. For me and Malcolm, the only way we could get through it was by just keeping our heads down and working. If we'd tried to go through loads of tapes of Bon's stuff just after he'd died, I don't think we'd have made it.

Angus also explained to Wall what he missed most about Bon: "His wit and his sense of humor, I think. He was a wild man but he wasn't stupid. And having him in the band was just a fantastic time in our lives. After he died, it was like we were forced to grow up a bit. It changed things, for sure. Not so much musically, 'cos we've always known what we're doing there, but in our lives, the way we looked at things. But then nothing stays the same forever, does it?"

Commenting on how the loss of Bon affected the band, Tony Platt, who worked on *Back in Black*, said, Bon "was the real spirit of AC/DC, the glue that held the band together. It was such a tragedy because he had everything to live for . . . but the strange thing was, someone told me he had visited a clairvoyant shortly before [his death], and she told him he would die in his thirties. Malcolm said to me, 'Sometimes Bon would disappear right after a show and we wouldn't see him until just before we were due on stage the next night. The hardest thing will be getting used to him not being there.'"

Angus added,

> We could be somewhere where you would never expect anyone to know him and someone would walk up and say, "Bon Scott," and always have a bottle of beer for him. It was uncanny. One time we were broken down in a bus outside this little town in Australia and some guy came along carrying a surfboard and a whole crate of beer. And it was really hot and we were dying for a drink. Anyway, he walked by the bus and looked in and yelled "Bon Scott!" and came running in and handing out all his beers, and everyone was there having a party while the bus was being fixed. He made a lot of friends everywhere and was always in contact with them, too. Weeks before Christmas he would have piles of cards and things, and he always wrote to everyone he knew, keeping them informed. Even his enemies, I think.

The Bonfire box set was truly a celebration of the band's time spent with Bon, and they were very proud of it. Angus commented to *Guitar World*, "I must admit, though, that while we were digging through the material, a few times, even we were shocked at what was coming back at us off the tapes—blown away. We felt humbled by our own machine."

Malcolm also stated to author Murray Engleheart in the *Bonfire* boxset, "Bon was the biggest single influence on the band. When he came in, it pulled us all together. He had that real 'stick-it-to-'em' attitude. We all had it in us, but it took Bon to bring it out." Angus more pointedly said, "I don't think there would have been an AC/DC if it hadn't been for Bon."

Stiff Upper Lip

Members: Angus and Malcolm Young, Brian Johnson, Cliff Williams, Phil Rudd

Produced by: George Young with coproducer Mike Fraser at Bryan Adams' Warehouse Studio in Vancouver.

Released by: EastWest Records on February 28, 2000

Cover art: A giant bronze statue of Angus holding his SG with a fist in the air.

Warehouse Studios is located in Gastown, near Vancouver, surrounded by restaurants and nightclubs. It was built during the gold rush in the 1800s by the Oppenheimer family. The inside of the studio itself started out in 1987 in the basement of the home of Canadian multiplatinum rocker Bryan Adams. On July 9, 1997, the doors opened at the Powell Street location. Studio 2 was completed one year later, and Studio 1 was finished on October 18, 1999. Ron O. Vermeulen designed the acoustic and technical layout, which includes three floors, each with a private lounge and kitchen area. Bob Clearmountain, who has produced Kiss, David Bowie, Bruce Springsteen, and Bon Jovi, has worked there for more than twenty years.

Stiff Upper Lip. With the cover showcasing a massive statue of Angus, which was featured in their live shows, *Stiff Upper Lip* returned to a more bluesy feel, including bringing back big brother George to produce. This album didn't receive as much airplay as past projects, with the title track getting most of the attention. Eerily, *Stiff Upper Lip* included the song "Safe in New York City," and the *Stiff Upper Lip* tour ended in May of 2001, just months before the attacks on 9/11. *Jim Johnson Collection*

Bryan Adams claimed the birth of the studio itself was a way of getting out of his own basement. Adams added an SSL 9080 console in Studio 2, and the band tracked *Stiff Upper Lip* in Studio 1, using a Neve 8078 console. The Neve originated from Air Studios in London, and was designed by Rupert Neve, legendary Beatles producer George Martin, and engineer Geoff Emerick.

This album was released very close to the twentieth anniversary of Bon's death, and Angus was asked if it was intended that way. He replied, "I've never done anything. I don't sort of sit and celebrate. See, the time Bon passed away I had also just got married. So you've got a period you remember and there's also my anniversary. And, if you forget that, there could be another death! [Laughing] I'd be seeing Bon quicker than I thought!"

Regarding George Young's return as producer, Angus said, "He helped us when we were doing the *Bonfire* box set, and from that we thought it would be great to work with him again. He had actually stopped producing for the past five years and taken a back seat, but even when we worked with other people we always liked him to hear everything before it was released. Being his younger brothers, I suppose we still look even now for his stamp of approval.

"I always think we did the great rock tunes when we worked with my brother George. The whole thing is not to get too serious and hung up about things. It's about having fun and a good time."

Engineer Mike Fraser confirmed that this time around, the band wanted a more bluesy feel versus a harder rock sound. He also stated to witness having the three brothers working together again, there was an intuitive dynamic between them that didn't require words.

Angus confirmed their approach by saying, "Just two guitars and your bass and drums, and really the only color they use is me for a bit of the guitar work. You try to keep everything minimalist, I suppose, if you're thinking in an art way—you keep it basic. The good rock 'n' roll bands are always the bare bones stuff. I always think the best rock out there is stuff that has got the blues element in it. They're sort of bombarding us these days with image, and that seems to be more and more the case. I think they're all sort of losing track."

Out of the seventeen songs recorded for *Stiff Upper Lip*, only twelve made it onto the album. The tracks that didn't make it were "Rave On," "Let It Go," "The Cock Crows," "Whistle Blower," and "Cyberspace." The working title of the album was *Smokin'*, but the band ended up going with an idea that Angus had come up with. While sitting in traffic one day, he was pondering the early images of rock 'n' roll. When Angus thought of Elvis and his infamous sneer, the phrase "stiff upper lip" came to mind.

The band only took six weeks to record *Stiff Upper Lip*. Angus explained, "We don't like to spend more than six weeks on an album. We don't want to lose the freshness. Our musical ambition had always been to put down a whole album like it was done by Little Richard and them back in the fifties."

Confirming that by the time they are ready to record a new album, most of the songs have already been written while on the previous tour, Angus stated, "We strive for consistency. We spend a lot of time working on it, but (you have to) come up with something that's a little bit different from what you've done before. You don't want to be a clone of what you were before."

Recording live off the floor as they always do, this time George added a click track for Phil to play along to, which had never been done before. Phil explained, "We've never used a click on any song, on any album while I've been in the band. When we got George Young back as producer, we both rose to the occasion and there was huge admiration right around the camp."

Fraser told Jake Brown, "They like to do it live—they don't like to manufacture it. There's nothing faked, and the only overdubs are Brian's vocals and Angus' leads or flourishes. They never go back in and redo their performances again—it's all live off the floor, and that's the great thing about the band."

A review in *Rolling Stone* stated, "With older brother George Young back onboard as producer, *Stiff Upper Lip* wisely sticks to its time-tested formula of no-frills riffing . . . confirming AC/DC's status as one of the most enduringly popular hard rock bands on the planet."

Being particularly proud of this album, Phil stated, "I love the album, I really do. I play it all the time if I'm home or in the car. All the songs are really good."

Brian eloquently explained the band's success by saying, "AC/DC has survived because we've never changed direction, never given in to trends. That's why there haven't been any solo projects from within the band. No one has ever wanted to. Our music doesn't go out of fashion because it isn't about fashion. I hear about all these different kinds of music—grunge, hardcore, death metal. And all it is is rock 'n' roll. Our music comes from the heart. It's always been there. People put you down for playing rock 'n' roll, you know? Well, fuck those people. You have got to do your own thing."

Stiff Upper Lip entered the *Billboard* charts at #7, and was certified platinum within six months. It also hit #1 on *Billboard*'s Mainstream Rock Tracks chart. The new album was certified gold in the United States, and platinum in Europe, less than three months after its release.

Request magazine interviewed Angus and Brian in June, asking them what Bon would think of the band now. Angus said, "I think he would've been proud, just knowing how he was as a person. Bon's biggest idol was actually George, going back to when he was in the Easybeats. And when he came to see us for the first time, he said, 'Well, I get to work with these two guys, and I get to work with their brother.' So I always think he would look well on what we've done, and I believe he does know, in a way."

On June 18, VH1 featured the band on the *Behind The Music* series. After its premiere, the *Boston Globe* interviewed Brian, where he openly slammed VH1's sensationalizing the darker part of the band's history. Due to his complaints, the show was re-edited, this time including Cliff (who had been left out of the original broadcast), and aired on August 12, 2000.

Stiff Upper Lip Tracks

"Stiff Upper Lip"
"Meltdown"
"House of Jazz"
"Hold Me Back"
"Safe in New York City"
"Can't Stand Still"
"Can't Stop Rock 'n' Roll"
"Satellite Blues"
"Damned"
"Come and Get It"
"All Screwed Up"
"Give It Up"

Black Ice

Members: Angus and Malcolm Young, Brian Johnson, Cliff Williams, Phil Rudd

Produced by: Brendan O'Brien at the Warehouse Studio, Vancouver, B.C., Canada.

Released by: Sony Music in October 17, 2008

Cover art: The AC/DC logo in red on a black and gray background, with a small silhouette of Angus, guitar in hand and fist in the air. On the back cover, there is a silhouette of Malcolm. The deluxe edition featured a blue logo, and there are also limited editions, one with a white logo and one done in yellow.

After the release of *Stiff Upper Lip*, AC/DC left their longtime label Atlantic Records and signed a multimillion dollar deal with Sony. For the first time in the band's career, they also signed an exclusive deal with Walmart, making it the only US outlet to sell the album. The decision was simple. According to Malcolm, Walmart pre-ordered 2.5 million copies and cut out all distribution costs. Upon release of *Black Ice*, Walmart stores across the country set up a merchandise section dedicated to the band, featuring everything from the new album to AC/DC T-shirts and pajama bottoms.

Working with Brendan O'Brien, a brand new producer for the band whose credits include Korn, Stone Temple Pilots, Pearl Jam, and Rage Against the Machine, was summed up by Brian Johnson when he said, "There was a little awkwardness when you first get in the studio with a new guy because he's butting into your little gang. But, by Christ, after five minutes with this guy we could see how wonderful he was. Brendan was fantastic."

When the band entered the studio in 2008, it had been eight years since they last recorded together, but engineer Mike Fraser stated that it seemed like no time had passed at all. Angus agreed that it was a good experience to work with Mike again. "It was also very good to work with Brendan O'Brien, who has a musician's background. Communicating with someone like that is also very good, because he knows exactly what you need. He knows what you're talking about. He is very sharp." Angus also stated that he had been impressed with O'Brien's skills, so they told him to be brutal. The band wanted a departure from the bluesy sound of *Stiff Upper Lip*, and aimed for their original full-on attack with *Black Ice*.

O'Brien told an Atlanta newspaper that he had no expectations, literally meeting the band for the first time on the day they started recording. As they hadn't done an album in over eight years, he was pleasantly surprised listening to the demos of their new songs, and was fully confident that they could "return them to form a bit."

Angus confronted the critics who claim they record the same album over and over again. He declared, "A lot of times we get criticized for it. A lot of music papers come out with 'When are they going to stop playing these

Black Ice: After a seven year break, the band went back into the studio in Vancouver in the spring of 2008 and recorded one of their best albums, some say, since *Razors Edge*. The opening track, "Rock N Roll Train," inspired their stage set, which featured a life-size locomotive complete with fireballs and red horns. Different versions of the album cover feature their logo in four different colors, and the single "War Machine" finally garnered them a Grammy. The tour lasted from October of 2008 until the end of the summer of 2010, making it the second-biggest selling tour in history, generating over 400 million dollars. Thirty-seven years after the band started in 1973, *Black Ice* proved that AC/DC still had it, in spades.   *Jim Johnson Collection*

three chords?' If you believe you shouldn't play just three chords, it's pretty silly on their part. To us, the simpler a song is, the better, 'cause it's more in line with what the person on the street is."

Citing their appeal to the fans, Angus claimed much of their success was due to Malcolm's rhythm guitar playing, telling *Guitar World*, "I'm just like a color over the top. [Malcolm's] the solid thing; he pumps it along. His right hand is always going. In that field I don't think anyone can do what he does. He's very clean, he's very hard. It's an attack. Anyone that sees him or knows about guitars can tell."

Angus explained that their big guitar sound comes from Angus being in one speaker and Malcolm in the other, and by using the shortest cables to their amps as possible, thus creating a bigger bottom end and a nice top end to the sound without losing its forceful crunch. To keep their energy up, the album was recorded three songs at a time, with Brian adding his vocals and Angus adding his solos before preceding to the next batch of songs.

After years of time off in between albums, Brian was concerned that he wouldn't be able to sing again, and pointedly told O'Brien, "'Brendan, will you make me a promise? If I'm not up to scratch, if I'm not up to the job, please tell me! I'm a big boy, I won't cry, I'll just disappear. I'll just say goodbye to the boys, and they can get somebody else in to do the job.' And I really, really mean it. Because the last thing I want is to be the member in this band that holds it all back. So Brendan looked at me and he went, 'OK.' But he never said anything, so I was very lucky."

Giving credit to Brian's keeping in shape and owning his own race car team where he races at almost the Formula 1 level, his worries over his vocal ability were unfounded. Being mindful of Brian's singing style, Fraser recorded Brian for an hour to an hour and a half at a time to avoid burning out his throat.

As Brian didn't care to be isolated in a recording booth by himself, O'Brien set him up to record in an office behind the reception desk in the studio. Brian explained how O'Brien gathered some speakers, a mixing desk, and a Shure 56 microphone. He joked that he sang along to the backing track the band had recorded the night before, and the receptionist immediately quit! When he first heard the album, Brian was stunned. "It was almost like listening to myself thirty years ago. It honestly feels like a young band who have just come on the scene."

On taking their first long break between albums, Angus told journalist Paul Cashmere, "AC/DC have made more albums in our career than a lot of bands have done. We are now lucky we get a lot more time to sit back and spend time writing, which is great for us. You can really concentrate. Sometimes in the past you got the deadline coming into it, especially when you commit yourself to a tour. A lot of stuff in the early days was written and recorded while we were touring. Nowadays, it's good to be able to sit back and pick what we want to do."

When *Black Ice* was released on October 17, 2008, it debuted at #1 on the *Billboard* chart, selling 1,762,000 copies worldwide, with US sales coming in at 784,000. The *LA Times* reported, "AC/DC topped the one-million sales mark for its new *Black Ice* during the album's second week of release, holding on to the #1 spot on the national sales chart with 271,000 copies. At the same time, the album also debuted at #1 in thirty-one countries." As of 2014, the album has gone on to sell eight million copies worldwide.

Black Ice Tracks

"Rock N Roll Train": Originally, this song was titled Runaway Train, and once the title was changed, it inspired the creation of the massive locomotive that was built for their live shows. Reportedly the entire production came in at around four million dollars.

"Skies on Fire"

"Big Jack"

"Anything Goes"

"War Machine": This song finally garnered the band their first Grammy award for Best Hard Rock Performance.

"Smash 'n' Grab"

"Spoilin' for a Fight"

"Wheels"

"Decibel"

"Stormy May Day"

"She Likes Rock 'n' Roll"

"Money Made"

"Rock 'n' Roll Dream"

"Rocking All the Way"

"Black Ice": This title, Angus told me, was inspired by something hard and dangerous. Those who have hit black ice while driving and lived to tell about it couldn't agree with him more.

Rock or Bust

Members: Angus Young, Stevie Young, Brian Johnson, Cliff Williams, Phil Rudd

Produced by: Brendan O'Brien at the Warehouse Studio, Vancouver B.C., Canada.

Released by: Sony Music on November 28, 2014, in Australia, and worldwide on December 2, 2014.

Cover art: Features the AC/DC logo carved in stone in front of a black speaker with the title below in gold lettering. The logo itself was presented as a special lenticular 3D display on vinyl copies and on CD. When animated, the band's logo perpetually shatters and then reassembles itself—quite appropriate considering how many times AC/DC has come back from the brink of disaster, stronger than ever.

This is the first and only album recorded by AC/DC without founding member Malcolm Young, who officially left the band in April of 2014 due to ill health. At first it was announced on April 16 that Malcolm was taking a

Rock or Bust: Recorded in just ten days in May of 2014, *Rock or Bust* had the band in the studio for the first time without Malcolm. It was announced in April that due to ill health, Malcolm would be taking a break. Their nephew Stevie Young filled in for him, and on October 4, 2014, they shot videos in London for two singles, "Play Ball," and "Rock or Bust." The cover features a picture of their logo carved in stone, in front of a black speaker with the title below in gold lettering. The logo itself is a special lenticular 3D display that perpetually explodes and then reassembles itself. The album was released on December 2, 2014.   *Jim Johnson Collection*

break. Eventually, reports were confirmed that Malcolm was suffering from dementia and would not be able to return to the band.

This is also the shortest AC/DC album ever recorded coming in at just under thirty-five minutes. While the band has previously taken up to six weeks to record an album, *Rock or Bust* was done in just ten days. On October 4, 2014, videos for singles "Play Ball" and "Rock or Bust" were filmed in front of hundreds of contest winners who converged in London to appear on camera with their idols. At the last minute, drummer Bob Richards, formerly of the band Shogun, filled in for Phil Rudd, who was called back to New Zealand for a family emergency.

Brian Johnson told *Classic Rock*, "We missed Malcolm, obviously, Stevie was magnificent in his stead, but when you're recording with this thing hanging over you, and your work mate isn't well, it's difficult. I'm sure he was rooting for us the whole time we were over in Canada."

Proving the fans felt the same way, *Rock or Bust* debuted at #1 in 42 countries. *Rolling Stone* declared, "Tried and true . . . AC/DC remain hard rock's masters."

Rock or Bust Tracks

"Rock or Bust"

"Play Ball": Fans were treated to an advance listen to AC/DC's new single on September 24, 2014, when this song was played in the promotional television campaign for Major League Baseball's postseason playoffs.

"Rock the Blues Away"

"Miss Adventure"

"Dogs of War"

"Got Some Rock & Roll Thunder"

"Hard Times"

"Baptism by Fire"

"Rock the House"

"Sweet Candy"

"Emission Control"

AC/DC Singles

Below is a listing of singles that were officially released from each of AC/DC's albums.

High Voltage: "Can I Sit Next to You Girl" and "Baby, Please Don't Go" (Australia) *T.N.T.*: "High Voltage," "It's a Long Way to the Top (If You Wanna Rock 'n' Roll," and "T.N.T." (Australia)

High Voltage (International): "It's a Long Way to the Top (If You Wanna Rock 'n' Roll)" and "High Voltage"

Dirty Deeds Done Dirt Cheap: "Jailbreak," "Dirty Deeds Done Dirt Cheap," and "Love at First Feel"

Let There Be Rock: "Dog Eat Dog," "Let There Be Rock," and "Whole Lotta Rosie"

Powerage: "Rock 'n' Roll Damnation"

Highway to Hell: "Highway to Hell," "Girl's Got Rhythm," and "Touch Too Much"

Back in Black: "You Shook Me All Night Long," "Hell's Bells," "Back in Black," and "Rock 'n' Roll Ain't Noise Pollution"

For Those About to Rock (We Salute You): "Let's Get It Up" and "For Those About to Rock (We Salute You)"

Flick of the Switch: "Guns For Hire," "Nervous Shakedown," and "Flick of the Switch"

Fly on the Wall: "Danger," "Sink the Pink," and "Shake Your Foundations"

Who Made Who: "Who Made Who"

Blow Up Your Video: "Heatseeker" and "That's the Way I Wanna Rock 'n' Roll"

The Razors Edge: "Thunderstruck," "Moneytalks," and "Are You Ready"

Live: "Highway to Hell" and "Dirty Deeds Done Dirt Cheap"

Ballbreaker: "Hard as a Rock," "Hail Caesar," and "Cover You in Oil"

Stiff Upper Lip: "Stiff Upper Lip," "Safe in New York City," and "Satellite Blues"

Black Ice: "Rock N Roll Train," "Big Jack," "Anything Goes," "Money Made," and "War Machine"

Rock or Bust: "Play Ball" and "Rock or Bust"

Non-Album Single: "Big Gun." This song was released in 1993 and is featured in the movie *Last Action Hero*, starring Arnold Schwarzenegger, who also appeared in the video with the band, directed by David Mallet. The storyline includes Arnold kicking down the door to an AC/DC concert and busting his way through the crowd. He ends up on stage dressed in an Angus schoolboy uniform, complete with a Gibson SG and his best Angus moves. Brian Johnson tells his side of the story in his book *Rockers and Rollers*, including how Arnold almost mowed them down in his (real military style) Humvee and laughingly told them the vehicle was the only ride that fit his shoulders.

AC/DC Bootlegs

AC/DC bootlegs literally number in the thousands and can be found for sale on dozens of websites on the Internet. Below is a list of some of the fan favorites.

AC/DC in the Beginning: Live at Hampton Court Hotel in Sydney, Australia 1974

AC/DC in the Studio: Live Radio Broadcast Atlantic Studios in New York City July 12, 1977

AC/DC from the Vaults: A collection of Bon and Dave Evans tracks with their former bands and some of their early recordings with AC/DC, including live cuts. Released in 2007.

AC/DC Superstars in Concert: Radio broadcast, Westwood One, BBC Radio Sessions, London, England, 1976–79

Apollo in Glasgow: Scotland, April 30, 1978

At the Roseland Ballroom: Recorded in New York City on March 11, 2003

Blues Booze 'N' Tattoos: In Nashville at the Atlantic Record Bar Convention recorded by local radio station WKDF on August 8, 1978

Bon Scott's Last Oui Oui: Pavillon de Paris, September 12, 1979

Chequers: Sydney, Australia, December 31, 1973

A Giant Dose of Rock & Roll: Recorded live at Hurstville Civic Center in Sydney, Australia on February 5, 1977

Hammersmith Odeon: London, December 17, 1979

Live in Adelaide: Australia, 1976

Live at the Agora Ballroom: Cleveland, Ohio, August 22, 1977

Live Milwaukee: Recorded at the Bradley Center in Milwaukee, Wisconsin, on August 30, 2000

Lock Up Your Daughters: Recorded live at the Gustav Siegle Haus in Stuttgart, Germany, on September 28, 1977

Monsters of Rock: Recorded live in Stockholm, Sweden, on August 25, 1984

Myer Music Bowl: Melbourne, Australia, F ebruary 27, 1981

She's Got Balls: Live at the Old Waldorf in San Francisco, January 1, 1977

The Paradise Theater: Boston, August 21, 1978

Trip Wires: Recorded live at Essex University, Colchester, England, on October 28, 1978

DVDs

Listed below are some of their most popular DVDs, among almost 200 titles. If you can't see AC/DC live, this is the next best thing. Don't forget to turn up the volume!

Let There Be Rock: Warner Home Video, July 1985
Fly on the Wall: Atlantic, September 1985
Who Made Who: Atlantic, November 1986
AC/DC: Albert Productions, 1987
Clipped: Atco, June 1990
For Those About to Rock: Monsters in Moscow: Warner Home Video, October 1992
Live at Donington: Atco, October 1992
No Bull: Warner Music Vision, November 1996
Stiff Upper Lip Live: Elektra, November 2001
Live at Donington (Remixed): November 2003
Live '77: VAP Video, January 2003
Family Jewels: Epic, March 2003
Toronto Rocks: Rhino, June 2004
Plug Me In: Columbia, October 2007
Backtracks: Sony Legacy, November 2009
Let There Be Rock: Warner Home Video, June 2011
Live at River Plate: Columbia, May 2011

12

Picking Up the Mantle

How Brian Johnson Was Born to Fill Bon Scott's Shoes

Brian Johnson and Bon Scott had crossed paths in the days before either one of them sang for AC/DC. In the early 1970s, Brian was playing in the band Geordie. They performed two shows with a band called Fang, formerly Fraternity, featuring Bon Scott on vocals.

On the second night Bon saw Brian perform, Brian ended his set writhing around the stage in pain. It was first thought to be an appendix attack, but was actually food poisoning. Bon took this to be a passionate performance, and was quite impressed with Brian's stage presence. On their last night in town, Fang was going to spend the night in their broken-down bus until Brian waited until his landlady was out of sight to smuggle Bon's band into his room, sharing a few beers in front of a gas heater. The next day Fang's bus got towed away, and that was last time Brian and Bon would see each other.

The fact that Bon got to see Brian perform years before his own death was eerie enough, but Bon actually told the band that if they ever needed to replace him, they should consider Brian Johnson.

By 1975, Geordie broke up and Brian worked replacing vinyl roofs on cars. Missing the stage, he talked his bandmates into rejoining in 1978, under the same name. Brian was a huge fan of AC/DC's and added "Whole Lotta Rosie" to Geordie's song list.

Once Bon was gone, the band didn't automatically call Brian. It was a fan over in the States from Ohio who sent a cassette tape to AC/DC's management. When Brian first got the call from Ian Jeffery to come to an audition, he thought it was a joke. After some convincing, Brian arrived at the rehearsal studio on March 29, 1980, and immediately

Brian Johnson, 1980.   *Getty Images*

started playing pool with a couple of the band's friends, thinking they were auditioning, as well. He assumed when the band was ready for him, they would come downstairs and get him.

An hour and a half later, Malcolm came downstairs, frustrated that the singer they were waiting on had apparently stood them up. They all had a good laugh when they realized Brian never got past the pool table! The band brought him up to the studio and he performed only a few songs with AC/DC, including "Whole Lotta Rosie," "Highway to Hell," and Ike and Tina Turner's hit "Nutbush City Limits."

Ian Jeffery, who was at Brian's audition, stated, "The first fucking strain (of Brian's vocals), you could feel the hairs on the back of your neck stand up. Angus gets out of his seat from his cross-legged position and his right leg's on the go. We're off and racing!"

Brian was called back two more times to play with the band. The second round he was asked to come up with lyrics to "Given the Dog a Bone," and on March 29, Malcolm called Brian to come back and jam with them for the third time.

On April 8, 1980, AC/DC announced that they had found their new singer. Immediately after being hired, AC/DC switched from recording *Back in Black* in London to Compass Studios in the Bahamas. It was a great hideaway for the band, and culture shock for Brian, who had problems recording in shorts and a T-shirt. Once he discovered he recorded better in his stage clothes, all went well.

However, the weight of writing lyrics for the new album was no small feat, and one night Brian claims something or someone woke him up in the middle of the night, and he was up into the wee hours writing lyrics as fast as he could get the words out. That's where "Hell's Bells" was born, and the new album, *Back in Black*, would go onto to become one of the biggest-selling albums in rock 'n' roll history.

Perry Cooper had his own doubts about anyone replacing Bon.

> I said to myself, how are they going to replace him? He had such a weird voice. Nobody ever said if it was good or bad, but it was different. And then I met Brian, and just fell in love with him. He is such a nice guy. Bon was, too. Yes, he liked to drink, he liked to party. But he was the sweetest man in the world. I really, at one time, considered him my best friend. From what I hear, in his passport, where you have a next of kin to call in case of an emergency, he had my name in it. This is what I was told. Whatever. I miss him to death. Brian just took it up, when he took over in *Back in Black*, he just picked up the mantle. And I never thought anybody could ever pick up the mantle.

And he did, he really did. And that's been the reason for the band's success all these years.

Perry and I both agreed that AC/DC's music is timeless. Perry declared, "And their material, Angus and Malcolm come up with such classic riffs. [The songs] are anthems, absolute anthems. Now when can you watch a

Bon Scott's bronze statue with Ted Ward, original guitar player from the Valentines; John D'Arcy, one of Bon's best friends and roadie for the Valentines; and Vince Lovegrove, also a member of the Valentines and a very close friend of Bon's. *Photo by Doug Thorncroft*

football game or a baseball game, and you don't hear 'Hell's Bells,' or any of those? They're anthems!"

On February 13, 1981, almost one year to the day after Bon's death, AC/DC played in Perth, Australia. It was their first time performing there in over three years. Many of Bon's family and friends were present, making Bon's heir feel like a member of the family. Brian was also completely surprised by the audience's reaction. He said, "I remember the first night after we played. I'm not an emotional person by any stretch of the imagination. But the kids had this forty-foot-long banner right across the audience, and it had 'The king is dead; long live the king.' And it was smashing. It was great. And then we went to England and the kids were chanting because they knew how I felt. They knew I was scared." That night, Brian dedicated "High Voltage" to Bon's mum, Isa.

Commenting on singing Bon's songs, Brian said, "The amazing thing about the older stuff, is that when we do a song like 'Let There Be Rock' on stage, sometimes it seems like Bon's ghost is right up there with us. It's a very strange feeling. But we're sure that Bon would have wanted us to keep playing those numbers, and when you see the reaction from the fans, you know that they want us to keep playin' 'em too."

13

The Second-Highest Grossing Tour in Music History

The *Black Ice* Tour

After a seven-year break, AC/DC went back into the studio in the spring of 2008 to record their new album, *Black Ice*. An extensive worldwide tour was planned, and 3,000 very lucky fans got to attend a dress rehearsal at the Wachovia Arena in Wilkes-Barre, Pennsylvania, on October 26, 2008. Two nights later, the band opened the tour in Wilkes-Barre.

Tickets to the dress rehearsal were won over the radio, and some were sold to the highest bidder. Fans flew in from all over the world to see AC/DC for the first time since 2001, cementing the fact that AC/DC fans are some of the most dedicated fans in the world. It was now almost forty years since their first performance, and fans would show up anywhere at anytime for a chance to see them play live.

During AC/DC's seven-year hiatus, they left their longtime label, Atlantic Records, and signed a new deal with Sony Music. To whet their fan's appetites, AC/DC released a double and triple DVD entitled *Plug Me In*, which was released in October 2007. The different DVD versions included five and seven hours of rare concert footage, including AC/DC performing "School Days," "T.N.T.," "She's Got Balls," and "It's a Long Way to the Top (If You Wanna Rock 'n' Roll)," which had been filmed in March of 1976 at St. Alban's High School in Australia.

The band also jumped on the video game wagon by announcing their debut in *Rock Band 2*, with the song "Let There Be Rock" as a playable track. This was followed up by *AC/DC Live: Rock Band Track Pack*, including their entire set list from the *Live At Donington* album. The pack featured eighteen songs and was specially remixed by Mike Fraser.

To celebrate the release of AC/DC's first album in seven years, Sirius/XM Satellite Radio launched AC/DC Radio, a channel that aired AC/DC music 24/7 from September of 2008 through January of 2009.

The band recorded fifteen tracks in just six weeks, and *Black Ice*, AC/DC's eighteenth studio album, was released on October 18, 2008, in Australia and October 20 in the US. A video for their first single, "Rock N Roll Train," was filmed on August 15 in London in front of several hundred fans who won a chance to be part of the audience. The single debuted on the radio on August 28, and three months later, "Rock N Roll Train" was nominated for a Grammy for Best Rock Performance by a Duo or Group with Vocals.

Surprising some of their fans, AC/DC signed an exclusive contract with Walmart and Sam's Club to be the only outlets to sell the new album, aside from their official website. Answering the question of the bold move, Malcolm simply stated to a mutual friend that Walmart preordered 2.5 million copies and eliminated all the distribution costs. Always the straight-forward businessman, Malcolm made a sound business decision.

After waiting seven long years, AC/DC fans around the world rejoiced in their announcement of a worldwide tour. Including forty-two dates, the first leg of their North American tour would end in Nashville, Tennessee, on January 31, 2008. From there the band toured through Europe, Asia, South America, Australia, and all points in between, keeping them on the road until the end of the summer of 2010. *Billboard* reported that AC/DC's *Black Ice* tour ended up the second-highest-grossing tour of all time, generating over 441.6 million dollars in sales.

To coincide with the US release of *Black Ice*, Columbia Records (Sony Music) and Walmart created "Rock Again AC/DC Stores." It was a first for Walmart to dedicate such a large area of their floor space to the release of a new album. Columbia also teamed up with MTV to Create "AC/DC Rock Band Stores" in Times Square in New York City and Los Angeles. To celebrate the event, *Black Ice* trucks drove through both cities blaring AC/DC music, stopping at random places to sell merchandise.

Selling more than 784,000 copies in the US in the first week of its release, *Black Ice* debuted at #1 in thirty-one countries, becoming platinum within days. It also marked the first time an AC/DC album debuted at #1 here in the States.

AC/DC also broke records for ticket sales for the new tour. Within minutes, their appearance at the Allstate Arena in Chicago sold out, forcing them to add a second show. Both nights at New York City's Madison Square Garden sold out in minutes, and their show at the General Motors Place in Vancouver broke records by selling out within just four minutes of the tickets going on sale. AC/DC also set records in Australia for selling 212,729 tickets for their three concerts in Sydney's ANZ stadium.

As the band took to the road, their first tour in seven years brought an avalanche of rave reviews from the press. The *Boston Globe* declared, "AC/DC is the greatest band ever"; the *Chicago Tribune* stated, "'AC/DC: Rock 'n' Roll that outlasts time;" and the *Associated Press* confirmed, "Critical acclaim escaped them . . . until now."

After thirty years, *Rolling Stone* finally featured AC/DC on the cover of their November 13, 2008 issue. Executive editor Jason Fine said, "It's their best record since *Back in Black*, since 1980. Unlike some of the records they made over the last twenty years, this one really sounds alive."

Brian Johnson told the *Associated Press*, "The critics have always been a little flippant with AC/DC about Angus and the school suit, and it's always easy to have a quick little joke or a dig at the expense of it, the easy riffs, and such and such, and they're all dead wrong. The easiest riffs in the world are the hardest ones to write, because they are very few."

Due to the band being off the road for seven years, this tour would be very different. The band were only doing a select amount of interviews, and for the first time ever, there would be no meet and greets after the show. Regardless, I still requested an interview with Angus, and asked for a chance to come backstage and say hello when they played Chicago on November 1, 2008.

Brian Johnson belting it out on the *Black Ice* tour. The massive locomotive and stage design reportedly cost four million dollars to create.   *Photo by Henri Lassander*

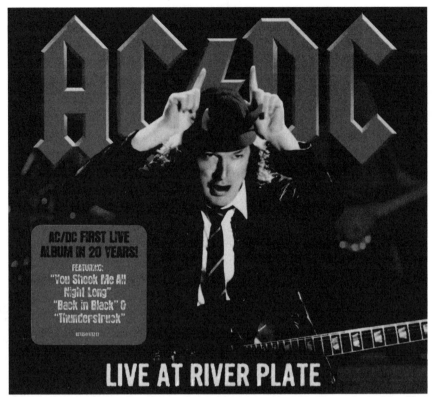

AC/DC FIRST LIVE
ALBUM IN 20 YEARS!

FEATURING:
"You Shook Me All
Night Long"
"Back in Black" &
"Thunderstruck"

LIVE AT RIVER PLATE

The double DVD *Live at River Plate*, recorded and mixed by Mike Fraser during the *Black Ice* tour, was filmed over three concerts at the El Monumental "River Plate" Stadium in Buenos Aires, Argentina. Reportedly the band played to over 200,000 people over those three dates. The live footage includes interviews with the band, fans, and road crew members. *Live at River Plate* debuted at number one in seventeen countries, selling 19,000 copies in the US in the first week and 40,000 copies in Brazil in just two weeks. The world premiere of the film was held at the Hammersmith Apollo in London on May 6, 2011.

Giving me one of the biggest rock 'n' roll surprises of my life, AC/DC's tour manager called me the day before the tour started to tell me that not only would Angus be happy to give me an interview, but I also had tickets and after-show passes waiting for me in Chicago. Even though they were limiting interviews, when Angus heard that I wanted to talk to him, he said, "If Sue wants an interview, Sue gets an interview." I guess you could say that there are some perks to having known the band for over thirty years!

When they hit the stage at the Allstate Arena, there were no doubts that one of the most successful bands in the world hadn't lost their rock 'n' roll Midas touch. In front of 17,000 screaming fans, AC/DC's show opened with an animated cartoon of the band traveling on what else, but a rock 'n' roll train. Surrounded by devilish girls trying to "distract" them, the boys barely manage to overcome them when Angus narrowly escapes the train before it crashes off the tracks. As the cartoon ends, a life-size black locomotive comes barreling out over the stage, halting just above the drum riser amid flying sparks and a thunderous roar from the audience. Suddenly Phil appears behind the drum kit, and Brian, Malcolm, Cliff, and Angus stride out onto the stage, launching into "Rock N Roll Train," heralding the return of the greatest rock 'n' roll band in the world.

For the next hour and forty-five minutes, AC/DC played five songs from their new album *Black Ice*, including the title track along with "Big Jack," "War Machine," "Anything Goes," and "Rock N Roll Train." The rest of their show featured an amazing string of rock 'n' roll anthems, including "Hell Ain't a Bad Place to Be," "Dirty Deeds," "Thunderstruck," "The Jack," "Hell's Bells," "Shoot to Thrill," "You Shook Me," "T.N.T.," "Whole Lotta Rosie," and "Let There Be Rock." Their performances were incredible, and I can't say I have ever heard them sound better.

As they closed the show with "Let There Be Rock," Angus careened out onto a walkway that led to a circular stage that rose at least twenty feet above the crowd. From his perch, he ripped through a scorching solo while spinning around on his back. Generating enough energy to power an entire city, after thirty-four years Angus proved that he could still bring it. The whole crowd, many of them sporting glowing red devil horns, went completely wild for the diminutive schoolboy, who barely stands five foot two. That's Angus Young; the real live Guitar Hero.

Just minutes after leaving the stage, AC/DC returned for a two-song encore of "Highway to Hell" and "For Those About to Rock." During "Highway to Hell," pictures flashed above the stage of days gone by with singer Bon Scott. Singing along to Bon's lyrics, the audience and the band always celebrate the legendary frontman. Bon has had a lasting impression on the band and their tongue-in-cheek image. Fond memories of Bon, always the life of the party, will forever be honored by the band.

After the show, my fourteen-year-old son Jamey and I had the privilege of visiting with Angus and Malcolm in their dressing room in the basement of the Allstate Arena. Sitting together sipping tea and smoking cigarettes, it was amazing to see how relaxed and down to earth they both were, considering they had just gotten done tearing up the stage in front of thousands of people. As always, it was like we had just seen each other last week, and we had fun joking about their ability to make it through the show. I know I was tired and sweaty from just watching them!

I asked Malcolm if he starts counting how many songs are left by the time they get to the middle of their set. He laughed and said, "Yeah, I do!" When we talked about the fans fearing that they would never tour again, Malcolm assured me that they always intended to go back out on tour. Then he looked over at Angus and said, "Well this has been the first real break we've had since 1974, right?" I also asked Angus if he would ever consider having an art show to display his paintings, and he immediately told me no. Then Malcolm laughed and said, "He's saving that for his old age!"

During our visit, we talked about how well the album was received and how devoted their fans are. I couldn't help bringing up the first night we met in 1977, when I predicted that someday they would be as big as the Rolling Stones. At the time the band thought that statement was outrageous, but Malcolm smiled and said, "Well, we did blow them off the stage at the SARS Benefit in Toronto, I know that much!"

Angus and Malcolm were both especially kind to my son, asking him all about school and what his interests were. When Angus mentioned how tall he was for fourteen years old, he quickly added, "Well then, everyone's taller than me." As we said our good-byes, Jamey got some posters signed, and we got our pictures taken. If that wasn't enough to give my son memories of a lifetime, Angus reached into his pocket (at his wife Ellen's suggestion), and gave Jamey the guitar pick he had used that night.

A few days later on November 4, 2008, Angus was generous enough to call me to talk about *Black Ice* and the incredible longevity of AC/DC.

It's been a long time in between albums. How long did it take you to put together the songs for the new album?
It starts with the last tour, you get some ideas then. It might be a song title or something, or a riff that you would get at a sound check, or backstage, and you keep a log of it. And that kind of becomes the basis of when you start to write. And also you do a lot of writing at home, when you take a break off the tour and have a rest.

After writing songs for over thirty years, does it get any easier?
Does it get any easier? Sometimes you rely on a lot of things through experience. But I think writing songs is something you learn, but it's a kind of learning through a kind of experience. Then after a while, you hope you get better at it.

Well, I don't think you have to worry about it. I think you have that down!

Yeah, but sometimes you wish you could write like I did when I was really young. You always want to write something that strikes a chord with a lot of people. I think that's the magic.

Well, I think you did that with the new album. I think you have some classics on here.
All right, good! (Laughs)

I heard that you wanted to come up with a title for the new album that would be tough, something that sounded hard. Who came up with the title Black Ice *?*
Well, it was me that came up with it. But we had already had a song called "Black Ice," and at the end of the day, we thought it would make a good album title.

Do you have a favorite song on the album?
I like a lot of them. But when you're writing and playing them, they all become your babies. Usually you do a lot of demos of the songs, and try to pick the ones that capture the spirit of the band.

Everything was written by you and Malcolm. Do you write the lyrics together or do you write one song and then Malcolm writes another?
Well, you kind of bounce off each other. I might come up with a line or he might come up with a chorus.

Who decides on the design of the album and the staging for the tour?
We come up with the album title, and then the artists bring you their ideas for it. They come up with things trying to see what matches your ideas best.

Well, I love the way the stage looks with the big locomotive. It all looked so cool!
Yeah! Well, a lot of it, again, we had enough time, and sometimes you get very rushed. A lot of things fall into place, and sometimes you have to sacrifice some things because of the time factor. This time we were very lucky because we already had all the songs that would definitely be on the album. Again, they [the artists] took the songs and came back with different ideas.

I realize you've only done about four shows so far, but what part of the show is your favorite, and why?
Favorite part? I think probably for me, it would be the anticipation. You get ready, and then you think, "I wish I was on now. I'm ready to go now!" I guess it would be for me, waiting to go out there and get wild.

Were you surprised by the fans and how much they wanted the band to come back out on tour?

Cliff Williams and me backstage at the Allstate Arena in Chicago, Illinois, on the *Black Ice* tour, November 1, 2008. I also got to meet Cliff's son Luke, who was there with a group of friends.

I suppose, you hear a lot of it. People around the band tell us what's going on. There's always a lot of people talking, but no one takes the time to check with the band. So sometimes we're the last to hear about something. Even when we went up to Vancouver to record, it was several weeks before anyone knew about it.

Back when we first met, some of the band talked about being rich and famous. Do you miss those days when you could go out and not be stopped by people everywhere you go?

I don't think I ever thought about being rich and famous. I think when you're young, and at that age, everything is an adventure. When you're living it at the time, you don't think that far ahead. Even today, I try to take things day to day. When someone asks me about something six months from now, I don't think that far ahead. I think at the time, I was happy to be doing what I was doing. It was an education, in a way.

Of course when I watched the show the other night, you can't help but think about Bon and how much he contributed to the band. What do you think Bon would have to say about how successful AC/DC is today?

He would love it! He would be living it to the hilt. It was just the nature of his character. He always used to say to me, "Whatever I do, don't do!"

When you're on stage playing some of the older songs, do you feel his presence around you?

Yeah, of course. Even sometimes when I'm just walking around, I think, Am I walking like him? The way Bon walked, with kind of a swagger. (Laughs)

It's amazing how well Brian was able to fit into the band.

Brian is his own character. He has such a good time. He was a fan of the music and brings something to it which is totally different from Bon. He's definitely his own character.

He is so funny, always cracking jokes.
That's right. For us, he keeps us highly entertained. And he brings a lot of things down to earth.

I know when I interviewed Perry Cooper, who was with Atlantic Records and very close to Bon, he didn't think it was possible for you to replace him. Then he went out on the road with you after Back in Black came out, and he was floored by how funny Brian was. I can't imagine during the recording of the album, being in so much pain, that you knew at the time that it would become one of the top ten biggest selling albums in history!
Yeah, I think at the time, you really don't know. But we had some strong songs, and we wanted to finish them. In a way, the recording was very therapeutic for us, because after a while you can start wallowing in it. It's always harder for the people left behind. The hardest part when you lose someone very close to you, is how do you do this? How do you go on?

To Brian's credit, look how great he did, and how loving and respectful he's been toward Bon's memory.
That's right! He's also a fan of those songs, and every time we get together to tour, he always wants to do one of the old tracks—"Let's try this one!" And he always does it in his own way.

It's funny to be talking about him like the new guy, considering he's been in the band now for twenty-eight years.
Yeah, well I'll always be the youngest! And I always say, don't have birthdays!

After seeing the band close to twenty times over the years, I don't think I have ever heard you sound better! It was so perfect, it was like listening to the album!
Good to know. Then the sound system was worth the money! (Laughing)

How do you feel about how the band is playing? Have they surprised you at all?
Yes, they have. I was in shock that they had done the album! (Laughing) From that point on, how everyone sounded, and that we did it in a very short time. It was a good experience also working with Mike Fraser again. It was also very good to work with Brendan O'Brien, who has a musician's background, and communicating with someone like that is also very good, because he knows exactly what you need. He knows what you're talking about. He is very, very sharp.

You didn't take that long to record the new album. How long were you actually in Vancouver?

About six weeks. You've got to do your homework first. Get all of that done before you go in. Then once you go in, it's all about getting the right sound. And then it's all about capturing the moment.

If there was one thing you are most proud of AC/DC, what would that be?

I think it's just the band being able to keep going. It's probably surviving this long. And playing what we've always played. From the moment I joined the band, Malcolm asked me to come along and play second guitar. And I asked him what we were going to play, and he said, "That's obvious. We're just going to play rock 'n' roll!"

Some describe AC/DC as a metal band, but I love the fact that you always claim to be a rock 'n' roll band.

That's what we are, and that's what we do best!

14

They Won the Title, But Lost the Cover

Highway to Hell

T he first time the phrase "highway to hell" was used was when Angus was asked by a reporter how the tour was going. At that point, AC/DC had been touring nonstop for several years, and their American booking agent had no mercy on how many miles the band racked up crossing the United States more than once. Angus stated in the *LA Times*, "We toured for four years at a stretch with no break. A guy asked how you would best describe our tours. We said, 'A highway to hell.' The phrase stuck with us. All we'd done is describe what it's like to be on the road for four years."

After three long years of constant touring, AC/DC went into the studio at first with Eddie Kramer, who was to produce *Highway to Hell*. Kramer and the band never clicked, prompting Malcolm to call their manager Michael Browning for guidance. Browning just happened to be hanging out with the legendary producer Mutt Lange, who quickly took over the position.

The new album contained some of their best work up to this point, and would unfortunately be Bon's last official recording with AC/DC. The ten explosive tracks were "Highway to Hell," "Girl's Got Rhythm," "Walk All Over You," "Touch Too Much," "Beating Around the Bush," "Shot Down in Flames," "Get It Hot," "If You Want Blood (You've Got It)," "Love Hungry Man," and "Night Prowler." The last cut features Bon's best impression of Robin Williams as Mork, his television character from the show *Mork & Mindy*. You can hear him say at the end of the song, "Shazbot . . . nano, nano."

Malcolm summed up *Highway to Hell* in *Metal CD*:

> That was a definite change for AC/DC. Atlantic Records in America were unhappy because they couldn't get the band on the radio, and they were desperate for us to come up with something more

Band glossy used for the *Highway to Hell* album cover. The record company rejected the original cover for the album, which was supposed to be the Devil behind the wheel of a car, looking into the rearview mirror with the band sitting in the back seat. At the last minute, they used this publicity glossy and superimposed horns and a tail on Angus, making it the first time Angus was portrayed as the "Little Devil."

accessible. We'd had our own way for a few albums, so we figured, "Let's give them what they want and everyone will be happy."

'Touch Too Much' was a hit off that record, but the one song that stands out head and shoulders over everything else was the title track. If certain people had their way, it wouldn't have been called "Highway to Hell," because the Bible Belt was very strong in America at the time and they made a fuss once the record came out. But even though we were under pressure, we stuck to our guns.

As soon as the album was finished, the band went back out on tour and opened their *If You Want Blood (You've Got It)* tour here in Madison, Wisconsin. Phil was very excited about the new album, and told me they were convinced that this was going to be the record that would put them over the top. I was stunned by the new songs, and the polished sound of the new record.

Phil also told me all about the photographs that were taken for the album artwork. One night they went out on a dark road in Staten Island to photograph the band hitchhiking. The artwork was to depict the band getting into a car, and the cover picture was going to be the band riding in the backseat, with the devil behind the steering wheel driving, while smiling at them in the rearview mirror. Kind of creepy, actually. Phil thought it was hilarious that these kids had followed them out to the shoot, and threw rocks at them while they were trying to pose. He was also defiant about how upset the record company had been over their choice of album titles.

The album title stuck, but the cover art didn't. When I received a copy of the album, I was shocked to see the cover photo. Apparently the band had won the battle over the album's title, but lost the war over the cover pictures. Instead of using the shot of the devil driving a car while smiling in the rear view mirror at the band in the back seat, the record company used an already-released publicity shot of the band. The only change they had made to it was superimposing horns and a tail on Angus. This is the first time AC/DC's marketing portrayed Angus as a little devil.

Contrary to popular belief, the necklace that Bon is wearing in the picture is not satanic. Yes, he is wearing a pendant with a pentagram on it, but the pentagram is pointing up, which means white magic, or positive energy. They did end up using one shot of the band standing on the road from that photo session for the album's back cover.

15

Bells, Babes, Cannons, Wrecking Balls, Statues, and Locomotives

AC/DC and Their Toys

T he opening track on *Back in Black* features the haunting sound of a church bell chiming a death knell, signaling the beginning of "Hell's Bells." To create the proper mood for the song, the band decided to record an actual church bell. They also commissioned a $14,000 replica of the four-ton Denison bell to take out on tour with them. Luckily for the roadies, they settled on a lighter version, at one and a half tons.

Engineer Tony Platt took the Manor Mobile recording unit out, and surrounded the carillon, which stands in the middle of Loughborough's War Memorial in Leicestershire, England. Armed with twenty-four microphones, they were still unsuccessful. The live recording had to be scrapped, and the band decided to capture the sound of the bell right in the foundry. Steve Cake's father was working at the John Taylor Bell founders back in 1980 when the call from the Bahamas came in. Cake said, "The traffic and birds chirping made that recording unusable. So the work (on the AC/DC bell) was speeded up, and what you hear on the album was definitely recorded at our factory." The actual person who forged the bell rings it on the album.

Starting out with just two cannons, their stage design has changed with every tour. Having someone who knew how to handle the pyrotechnics was crucial, and that's when "Pyro" Pete was hired. Pete Cappadocia excitedly recalled getting the opportunity to work with AC/DC. "I was working for Def Leppard, and their production manager was friends with Jake Berry, who was AC/DC's production manager at the time. They wanted to make some changes with the cannons, in 'For Those About to Rock.' So I think Jake was off at the time, and he came to one of our shows, and I met him and we talked. He said the next time they were ready to go back out on tour, they would call me. So they called, it was about 1983. We made a few changes with the cannons, and then I headed off with the band. And then we were off and running. Every tour since 1983, they've called me, and we've either made changes, or built new cannons."

Delighting fire marshals around the world, AC/DC would roll out two cannons for their encore, "For Those About to Rock (We Salute You)." It was a constant battle to get the clearance to use them every night. Sometimes the road crew would be backstage handcuffed during the song, and at other times, Ian Jeffery would provide the cannon blasts courtesy of a Prophet synthesizer. Perry Cooper laughed about what happened in Connecticut. "I remember when the fire marshal came up and said they couldn't fire the cannons. Well, they did and we got arrested that night. At least they gave us a good talking to. Years later, the roof caved in on that place!"

Aside from the cannons and bell, shows on the *Who Made Who* tour opened with the title track, which featured local fans dressed as Angus. You would think a one and a half ton bell would pose some problems, but according to "Pyro" Pete, Angus impersonators were much more hazardous. He explained,

> When you get the show up and running, it becomes like a machine that just runs. It's like one of those huge printing presses that you can't just turn off or it will rip itself apart. Or a locomotive, that can't stop on a dime.
>
> For the *Who Made Who* tour, there were winners for an Angus look-alike contest. The show would start, and it would be however many they could get, whether it was ten, twenty, or even thirty, they would be up along the back line of the stage with their cardboard guitars, doing their best Angus impersonation. And then the real Angus would rise up on an elevator in this tube in the center, and come up about six or eight feet higher than the fake Anguses. We had a signal where we would grab the first fake Angus, from behind, and they would turn around and come off the stage back down the same way they went up. Well, not always would these guys want to come off the stage!
>
> So you would get these fake Anguses running around, and sometimes it would be like trying to catch a chicken or something. Where everyone else would leave, you would always get this one guy who is still throwing his arm up. And we're back there hitting him with balls of rolled up tape, or poking him with a yardstick, trying to tell him to get the hell down! We didn't want to ruin the illusion by having

somebody on the crew just jump up and grab this guy and wrestle him off the stage!

The band was always like that, too. [They always said] if a fan got up on the stage, don't run out and tackle him and beat the hell out of him. I never figured out that mentality, either. Some bands are like that. If a fan gets up on the stage, and if I'm in a position where I see it happen, I'll run out and put my arm around them, and escort them off the stage. If they start to fight, then you have to drag them off. So the band didn't want us pummeling the fake Anguses during the show!

But more than once, we had to resort to poking them fairly hard to get their attention. I remember one time we grabbed this one guy by his ankles, and we were trying to get him off to the side and he fell down. So then he started rolling around on the floor doing Angus' whole solo. The rest of the band didn't even know what was going on! Cliff walks front to back, front to back, and looks down at his feet, and looks at the microphone. Angus runs all around, and Brian runs all around. And Malcolm does the same as Cliff, he walks up to the microphone and walks back, he doesn't really look, he looks down at this feet or at the microphone.

So Simon was the only one who saw what was going on, and he was really laughing watching us trying to get this guy off the stage. Finally it came to a point where somebody had to go up and grab him, and even when we were pulling him off the stage, he's still throwing his arm up into the air! Stage crews always cringe whenever we hear the two words "contest winner."

For a while, MTV and all the local radio stations and promoters used to hold contests. I remember when they came up with "Roadie for a Day." Which meant that you got some kid who was a fanatical fan who was just insane about it. Another "roadie for a day" guy, and he wanted a cleaning job, like cleaning the bell. And the guy says, "Oh my God, not the bell!" We told him he didn't really have to clean the whole bell, we just gave him some brass polish and a rag and asked him to just clean around the AC/DC letters. He must have taken a toothpick, a Q-tip, and a toothbrush and gotten every molecule of dirt off of the bell. When it came down that night, and the lights hit it, it looked really good!

Each time AC/DC goes out on tour, they make a special effort to keep the stage show new and exciting for the fans. The *Ballbreaker* stage featured a very large gray, industrial-looking building, which ran across the entire stage. Along the top were thin rectangular windows, with several garage doors running along the bottom. The show opened with a video flashing

AC/DC and their Rock 'n' Roll Train at the Partizan Stadium in Belgrade, Serbia, on May 26, 2009.
Photo by Brian Rasic

across giant projection screens that hung above the stage. It was a cartoon feature of Beavis and Butthead backstage, looking around for chicks.

After they knock on AC/DC's dressing room door, Angus answers and presents them both with one hell of a mighty rock chick who cracks a whip, and starts the ball rolling. Or should I say, the wrecking ball, a very large one at that, which lowers down from the ceiling. Accompanied by flashing lights and the sounds of roaring engines and screeching metal, the ball proceeds to swing back and forth, demolishing the building. Among pieces of flying debris, the garage doors open to reveal the band, who immediately break into "Back in Black." The set list, completely new for the tour, included songs originally recorded with Bon Scott, like "Dog Eat Dog," "Shot Down in Flames," "Girl's Got Rhythm," and "Down Payment Blues," plus two songs they hadn't played since 1978: "Gone Shootin'" and "Riff Raff."

"Pyro" Pete explained to me how the tours have changed over the years.

When I first started, we had two cannons, which we used for a couple of tours. And then they went to a different stage set and they built cannons into the stage set that had big deck guns which looked like they were off a battle ship. They came up and telescoped out. That was one of the first real departures from the original cannons.

And then we did the *Monsters of Rock* in 1991, where we had twenty-one cannons. We had seven up each side for an outdoor stadium show, and seven across the middle, for a total of twenty-one guns. We actually had a whole truck just for these fiberglass cannons, but they had to be made a little bit shorter, and a little bit squattier, so we could fit them all in the truck.

Then on another tour, we revamped those cannons, and actually put a recoiling mechanism on them so when we shot them, they would jerk back. So every year, they wouldn't want to replay it. It was always fun, because it would be like a subtle difference, but it would just change the vibe of the thing. It was kind of cool, because it wasn't the same old thing. The bell went through as many variations as the cannons. Every tour was like, "What can we do to the bell this time, how can we make the bell's appearance look different?" One tour, Brian used to like the bell to come down, and he would grab a big clanger. It was an actual bell clangor that should have been on the inside of a bell, but we had a wooden handle put on it, something the size of a sledgehammer. But it was made specifically for hitting a bell, so it wouldn't break. So Brian would hit the bell with this thing, and that's what he really enjoyed, he really liked that.

But one year we decided to build a mechanism that would swing the bell, so it looks like the bell is swinging, like in a bell tower. Brian had a button at the end of the rope that would actually activate the clanger. So they would lower down this big black metal structure that was like a frame, and you really couldn't see the frame around it, because it was painted flat black. So one of the carpenters would turn on the mechanism to swing the bell, as Brian would pull on the rope.

Brian had a bit of a bungee cord at the top so he could look like he was pulling on this thing. Which he was, so the bell would start swinging back and forth, and when he pressed the button, the bell would clang. So fine, we've got everything going, and he gets out and the bells swinging, and he's having fun with it, and he's deciding he likes it, and he jumps up really high and grabs the rope, and comes down on it with all his weight! The bungee cord snaps, and Brian lands on his back! And the whole rope, all forty feet of it, landed on his chest. He immediately got up and started prancing around on stage, and all he said was, "Cheap fucking rope!" He never missed a beat!

One time we had the cannons on these electric lifts that would lift them up, and one night only one side would rise, because the other side had gotten unplugged or blown a fuse, or any of the million things that go wrong at a show. We're trying to lift this thing manually, and Brian is singing away, looking at the one that wasn't working, and right in time with the music, he sings, "Come on, you bastards!" It's so much fun, when things go wrong, it's not like someone is stamping their feet, or there's a meeting where heads are going to roll. Which is so unusual. Any other rock star, where the bungee cord broke, would have wanted to know who was responsible. He was used to being able to swing on the rope, because another incarnation of the bell, we had the clanger installed inside the bell, and Brian could pull on the rope to make it clang, and that rope he could swing on, which he used to do all the time. Needless to say, the bungee cord/electric clanger mechanism did not see too many tours. I believe we went back to pulling on the rope clanger, fairly quickly.

"Pyro" went on to explain the difficulties of firing off cannons every night.

Outside the United States, I've set up the cannons and left for the next city. Sometimes we weren't exactly cleared to use them, and I was the only one who knew how to set them up. Shooting the cannons involves a trigger or a pickle, as it's known in the demolition business. A button in a handheld device that goes through a firing system. Once you press the button, it would shoot a concussion mortar, from the backstage area, and simultaneously it would shoot a flash device in the cannon. So the cannon would do the puff of smoke, and a big flash, but the loud bang comes from a device next to the cannon.

That's one of the great things about the band. They know they're a rock band, and they know they could go out with no stage set, no nothing and just play, and the people would be happy. But they want to do a different look without being overly theatrical. They at least wanted to make it so each time they went out their stage set mimicked the album cover, or the art. Although they didn't need any of these things, unlike a lot of groups that need the production because the band isn't that good, or the music isn't that good. Some acts need the production to hide the flaws. These guys don't need the production, but they think the fans enjoy it. You get a double bonus: you get an excellent band, and a good stage production to watch, as well.

They would never have an effect just for having an effect. If an effect didn't have a point, it wasn't used for no reason. The band wouldn't allow that. We finally got them to use flames for "Highway to Hell." After they saw them, they agreed to use them. They also never wanted their effects to appear as effects, they wanted it to appear mechanical, as in the wall getting torn down for the *Ballbreaker* tour. It all had to look functional.

The stage design for the *Stiff Upper Lip* tour featured a forty-foot bronze statue of Angus, complete with billowing smoke and glowing red horns. Or as Angus said, "There's lots of surprises. It's a big show. I know, because I'm paying the bills!" Adding another visual treat, along with the cannons and bell, was not without its challenges.

"Pyro" Pete explained,

> When we used the statue for *Stiff Upper Lip*, it didn't quite come apart like it was intended to. It was supposed to fall apart during the show, and there were guidelines to keep falling in the right places. I remember during one of the rehearsals, the head almost coming down and barely missing Phil. It landed right next to the drum kit with a huge thud. And everybody just stood there and said, "Wow! Now that's not good!" Then we had to slow down the falling apart of it. We added pyrotechnics to it, so it looked like it was blowing apart. It used to blow smoke out of its mouth, the horns would light up, and then it would fall apart. We added all the pyro to the joints, so when the arm fell off, it would blow a bunch of sparks. It would also throw sparks, and flash and smoke. That way we could use the ropes to pull the arm in a little slower.
>
> There were actually air bags for these pieces to land on. The real reason for the ropes was in case you had to, you could stop a piece. Even though they had something to land on, these were pieces of two hundred pounds each of Styrofoam, fiberglass, and fire coating. It took quite a bit to make it work right. The real fun about that was backstage when the statue fell apart. Now that was the place to be!

Waiting for seven years after the *Stiff Upper Lip* tour to be called back to duty, "Pyro" Pete was ready more than ever to see what the theme of the new tour would be. The opening track on the *Black Ice* album, "Rock N Roll Train," inspired the creation of a massive locomotive designed and produced by Brilliant Stages in London.

Dealing with the bell, the cannons, Rosie, tons of pyrotechnics, and now a locomotive, the most eventful mishap for the crew happened before the *Black Ice* tour even started. For one month the band rehearsed at the Center Stage in Wilkes-Barre, Pennsylvania, in September of 2008. "Pyro" Pete explained the process:

> Actually the best tale I have for you was during the rehearsals. We're in rehearsals with the train, the inflatables, and all the props and everything, and we're trying to figure out what to use, when, where, why, and how.
>
> We were rigging up all the flames for the train, practicing with that, and they had the "Doris" inflatable out, which is English slang for an "easy" woman. We have several different names because there are actually several different Rosies. To keep from getting confusing,

let's just call her Rosie. So we had Rosie out, and typically during the day, the carpenters, the effects guys, the sound guys, we're all in there doing our thing. Then at night, the lighting guys will have it. So they need to turn all the lights off so they can play with them.

So we go back to the hotel, and after a nice hard twelve to fourteen hour day, I'm just getting to bed when I get a phone call from Opie [production manager Dale Skjerseth, known throughout the industry as 'Opie']. I get a frantic phone call, "There's a fire on the stage! There's a runner coming to get you guys, so get your crew!" And then he hangs up. So I grab all my guys and run downstairs and there's a runner there, so we shoot back to the venue, and we get there just as the fire department is getting there.

We go inside, and the stupid inflatable [Rosie], the lighting guys were playing with the inflatable, testing it with lights and everything, they deflated it, and then it was laid down on top of some lights. And they went off on focusing some of the lights, and as the inflatable laid there, it caused a fire backstage, which had nothing to do with us!

Then we were told, "You're here, so you're going to help clean up." So we were there for several hours because they had discharged the fire extinguishers and they had some CO_2 fire extinguishers, which are fairly clean, but they also had some dry-chemical fire extinguishers, which put out this lye-like sprinkle that spreads real thin and when you sweep it up, it gets everywhere.

We were rustled out our hotel in the middle of the night for an emergency, and we just about split our guts laughing when we see these lights that are totally melted and Rosie has a big hole melted into her. Then we had to get on the phone and get the guy in storage, because they have several different Rosies from several different tours. So we got a replacement Rosie sent down there, but it was all pretty hectic.

This one we had to modify, because this Rosie [the one that melted] was the one who looked like she was sitting on the train. The one they sent was one where she was laying on her side, so it involved new platforms and moving some of the pyro and lights around to make it work. And this happened just days before the tour started, so we had to have the replacement Rosie FedExed out!

The stats on AC/DC's Rock 'n' Roll Train were included in an official press release from Brilliant Stages, which was issued on November 26, 2008. It stated:

> Brilliant Stages has designed and manufactured the infrastructure of the spectacular focal point of AC/DC's *Black Ice* tour 2008, the "Rock 'n' Roll Train." Conceived by Fisher Studio's Jeremy Lloyd and Mike

Fisher, the centerpiece is inspired by the first track on AC/DC's new album and requires a "life-size" steam locomotive which appears to have crashed onto [the] stage.

The locomotive needs to be hidden upstage at the top of the show before, self-supported and powered by crew alone, moving 4.5 m downstage to slew round into its final position between two video walls and over the walkway.

Various effects needed to be incorporated into the design, including lighting, pyrotechnics, smoke, CO_2, headlights, a brass bell, a deployable, and light-up devil horns, not to mention concealing—and then supporting—a huge inflatable known as "Rosie!"

The complete centerpiece, as always, has been designing for touring needs with all parts fitting into 10′ long, 8′ high, 44″ carts for trucking and upper deck air freight.

Stufish enhanced the dimensional effect by adding an exaggerated perspective to the design, a maquette of which was made before being handed over to Brilliant Stages to work on full-size fabrication.

Rod Edkins' team at 2D3D created the strong, lightweight panels of the locomotive's skin from thin-sectioned GRP, which the ever-strong CAD team at Brilliant Stages had to marry, along with the other effects, to a suitable rolling and slewing sub-structure. . . . Surprisingly, at a total of 6,000 kg, the locomotive can be pushed up and downstage by only two stagehands and takes just three people to rotate it to its show position.

Tony Bowern of Brilliant Stages commented, "We enjoy the challenges which this kind of project brings. Richard Hartman as project coordinator and Mo Hale as head carpenter have been great to work with. We have worked successfully with Stufish on a number of projects over the years and always look forward to the next creation they will bring!"

Spectacularly lit by Patrick Woodroffe and Dave Hill with Dale "Opie" Skjerseth as production manager, the *Black Ice* tour marks the first appearance of AC/DC in eight years. . . .

Woodroffe told Live Design Online that the band brings a different perspective to the normal rock tour. "AC/DC is an interesting hybrid in that they are a very straightforward rock band, but they also have a real sense of theatre, and they always have," he says. "Angus [Young] dresses like a schoolboy; they use cannons and bells and all these iconic effects that they have for years. So the idea has always been to give them a great opening to the show that then becomes the background to the rest of the performance. Once the look is there, we don't ask them to interact with it too much but simply give them a great space in which to perform."

Opie explained the train concept to *TPI* magazine in March of 2009: "It came directly from the new album and the track, both of which were originally going to be called 'Runaway Train'. Then the album title changed, and the song became 'Rock N Roll Train,' but the idea of having this huge, life-size train on stage was still as relevant. Mark Fisher did the design, we showed it to the band, and they went with it. We gave ourselves plenty of time, from Mark's first sketches last June through to manufacturing, to ensure that deliveries arrived within the deadline, and I always like to use these companies because there's no fuss and they're so great to deal with."

"Pyro" Pete concluded, "The train took a whole army of guys to run it, with the flames and everything, and I just love all the props, especially Rosie, because every tour they want to do something different. For a while it was just the cannons, but I think on the *Ballbreaker* tour, when the big wrecking ball took the wall down, and we they saw how cool that was, then they were all for using pyro, like, 'Yeah, let's use a bunch of it!'"

16

Twenty-Five Years Later

AC/DC Are Inducted into the Rock and Roll Hall of Fame

The Rock and Roll Hall of Fame is an eight-story glass pyramid built on the shores of Lake Erie in Cleveland, Ohio. Designed by I. M. Pei, who also designed the Pyramide du Louvre in Paris and the Javits Center in New York City, stated that he wanted the Rock and Roll Hall of Fame to "express the dynamic music it celebrates." The Hall of Fame houses some of the most iconic objects in rock 'n' roll music history, including one of Angus' schoolboy uniforms. To be inducted into the Hall of Fame, a band is only considered twenty-five years after their first recording. Then you have to gain the most votes and be included on more than fifty percent of the ballots.

Beating Black Sabbath and the Sex Pistols by two years, their induction into the Rock and Roll Hall of Fame was fitting for the band that toured nonstop for years. Or as Malcolm put it, "It was more like an abduction!" The ceremony was held on March 10, 2003, at New York's Waldorf Astoria, and their award was presented to them by Steven Tyler of Aerosmith. Representing Bon were his nephews Daniel and Paul Scott, who joined the band on stage. In his induction speech, Tyler referred to the band as the "thunder from down under."

Tyler ever so eloquently stated,

> Thank God for the power chord. That thunder from down under that grabs you in the lower forty and gives you the second-most satisfying surge that can run through your body. There is no greater purveyor of that power chord than AC/DC. The sparks that flew off the heavy metal of *Back in Black*, and the primal stink behind "You Shook Me All Night Long" lit a fire in the belly of every kid that grew up born to break the rules. And they're still out there touring; the fire rages on.

According to this shirt that's from way back when, AC/DC opened for us in 1979. I was talking to the guys about how they keep it going on these years, and Angus told me that–actually, hold on, I wrote it down. You gotta hear this.

Angus told me, 'Look, we hope to rage on, and over the years we put a lot of hard yacker with our no-worries-mate and fuck-all attitude and hair like a bush pig's ass. It's no wonder we had to give a gobful to a few bloody wingers.' It's like, wow, you know, I used to think I didn't understand them 'cause I was fucked up, but it's not just me, right?

On the journey from the pubs of Australia to the stadiums of the world, AC/DC became the litmus test of what rock does. You know, does it make you clench your fist when you sing along? Does it scare your parents to hell and piss off the neighbors? Does it make you dance so close to the fire that you burn your feet, and still don't give a rat's ass? Does it make you want to stand up and scream for something that you're not even sure of yet? Does it make you want to boil your sneakers and make soup out of your girlfriend's panties? If it doesn't, then it ain't AC/DC.

The official band glossy for the release of *Ballbreaker*, featuring Phil Rudd back on drums for the first time in twelve years. Up against bands like Alice in Chains, Metallica, and Guns N' Roses, this was as menacing as the band could look and still maintain their tongue-in-cheek attitude. The rock 'n' roll band fronted by a wayward schoolboy!

My ticket stub from Madison Square Garden for the second time AC/DC had played the Garden, on December 5, 1983. The ticket price was $13.50, and the band had just been featured in *People* magazine. That night backstage was filled with celebrities, including Gene Simmons from Kiss and the actor Matt Dillon.

These guys have dedicated themselves to the majesty of the power chord, ignoring the spoon-fed, "don't bore us, get to the chorus" fickle taste of pop music. Let's see, 1975, *T.N.T.* 1976, *High Voltage* and *Dirty Deeds Done Dirt Cheap.* 1977, *Let There Be Rock.* 1978, *Powerage*, and *If You Want Blood (You've Got It)*. 1979, the six-million-seller sensory assault, *Highway to Hell.*

But just as they reached to be their creative pinnacle, they experienced the worst kind of tragedy imaginable: the death of the great singer Bon Scott. But rather than collapse, they rose like a sweat-soaked phoenix from the ashes, with their nerves of steel, hand in a velvet glove, sledgehammer to the back of the head vocals of Brian Johnson. Then came *Back in Black*, which sold a crushing nineteen million. That's thirteen million more than the previous release, with more than a little help from brilliant Mutt Lange, who continues to blow minds and speakers all over the world. AC/DC is the ultimate middle finger aimed at the establishment.

Think about it. The monster meet-me-in-the-backseat backbeat, the shredding vocals, that 100,000-megaton guitar assault, and let's not forget about that schoolboy uniform, which begs the question, "How do such big balls get in such small pants?" So when you think of this planet and how it may be on the highway to hell in a handbasket, think about how some distant future civilization will stumble upon what's left. They may marvel at the paintings of Rembrandt, they may gawk with wide-eyed wonder at Michaelangelo's *David*, they may drink deeply of the panty soup, but when they throw on *Back in Black*, they will still clench their fists, they will still piss off their neighbors, and dance too close to the fire–then they will have wild, animal sex under the light of the moon, bathed in the tribal energies of a thousand power chords.

Here's to the Holy Grail of it all; here's to the highway to hell. May we have as much fun there as we had getting there. Ladies and genitals, it is my honor on behalf of Aerosmith and every kid who has ever rocked his ass off to induct AC/DC, this night and forever, into the Rock and Roll Hall of Fame.

Not known to frequent such formal affairs, the entire band accepted their induction with grace and gratitude. Brian Johnson followed with words from the late, great Bon Scott: "'In the beginning, back in 1955, man didn't know about a rock 'n' roll show and all that jive. The white man had the schmaltz, the black man had the blues, but no one knew what they was gonna do. But Tchaikovsky had the news. He said, "Let there be rock!"' Bon Scott wrote that. And it's a real privilege to accept these awards tonight."

Never one to conform to a black-tie event, Malcolm commented,

> When we got there it was like playing in front of a bunch of fucking penguins in a restaurant. The guys from the Clash were up before us, and the Edge of U2 got up to introduce them. Fuck, he made this forty-minute speech [about late Clash guitarist Joe Strummer]. He was the most boring bloke I've ever had the misfortune to witness. We were at the side [of the stage], waiting and getting madder and madder, even though we had sympathy [for the rest of the Clash]. So when they said to go, we fuckin' took off. It was an anger-fueled performance. We ripped the place apart. They were dancing up in the balconies in their tuxes. It was quite a moment for us. The rest of the bands were pretty mild in comparison.

Inducted with AC/DC that night were Elvis Costello and the Attractions, the Clash, the Police, and the Righteous Brothers.

The band played "Highway to Hell" and "You Shook Me All Night Long," with Steven Tyler doing his best to keep up with Brian. One CNN reporter declared the band was loud enough to peel paint. Former VJ Kurt Loder, who was in attendance, stated, "There's a tiresome sense of decorum that's built into most award shows, and it lends to mute all things rude and unruly. AC/DC are apparently unaware of this. They may be unaware of anything apart from what Steven Tyler called 'the majesty of the power chord.'"

On May 20 of the same year, Malcolm, Angus, and Bon Scott were awarded the Ted Albert Award for Outstanding Service to Australian Music. This award is given out to songwriters, and as Malcolm accepted, he said, "On behalf of AC/DC and Bon Scott, especially Bon as he's a big part of this, we're proud of the honor of receiving this award."

17

Synchronicities

AC/DC, Strange Coincidences, and the Number 17

AC/DC's history and my friendship with the band includes some odd and strange coincidences. Below is a list of funny and sometimes eerie synchronicities, especially involving the number 17.

- Bon Scott was born in Scotland, in the county of Angus.
- Bon's mother's maiden name was Mitchell, which is Malcolm's middle name.
- AC/DC's first album, *High Voltage*, was released on February 17, 1975.
- When they first came to America, their press kit said Angus was seventeen years old.
- They started recording their seventeenth album on July 17, 1999, recording seventeen songs.
- In the movie *Let There Be Rock*, Malcolm appears wearing a number 17 soccer jersey.
- *Highway to Hell*, Bon's last album, peaked at #17 on the US charts.
- *Bonfire*, the box set tribute to Bon, was released on November 18, 1997, seventeen years after his death.
- When I was signed the contract to write *The Story of AC/DC: Let There Be Rock*, AC/DC had released seventeen albums.
- When I met AC/DC roadie Barry Taylor in 1977, he lived at 17 Taylors Lane in England.
- When Bon died, he was living on the fourth floor, in apartment number fifteen. I met the band on the tour for *Let There Be Rock*, which was their fourth album, and Madison, Wisconsin was their fifteenth date.
- When I was eight years old, I found an authentic wooden boomerang, which I played with and lost in a field the following summer. The year I found it was 1963, the same year Angus and Malcolm moved from Scotland to Australia.

Lightning bolt from the Bon Scott Path in Fremantle Cemetery. When Bon was asked if he was AC or DC, he always replied, "No, I'm the lightning flash in the middle!"

Photo by Doug Thorncroft

- The original singer in the Velvet Underground, the band Malcolm played with before he formed AC/DC, was named Brian Johnson.
- A fire before their appearance at the Mayfair Ballroom in Newcastle in October of 1979 (which was postponed until January 25, 1980) was the only blaze the band had ever encountered in all the years they toured the world. It's rather spooky that it broke out in Brian Johnson's hometown, and it's also the same venue where Bon would perform one of his last two concerts with AC/DC.
- Bon Scott's first official night singing for AC/DC was on October 5, 1975, Brian Johnson's birthday.
- *Black Ice* was released on October 17, 2008.

Visiting with the band on the *Razors Edge* tour after their show at Alpine Valley, in East Troy, Wisconsin, as soon as I walked into the dressing room, Malcolm looked over at me and said, "Hey! We saw Barry right after we saw you last December!" This turned into a long conversation about Barry's chosen profession (he's now a minister), and the book he wrote which mentions the band.

My ticket stub from the *Ballbreaker* tour at the Bradley Center in Milwaukee, Wisconsin, March 5, 1996.

My ex-husband John was wearing a T-shirt from our favorite vacation place in Florida, and as soon as Brian saw it, he yelled, "That's where I live!" Then he pointed at his eye, and said he had just gotten a shiner down there in a local pub. Apparently no one in the press had gotten hold of that story. Then he quickly grabbed John and told him that they both needed a drink. Angus and Malcolm were now strictly teetotalers, but Brian travels with his own bar.

For the next hour, we got to hang out with the band. Angus and I ended up on a couch, comparing how small his hands were to mine. We both have extremely little fingers, and he laughed when he told me that's why he plays Gibson SGs. They have the only guitar neck that Angus can get his hands around! After enjoying a great visit, we said our farewells, and they vowed to somehow track down a phone number or address on Barry for me.

A few days later, I wrote Barry a long letter and mailed it off to the last address I had for him in California. When that letter came back to me, I put it in a new envelope and mailed it off to the last place he lived in England. A few weeks later, that came back undeliverable, as well. It made me sad, and I was starting to feel as if I wasn't meant to find Barry after all, so I ripped up the letter up and threw it away.

That very same night, I was sitting on the couch flipping through the TV channels, when I heard someone say the words "AC/DC." That usually makes me stop and listen, so I flipped back and right in front of me, on my "color TV screen," was Barry Taylor! He was on the Christian channel's *700 Club*, talking about giving up rock 'n' roll to follow religion. The next day I called the *700 Club* and left a detailed message for Barry. Just a few days later, Reverend Taylor called me back directly.

Barry and his wife Cathy were running their own church in the mountains of California. He hadn't completely turned his back on rock 'n' roll. Barry, a guitarist himself, had formed his own church band, and much of his service celebrated with music. He had also been traveling the world spreading God's word, particularly in the Soviet Union and Germany, during the time the Berlin Wall came down.

Ironically, Barry had just traveled through New Zealand, where he saw Phil Rudd. I was flattered when Barry told me that he and Phil had just been talking about me. Right after Barry's visit with Phil, the band played in New Zealand and that's when Phil asked Malcolm about "having another go."

18

Good Causes

Co-Headlining with the Rolling Stones

n the summer of 2003, AC/DC played five dates in Germany: two headlining shows, and three supporting the Rolling Stones. Also appearing with them were the Pretenders. There were rumors that the tickets for the Stones weren't selling that well in Europe, until they added AC/DC. It would be the first time since 1979 that AC/DC were billed as a supporting act.

Both AC/DC and the Stones made Canadian history when they played in front of 490,000 people in Downsview Park in Toronto on July 30, 2003. *Molson Canadian Rocks for Toronto*, a benefit for SARS, was hosted by Dan Aykroyd and Jim Belushi. Also appearing were Rush, the Guess Who, the Isley Brothers, Sass Jordan, and Justin Timberlake.

AC/DC whipped the crowd into a frenzy, ending their set with "Let There Be Rock" and "Highway to Hell." Later, Angus and Malcolm joined the Rolling Stones on stage to jam on the song "Rock Me Baby." There were lots of pictures of Justin Timberlake singing with them, as well. Brian had been asked to come out and sing too, but decided against it. It had to do with singing alongside a Backstreet Boy. I guess you have to draw the line somewhere.

Martin Popoff wrote in *Metal Hammer Special 2005*, "A definite highlight of the band's touring history occurred on July 30, 2003, when AC/DC put in a blistering seventy-minute set second to a show-closing Rolling Stones at the Toronto Rocks festival, before a crowd of 450,000. It is widely believed that the band stole the show that night. Later, Angus would jam with the Stones during their set, capping off the all-day event and resulting in AC/DC being raved about for months afterward. It was a fitting finale as now, we all wait for the new record, and the rabble-roused performances to come...."

When the Rolling Stones had appeared earlier that year in Sydney in February of 2003, Angus and Malcolm showed up on stage to play B.B. King's "Rock Me Baby" at the Enmore Theater. Always huge fans of the Rolling Stones, the Young brothers still took these performances in stride.

Ron Wood and Keith Richards of the Rolling Stones with Angus, Malcom, and Brian. Together in Toronto for the SARS Benefit in August of 2003.

KMazur/WireImage/Getty Images

Angus and Malcolm jammed one more time with the Rolling Stones on stage at their Twickenham Stadium show in London on September 20 to play "Rock Me Baby." Ronnie Wood even managed to get Malcolm to solo during the song.

For one night only, AC/DC played at the Hammersmith Odeon in London on October 21, 2003. The 4,000 available tickets sold out in just under four minutes. Released the same month, the movie, *School of Rock*, starring Jack Black, confirmed the band's place as rock 'n' roll icons, especially when Black appears on stage in a mail carrier's uniform altered to look like a schoolboy's outfit. The comedy hit #1 at the box office, and featured the AC/DC song "It's a Long Way to the Top (If You Wanna Rock 'n' Roll)."

"Pyro" Pete told me,

> I remember when we were doing the European Stones tour, and Angus and Malcolm came out and played a few songs with them. And everyone came out to watch, but Angus and Malcolm were the only ones who were going to play. They were standing on the side of the stage, and they were acting just like any of the stagehands' friends, except that they were going to go out and play! I was talking to Malcolm, and his guitar tech came over and told him he was going to go out right after the next song. And Malcolm just said, "All right, nice talking to you, Pyro," and that was it. Like it was an everyday

My ticket stub from the *Stiff Upper Lip* tour at the Kohl Center in Madison, Wisconsin, for May 1, 2001. Due to Brian having throat problems, they had to cancel the show and come back ten days later to make up the date. The tour had officially ended, so the band had to rent new buses and make last-minute travel arrangements to accommodate three dates that were postponed. They were a bit frustrated, because their families were all waiting for them to join them on vacation in Sarasota, Florida.

occurrence. Then afterwards you would see them with the crew in catering, and they would just be sitting there. Which is one of the coolest things about them.

Two years later in an interview with *Drum!* magazine, Phil Rudd declared,

The greatest thing I've ever done with this band was smoke the Stones into the weeds in Toronto in front of 485,000 people. It was for the big SARS benefit that they had there almost two years ago. A big event, I believe it was the biggest ticketed show in North American history. They closed off the motorways, and there was this big mass of people that walked in and out in one day. We did three shows in Europe with the Stones during the summer, and they said, "We're going to do this one in Toronto, do you want to come?" We said, "Yeah we'll come." So we went, and it was the Stones, us, the Guess Who, and Rush. The Stones gave us an hour—that's a dangerous thing to do. You don't give us an hour before you go on, mate. We're not going to leave much left. (Laughs) It was a great show; it was tremendous. Brian was rocking.

The whole band just nailed it. We got into the van offstage and went, "Yeah, fucking follow that!" Because we're an arrogant bunch of little pricks. We do take our command of the stage pretty seriously, in case you hadn't noticed.

19

The Loss of a Rock 'n' Roll Icon

The Death of Bon Scott

A C/DC had just finished the *Highway to Hell* world tour, which came to a close at the end of 1979. After a break for the holidays, AC/DC met in London, found places to live, and immediately went into the studio to start rehearsing songs for their next album. On the night of February 18, 1980, Bon Scott had an early dinner over at the home of tour manager Ian Jeffery. Then he went back to his apartment and placed three telephone calls: one to his ex-girlfriend Silver Smith; one to Coral Browning (Michael Browning's sister), who was living in Los Angeles; and one to the woman he was dating at the time, his Japanese girlfriend Anna Baba.

When Bon spoke with Silver, he asked her if she wanted to do something together. Silver already had plans, but when her friend, Alistair Kinnear, called to ask her to attend the launch party for the band Lonesome No More at the Music Machine (later called the Camden Palace), she suggested he ring Bon instead. Kinnear ended up fetching Bon to go to the club around midnight. For a couple of hours, both Bon and Kinnear partied heavily at the Music Machine, drinking at the free bar backstage, as well as the bar upstairs. Kinnear later said he saw Bon drink at least seven double whiskeys that night.

By the time Kinnear drove Bon back to his flat in Ashley Court in Westminster around 3:00 a.m., Bon had already passed out. Reportedly, Kinnear went looking for Bon's girlfriend, Anna Baba, who wasn't home. He opened the door to flat number fifteen on the fourth floor using Bon's keys, but was unable to rouse Bon enough to help him inside. He left the apartment door ajar, but during his struggle to get Bon out of the car, Kinnear managed to lock himself out of the lobby. The next day a note was found by the caretaker reporting that Bon's door was left open and a set of keys were found on the inside mat.

Calling Silver for help, she told Kinnear to take Bon back to his own flat at 67 Overhill Road in East Dulwich, South London. Once Kinnear got home, he wasn't able to move Bon at all. Taking Silver's advice, Kinnear laid the front seat down, so Bon could lie flat. He then covered him with a blanket, and left a note so when Bon woke up, he would know which apartment to come up to.

The next morning around 11:00 a.m., a friend by the name of Leslie Loads awakened Kinnear. Kinnear was so hung over, he asked Loads to check on Bon. When Loads came back claiming the car was empty, Kinnear went back to bed. That evening at about 7:45 p.m., Kinnear went down to his car, intending to visit his girlfriend who was in hospital. He was shocked to find Bon still lying there, in the same position he left him in, not breathing. Kinnear immediately drove him to King's College Hospital, where Bon Scott was pronounced dead on arrival.

Kinnear gave Silver as Bon's closest kin in London, so the hospital phoned her first and told her to come immediately. When she arrived, they ushered her into a little room and gave her a cup of tea. When Silver realized that Bon was dead, she gave them the phone number of the band's manager, Peter Mensch, and later claimed she then just shut down. She said she didn't remember it, but she also called Angus. He was quoted as saying, "Peter, our manager, got to the hospital as soon as he could to find out exactly what had happened and identify him, because everyone was in doubt at the time. I immediately phoned Malcolm 'cos at the time I thought maybe she had got the wrong idea, you know, my only thought was is it Bon. And Ian, our tour manager, said it couldn't be Bon 'cos he'd gone to bed early that night. Anyway, the girl gave me the hospital number, but they wouldn't give me any information until the family had been contacted. Anyhow, Malcolm rang Bon's parents 'cos we didn't want them to be just sitting there and suddenly it comes on the TV news, you know."

Rock singer dies

LONDON (AP) — Bon Scott, 30, lead singer of the Australian rock group AC-DC, has been found dead in a parked car where a friend had left him to sober up after a day's drinking.

Scott was born in Scotland but was reared in Australia where the five-man group was formed. AC-DC currently has a single, "Touch Too Much," at No. 34 in the British charts. The group's recent album, "Highway to Hell," reached high on both the British and American charts.

A small newspaper clipping from the February 1980 *Wisconsin State Journal* reporting Bon Scott's death.

Angus later stated, "I felt horribly grown up in a way because, when you're young, you always think you're immortal, and I think at that time it really sort of spun me round. He'd always been quite wild but, because I think we were young, that's the last sort of thing you think of someone because up until that time we steamed through everything. A lot of times we didn't even think."

Malcolm would say in an interview on VH1's *Ultimate Albums* in June of 2003 that this was the worst phone call he had ever had to make. Bon's mother, Isa, recalled how at first she thought the voice on the other end of the phone was Bon's. When she realized what Malcolm was trying to tell her, she just screamed. Isa would also say that at least her beloved Ronnie knew not to die on her birthday, which had been the day before.

Ian Jeffery went with Peter Mensch to identify Bon's body. Bon's death certificate stated that his demise was caused by acute alcoholic poisoning, or "death by misadventure." Without anyone looking, a few months short of his thirty-fourth birthday, Bon Scott slipped away, all alone in a cold, dark automobile in the early morning hours of February 19, 1980. Gone was one of rock 'n' roll's most original, unique, and endearing front men.

The BBC's Radio London would confirm, "Body of thirty-three year old Bon Scott was found dead last night in a parked car in Dulwich, South London." Angus later said in *Musician* magazine, "It was just like losing a member of our own family, maybe even worse, because we all had a lot of respect for Bon as a person . . . Malcolm and I were really looking forward to getting Bon in the studio. After the success of the last one it was going to be a really big challenge, you know. That the best thing he'd ever done on record, I think that's the real loss for everyone, especially the fans, 'cause they would've had a chance to hear him at his peak. That would have been the crowning glory of his life."

Malcolm was quoted in *Classic Rock*, August 2005: "We were so depressed. We were just walking around in silence. Because there was nothing. *Nothing.*"

An autopsy performed on Bon on February 22 revealed half a bottle of whiskey in his stomach. There have been many rumors and innuendo about what really happened to Bon that night, everything from murder to a heroin overdose. Bon was supposed to meet up with UFO's Phil Mogg and Pete Way, who were both known to have used heroin, but according to Kinnear they never showed up. The autopsy report showed no drugs were found in his system. Bon's ex-girlfriend Silver was involved in heroin, and Bon once overdosed after trying it for the first and only time years before in Australia. After that scare, he stuck with his trusty JD. Bon rarely drank heavily before his performances, and only really partied after his responsibilities for the band were met.

As for drinking until he passed out, Ian Jeffery once said that he roomed with Bon for five years on the road, and never once saw him sleep in a bed. Not that he never saw him in a bed, it's just that sleep didn't have anything to do with it. No matter how hard Bon partied the night before, he was always up and ready to make it to their next gig. The fact that he died all alone in a dark, freezing car in the middle of the night is completely unfathomable. The real tragedy was the fateful decision to leave him alone in the car.

Kinnear was interviewed the next day by the police, but for twenty-five years, no one had been able to track him down. Finally, in the fall of 2005, *Classic Rock* gained an exclusive interview with Kinnear himself, who had been living in Costa del Sol Spain since 1983. Kinnear denied previous reports that Bon choked on his own vomit, and was wrapped around the gearshift of his car. When he found Bon, he was lying in the same position he left him in.

Kinnear went on to state to *Classic Rock*,

> The next day Silver came around to see me. She told me for the first time that Bon had been receiving treatment for liver damage, but had missed several doctors' appointments. I wish that I had known this at the time . . . I truly regret Bon's death. Hindsight being 20/20, I would've driven him to the hospital when he first passed out, but in those days of excess, unconsciousness was commonplace and seemed no cause for real alarm . . . we should all take better care of our friends, and err on the side of caution when we don't know all the facts.

Condolences and tributes to Bon Scott came in from all over the world. Cheap Trick and Angel City did a version of "Highway to Hell," in Nice. Santers, a Canadian trio, covered "Shot Down in Flames." Bon's friends in the French band Trust dedicated their album, *Repression*, to him. The Scottish band Girlschool added "Live Wire" to their set, and over here in America, Nantucket, the band that played with AC/DC many times, chose to cover "It's a Long Way to the Top" as the title track for their new album. A pub in London called Bandwagon held a Bon Scott benefit night, and Ozzy Osbourne and the late Randy Rhoads wrote the song "Suicide Solution" for him. The international media ran stories, and George and Harry ran a full-page ad in *RAM* which said, "A great singer, a great lyricist, a great friend, one of a kind. We'll miss you."

Ozzy later stated, "I wasn't a chum of Bon Scott's, but I used to see him from time to time. I was trying to kick the alcohol and I know he had an alcohol problem, and when he died it gave me the shove I needed . . . It was so fucking sad because Bon was a great singer—Bon was just made for AC/DC."

The band accompanied Bon's body back to Perth in Western Australia on February 28, and Bon was cremated on February 29. Much to the relief of his family, only his close family members, the band, and a few select friends attended funeral services at a church in Fremantle, Australia. Bon's ashes were laid to rest in the Memorial Garden, under the gum trees, in the Fremantle Cemetery on March 1, 1980, with little fanfare. Perth, Australia, was just too far away for most fans to travel. Bon's mother expressed true appreciation that the fans that were present were very reverent. Angus described it: "The funeral itself was more or less quiet, though there were a lot of kids outside. It was better being quiet, because it could have been very bad if a lot of people had just converged there."

The Bon Scott Arch leading to his gravesite in Fremantle, Australia, which is now visited by thousands of fans every year. Faithful fan Doug Thorncroft should be commended for all the work he did to see that Bon's gravesite was upgraded and recognized as the national landmark it is now. Thorncroft was also instrumental in seeing that a bronze statue be commissioned in Bon's honor.   *Photo by Doug Thorncroft*

During the services, Bon's father, Chick, leaned over to Malcolm and told him they would have to find another singer and keep going. Bon would have wanted it that way. The band spent some time with Bon's parents, who were adamant that they keep going. Chick also told Angus, "You must continue with AC/DC. You are young guys, you're on the brink of major success, and you can't afford to give up now." Angus told *Classic Rock* in August 2005, "But to be honest with you—we weren't really listening; we were wrapped up in our grief. Bon's dad kept repeating his assurances. He told us time and time again: 'You should keep going, you've still got a lot to give.'"

In a press release from their record label, Atlantic wrote,

> Bon Scott was always the top joker in the AC/DC pack. The stories of his sexual and alcoholic excesses are legion and that part of his enormous fan mail that didn't involve tempting offers from young girl fans invariably berated him for "leading poor Angus astray." Sadly, Bon is no longer with us after he tragically went just one step too far on one of his notorious boozing binges. But if there is a crumb of comfort to be found in such a needless and premature death, it is that Bon probably went out the way that he would have chosen, never flinching as he went over the top just one more time.

Angus also stated, "I don't think there would have been an AC/DC if it hadn't been for Bon. You might have got me and Malcolm doing something, but it wouldn't have been what it was. Bon molded the character and flavor of AC/DC."

During all my research on Bon, I was unable to find a bad word said or written about him anywhere. Even his ex-wife and girlfriends still cared for him, and there aren't that many guys you can say that about! He was a born rock star, and loved people. And as Angus once said, Bon wasn't your typical rock 'n' roll singer. He started out as a drummer, and always acted like one of the band, never the star. In the movie *Let There Be Rock*, he was asked if he felt like a star. Bon laughed at the interviewer, and said, "No, but sometimes I see stars though!"

At the time of his death, Bon was writing lyrics for the new album. While Bon worked on lyrics, he boasted to photographer Robert Ellis, as quoted in Mark Putterford's book, *Shock to the System*. "All he kept talking about was how great this next record was going to be. He carried this pad full of lyrics around with him, and he'd read them out to you whenever he could. He just kept on about the new album, how it was going to be the best thing AC/DC had ever done, and he was so fired up about it you couldn't help but believe him."

While Angus and Malcolm were hammering out the basic tracks, Bon did come into E'Zee Hire, the rehearsal studio that they were working in, sometime between February 12 and February 15. He didn't record any vocals, but he popped in and offered to play drums for them, claiming, "Let me bash away."

Jamming to one of their trademark riffs, together they played "Have a Drink On Me." Later, Bon also helped formulate the drum intro for "Let Me Put My Love Into You." Angus later said, "It was kind of funny, the first time we ever sat down, here's this guy saying, 'I'm your new drummer.' Mal convinced him to sing, to get up to the front of the stage. Then he was there at the end again. The last you saw him, there he was behind the kit. He played the intro to one of the tracks. It turned out it wasn't one of the greatest songs but the intro was great; "Let Me Put My Love Into You," just the intro on it before it goes into Mutt Lange territory." Agreeing to meet the following week, with more lyrics written, Bon said his good-byes and left. It was the last time Angus and Malcolm would see him alive.

There has been much speculation on what happened to Bon's notebook of lyrics, along with the rest of his personal effects, after his death. Ian Jeffery has been quoted as saying he possessed a notebook of Bon's, which contained lyrics for fifteen songs for *Back in Black*. To this day, no one has ever seen the notebook, nor has it been substantiated that Bon's family did not receive it. Considering how private the band is, I can't imagine them alerting the media if Ian did hand them over. Angus heatedly denied these rumors in the August 2005 issue of *Classic Rock*, "No, there was nothing from Bon's notebook. [After his death] all his stuff went direct to his mother and his family. It was personal material—letters and things. It wouldn't have been right to hang on to it. It wasn't ours to keep."

The song titles for *Back in Black* were already in place, and Atlantic record executive Phil Carson went on record stating that the lyrics were written by Brian Johnson. "Rock 'n' Roll Ain't Noise Pollution" was the last song to be recorded and the phrase did come from Bon yelling at an angry landlord over the volume of his stereo.

After Bon's service, everyone around the band started to suggest finding another singer. Angus and Malcolm weren't as optimistic, but eventually agreed that they should hold auditions. After several weeks of moping around their separate households, Malcolm called Angus and suggested they work on songs, to keep busy and stay together. Without concern for managers, the record company, or anyone else, Angus and Malcolm locked themselves in their studio and poured their grief into their music. Angus

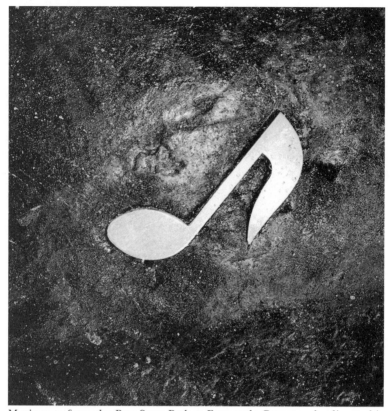

Music note from the Bon Scott Path at Fremantle Cemetery leading to his gravesite, which has also been declared a heritage-listed site by The National Trust of Australia.   *Photo by Doug Thorncroft*

told *Classic Rock*, "I guess we retreated into our music. At the time we weren't thinking very clearly. But we decided working was better than sitting there, still in shock about Bon. So in some ways it was therapeutic, you know."

When it came time to talk about finding a replacement, Angus stated "After a while, when we felt we were close to having all the songs together, we knew we had to confront the question of a new singer. But it wasn't like we put an advertisement in a music paper that said: 'AC/DC wants a new front man.' No . . . that would have been too over the top. It was subtler than that. People like Bon are unique. They're special. And we didn't want someone to come in and copy him. If anything, we wanted someone who was his own character."

Perry Cooper was stunned when he heard the news of Bon's death. He told me, "I was so hurt when Bon died. I actually got a Christmas card in

February, after he died. It was a dirty double entendre card, and he wrote, 'I never knew who to send this to, then out of the blue I thought of you. Merry Xmas Mate, Bon.' He had been dead for almost a month when I got it, so that was very upsetting. And I said to myself, 'How are they going to replace him?'"

Apparently Bon didn't put enough postage on his 1979 Christmas cards, and they were somehow delayed and delivered in late February. The insufficient postage explanation is plausible, but why weren't the cards returned to the sender? I think this was Bon's way of making sure all the people he loved knew it. No matter how busy he was while on the road, he cared very much about his family, friends, and fans, and always made the extra effort to show them. Not surprisingly, even after his death, Bon Scott would get the last word in.

No doubt a lot of AC/DC fans regard the years with Bon as their golden years. Good friend and vocalist Vince Lovegrove described Bon's appeal in the DVD *Life Before Brian* in November 2005, "What Bon contributed to rock 'n' roll is that he took away all the showbiz. Although he was a showbiz kind of guy, by the very nature of the fact he was on stage, he brought an ordinariness, a slight edge of 'amateur-ness,' about rock 'n' roll to the fore. Something that wasn't slick. Bon was certainly not slick, he was a rough diamond, and he brought that to AC/DC and he brought that to rock 'n' roll music, and I think that has to be one of the reasons why he's gone on and on and on."

Bon was often described as a "larrikin," which is Australian slang for a rascal or scallywag. Former manager Michael Browning told *Classic Rock* in 2005 that Bon "brought an enormous presence and character into the group. And I rate Bon as a lyricist up there with the greats, alongside Jim Morrison and the like. Bon was a poet first, and a lyricist second. He was a highly intelligent lyricist and poet. He really took the Aussie larrikin archetype to a whole different level. Bon knew exactly why they appealed to the audience so much, when he said, 'Rock 'n' roll is the channel to give us all a vent to those frustrations. Lack of money, lack of alcohol, lack of women, or whatever. Rock 'n' roll is just a damn good outlet for what's hurtin' inside.'"

Angel's guitarist Rick Brewster told me, "Bon was one of the true gentlemen of rock—well spoken, mostly quiet, often kept to himself. And funny—he was full of one-liners that kept the band laughing. There seemed to be a serious side to Bon too. He was a dedicated musician, proud of the band, committed to performance, and he cared about people. He handled success with grace, dignity, and perspective."

Bon Scott smiling on stage at the Stone Hearth in Madison, Wisconsin, on August 16, 1977. In tight jeans and no shirt, in all his glory, he was right at home under the spotlight.
Photo by Keith Wessel

Angry Anderson, lead singer of Rose Tattoo, composed a touching memorial for Bon in the February 2005 issue of *Classic Rock*. Anderson wrote, "He was the only singer I ever invited to sing with the Tatts, whenever he felt like it: we spoke quietly, we laughed loudly, and we drank hard, we were heading in the same direction at different speeds, for a moment we were side by side, then he was gone."

There aren't enough words to describe the impact Bon Scott had on AC/DC, then and now. His spirit fortified the Young brothers' heart and soul rock 'n' roll, and his lyrics molded their image to this day. Bon was an original character whose over-the-top attitude towards life gave their balls-to-the-wall, no-holds-barred music a rebellious voice that still incites hundreds of thousands to raise a fist into the air.

Bon Scott was the Albert Einstein of double entendres. He was the rare performer who had friends and fans from all over the world, including everyone from struggling reporters to superstars. You didn't need to be upper class to enjoy his company. Bon Scott was the original Dalai Lama of rock; he judged no one, and partied with all.

Angus used to say, "Bon didn't dwell on the meaning of life too much. He lived for the moment." He also enjoyed a lot of those moments, as Angus told *Sounds* in July 1986. "Bon joined us pretty late in life, but that guy had more youth in him than people half his age. That was how he thought, and I learned from him. Go out there and be a big kid."

Cheap Trick's vocalist Robin Zander told me, "I liked having breakfast with Bon, because he would always order a croissant or something with his glass of whiskey." Longtime Cheap Trick tour manager Kirk Dyer agreed, "Oh yeah, that's because he never gave a shit! His attitude was, 'I don't care if you know me or not, now where's the party?' That's how I remember him the most."

The last photograph taken of him was backstage at the Hammersmith Odeon in London, with his friend bassist Pete Way, at UFO's performance in February 1980. In the picture, Bon has a great big smile on his face, just the way everybody remembers him.

Almost two decades later, *Bonfire* has sold over one million copies, and continues to be a must-have for any AC/DC fan. Every day, somewhere, you hear Bon's voice on the radio, and every day he gains new fans. *Classic Rock* magazine gave Bon Scott second place in their Top 100 Rock Singers list, only edged out by the equally legendary Freddie Mercury.

Commemorating the twenty-fifth anniversary of Bon's death, nearly one thousand fans gathered for a memorial service in Fremantle, Australia. Reenacting their infamous ride through Melbourne, the tribute band Riff Raff traveled through the streets on a flatbed truck, playing "It's a Long Way to the Top." Bagpipers, dressed in black, marched into the cemetery playing songs that Bon learned to play as a child. Later that night, Riff Raff held a concert at the Leopold Hotel. On February 22, 2005, Bon Scott's achievements and contributions to rock 'n' roll were recognized by WAM, the Western Australian Music Industry Association, when they inducted him into the West Australian Music Hall of Fame.

One Seven-Year Break

Almost Forty Years of Touring

AC/DC hit the road in the beginning of January 1974. The band stayed on tour almost constantly, taking their longest break of seven years after the *Stiff Upper Lip* tour ended in 2001. For years, rumors flew that the band was done, that they were never going to tour again, and that was it for AC/DC. To the delight of millions of fans around the world, the band went back into the studio in the spring of 2008 and recorded *Black Ice*. The official *Black Ice* tour started at the end of October of 2008 and continued until the end of the summer of 2010. Following is a list of all of AC/DC's official tours and the number of dates they played.

From December 1973 through August of 1974, AC/DC played forty-three club dates throughout Australia, in Sydney, Liverpool, Caringbah, Newcastle, Gosford, Maroubra, Hornsby, French Forest, and Cronulla. In August of 1974, AC/DC supported Lou Reed for eight dates in the cities Sydney, Melbourne, Adelaide, and Brisbane. Dave Evans told me some of his memories of constantly traveling back and forth across the country. "In Australia the bands had to endure long hours on the road driving between towns and cities. It would take about twelve to fourteen hours to get from Sydney to Melbourne, depending on the weather. When we drove from Adelaide to Perth, it took two days to get there. Most times band members would try to doze off. There weren't many humorous moments really. We got to see the countryside as it passed by and of course there are some really beautiful parts of Australia, but we were on a schedule and had to keep driving."

The funniest thing that did happen to Dave while performing with the band was revealed to Brian Coles in *Electric Basement* in September 2000. "I remember falling off the stage at the Sydney Opera House. It was a free gig and it was packed with thousands outside who couldn't get in. I overbalanced at the front of the stage and made it look as if I had jumped off. You wouldn't believe it but right in the middle of the front row was an empty chair that I spun around and sat in, and watched the show along with the audience during Angus's lead break. Then I jumped up onto the stage in time for my cue for the vocals to begin again. People complimented me on a great stage act, but now I can reveal the truth."

1974: "Can I Sit Next to You Girl" Tour (Australia)

This tour included forty-six dates throughout Australia, including the cities Maroubra, Gunnedah, Leederville, South Gambier, Canberra, Leichhardt, Corrimal, Adelaide, Sydney, Perth, Melbourne, Rockdale, and Hurstville.

During 1975, from January through February, AC/DC played twenty-eight club dates in the Australian cities Liverpool, Hurstville, Sydney, Melbourne, Chadstone, Sunbury, Sorrento, Epping, Adelaide, Frankston, Ballarat, Geelong, and Thornbury.

1975: *High Voltage* Tour (Australia)

This tour started on February 24, 1975 and ended in September. The band played 115 dates and the set list included "Live Wire," "She's Got Balls," "Rock 'n' Roll Singer," "Soul Stripper," "Show Business," "High Voltage," "Can I Sit Next to You Girl," "It's a Long Way to the Top (If You Wanna Rock 'n' Roll)," "The Jack," "T.N.T.," and "Baby Please Don't Go."

1975: *T.N.T.* Tour (Australia)

The Australian *T.N.T.* tour included 113 dates from September of 1975 and until January 1976, covering all the major cities: Sydney, Adelaide, Perth, Melbourne, and all points in between.

1976: *Lock Up Your Daughters* Summer Vacation Tour (Australia)

Starting on January 2, 1976, at the Civic Hall in Portland, VIC, they played seventeen dates, ending in Adelaide on January 24.

1976: Club Dates (Australia)

On January 27 they started in Thornbury and played thirty club dates throughout Australia, with the last three nights at the Bondi Lifesaver in Sydney. Knowing they were heading overseas, the last night at the Bondi was the first time Angus dropped his drawers and mooned the crowd—an affectionate display that continues to this day.

1976: Club Dates and Backstreet Crawler Tour (UK)

Beginning at the Napier College Student Union in April, 1976, AC/DC played twenty-four dates, including London, Glasgow, Manchester, Birmingham, and Newcastle, ending in Portsmouth on June 8.

1976: *Lock Up Your Daughters* Tour (UK)

Returning to the City Hall in Glasgow on June 11, the band played nineteen dates through the UK, ending at the Lyceum Ballroom in London on July 7.

An AC/DC button from the *Lock Up Your Daughters* tour from 1976. This tour caused an uproar throughout Australia, causing the radio station owned by the church to refuse to play their songs and the vice squad to follow them around, prompting the band to want to leave the country. As soon as their manager Michael Browning could book them overseas, they were off to conquer the world!

1976: Tour of Sweden

The band played five dates in Sweden, starting on July 16, in Falkenberg, Malmo, Stockholm, and Vaxjo and ending in Anderstorp on July 24.

1976: Europe and UK Summer Tour

Starting at the Marquee Club in London on July 26, AC/DC were booked for twenty-nine dates through England, Holland, France, and Germany. Three dates were cancelled: Nimes,

France, on August 27; Folkestone, UK, on September 11; and St. Alban's, UK, on September 25.

1976: Rainbow Tour (Europe)

Their tour with Rainbow started on September 23 in Hamburg, Germany, and included twenty-one dates through Germany, France, Holland, and Switzerland.

1976: *High Voltage* Tour (United States)

The band was scheduled to play in Los Angeles and various American cities between September and November of 1976, but the entire tour was cancelled.

1976: *Dirty Deeds Done Dirt Cheap* Tour (UK)

Starting at the Southhampton University on October 27, the band played sixteen dates, which included Glasgow, Liverpool, Newcastle, and London.

1976: *A Giant Dose of Rock 'n' Roll* Tour (Australia)

Returning to their homeland in December of 1976, AC/DC played nineteen dates throughout Australia, where one date at the Town Hall in Tamworth on December 16 had to be cancelled due to the mayor refusing to give them permission to play.

1977: *A Giant Dose of Rock 'n' Roll* Tour (Australia)

From January 7, 1977 through February 15, the band were originally scheduled for twenty dates throughout Australia, including Sydney, Perth, and Adelaide. The first two dates were postponed and their January 12 date in Warrnambool VIC was cancelled altogether. Plus, their date at the Haymarket in Sydney was changed from January 27 to January 30.

1977: *Dirty Deeds Done Dirt Cheap* Tour (UK)

To support the Australian release of *Dirty Deeds Done Dirt Cheap*, the band headed back to the United Kingdom, starting at Edinburgh University on

February 18. The band was booked for twenty-eight dates and had three shows cancelled in Swansea, Leicester, and Hemel.

1977: European Tour Supporting Black Sabbath

In support of Black Sabbath, AC/DC started in Paris, France, on April 5 at the Pavillon de Paris and were booked to play eighteen dates through France, Denmark, Germany, Switzerland, and Sweden. The last two dates in Oslo, Norway on April 23 and Helsinki, Finland on April 24 were cancelled, perhaps due to the flick knife incident between Geezer Butler and Malcolm Young.

1977: Australian Club Dates

This leg consisted of two undercover club dates at the Bondi Lifesaver in Sydney to work in their new bass player, Cliff Williams. The first night they appeared as the Seedies and the second night they were billed as Dirty Deeds.

1977: *Let There Be Rock* Summer Tour (US)

Opening their first American tour at the Armadillo World Headquarters in Austin, Texas, on July 27, 1977, the band played twenty-nine dates, winding their way through Texas, Florida, Missouri, Illinois, Ohio, Wisconsin, Indiana, New York, Michigan, California, and back to Florida, ending on September 7 in Fort Lauderdale.

This first leg of their American tour was driven in a station wagon following a twelve-foot Ryder truck, with only a three-man road crew. It was also the beginning of the "highway to hell," according to Angus. This tour included their debut in NYC at CBGB and Los Angeles' Whisky a Go Go, where they were discovered by Gene Simmons, who invited them to open for Kiss.

1977: *Let There Be Rock* Tour (Europe)

Right after their dates in NYC and Hollywood, the band flew back to Europe for twenty dates including Sweden, Finland, Germany, Belgium, and Switzerland.

1977: *Let There Be Rock* Tour (UK)

AC/DC returned to England for eighteen dates, including performances in Sheffield, Liverpool, Glasgow, London, and Manchester, and ending in Cambridge on November 12 at the Corn Exchange. Their album *Let There Be Rock* was released on October 14 in the UK and became their first album to chart, peaking at #75.

Journalist Phil Sutcliffe gave them four stars in his album review in *Sounds* on October 22, 1977. He wrote, "So it's just as well I first heard *Let There Be Rock* in the bath: very handy for washing my mouth out with soup. Because I could hardly [deleted] usually believe the [deleted] audacity of the mother[deleted], the sheer [deleted] simplicity and [deleted] direct-ness of the little [deleted]. They [deleted] me totally . . . You know what AC/DC do live. Blow roofs off.

"Destroy walls. Steamroller the debris into a fine powder. Well this is the first time I've heard them pack all of that into a record. They broke the master after they pressed Ron [sic] Scott."

The following week he continued his support with a review of their show at Mayfair in Newcastle called, "Sex, Snot, Sweat, and School Kids (Or: AC/DC Are Back in Town)":

> The crowd was pogoing, roaring, and chanting, "AC/DC, AC/DC," after that first number. They basked in their own hell heat while soaking in Angus's flying sweat and snot as if it were Holy Water . . . With a superbly produced instrumental sound you could hear exactly how effective they all are. Phil Rudd on drums straight and loud, new bassman Cliff Williams unorthodoxly strumming a growling under-thrum, Malcolm Young emerging as a riffmaker of the most ferocious intensity, and Angus continuing to play hard and even imaginative lead while shaking himself about as if he had no further use for his head . . . Bon is vital. He's the spice and flavor with the heavy hard-tack. An appealing rogue and buccaneer, give him a wooden leg and a parrot on his shoulder and he'd be the image of Long John Silver.

1977: *Let There Be Rock* Winter Tour (United States)

Back for a second run at the United States, AC/DC started at the Mid-Hudson Civic Center in Poughkeepsie, New York, on November 16 and played twenty-four dates covering New York, Pennsylvania, Tennessee, West Virginia, Georgia, Illinois, Wisconsin, Indianapolis, North Carolina, and Maryland. This tour included the night I interviewed them at the Electric

Ballroom in Milwaukee, Wisconsin, on December 4 and ended on December 21 at the Stanley Theatre in Pittsburgh, Pennsylvania.

After the holidays, the band was scheduled to play some dates in Australia, but those were cancelled due to Cliff having trouble getting a work visa to enter the country. Once he was free to travel, the band convened in Sydney to record their new album, *Powerage*, at Albert Studios.

The poster advertising AC/DC's appearance at the Stone Hearth in Madison, Wisconsin, August 16, 1977. I never got one the night they played the club, but literally three years later, I was at the door taking money for a local band, and was sitting at a little podium with a chair and a small drawer. Out of sheer boredom, I opened the drawer, only to find it lined with a sheet of white paper. Curious, I peeled back a corner and saw that the flip side was a bright yellow. All my history with AC/DC includes some incredible synchronicities, and this is one of them. Guess who stole the drawer liner from the Stone Hearth that night?!

1978 *Powerage* Tour (UK)

The *Powerage* tour of the UK started on April 27, 1978, at Victoria Hall in Hanley and continued through the United Kingdom, including Glasgow, Manchester, London, Cambridge, Liverpool, Newcastle, Leeds, and Edinburgh, and ended in Oxford in early June of 1978. The band was originally booked for thirty shows, but four dates were either cancelled or postponed.

1978: *Powerage* Tour (US)

AC/DC brought *Powerage* to the States on June 24, 1978, starting at the Scope in Norfolk, Virginia. From there, the band covered sixty-three dates including almost every state in America. The constant zigzagging through America prompted roadie Barry Taylor to state at times they wanted to kill their booking agent.

This tour included the night they played the Riverside Theater in Milwaukee, Wisconsin, on September 12. That night is one of my all-time favorite memories of the band, and can be found in Chapter 26, "Always Smiling: Bon Scott and his Antics."

1978: *Powerage* Tour (Europe)

After a couple of cancelled dates over the summer in Germany and Belgium, the *Powerage* tour continued through Europe, starting in Malmo, Sweden on October 10, 1978, and ended in Belgium on October 27. The tour covered fifteen dates in cities across Germany, Sweden, Switzerland, France, Holland, Sweden, and Belgium.

1978–1979: *If You Want Blood* Tour (UK/US)

On October 28, AC/DC were back in the UK playing the University of Essex in Colchester, the first of seventeen dates, which ended with two nights at the Hammersmith Odeon in London on November 15 and 16.

Before landing back in the States, the band had booked four dates in Japan that were cancelled. Unfortunately, the road crew flew all the way to Japan before they found out the dates had been axed. Barry Taylor sent me a postcard from Japan and reasoned at least it gave them a few days to play tourist before boarding another plane.

Since their April 8, 1979, appearance in Los Angeles was cancelled, the *If You Want Blood* tour started on May 8, in Madison, Wisconsin. I had heard from Barry that he was quite surprised that the band and manager Michael Browning had discussed making it to Wisconsin just for him, and I was more than delighted to have them open their tour right in my hometown.

Right after their show, I got to listen to *Highway to Hell* on Phil Rudd's boom box in his hotel room: a true rock 'n' roll honor. Their *If You Want Blood (You've Got It)* tour covered fifty-three dates and ended on August 5 at the Spectrum Arena in Philadelphia, Pennsylvania. This is also the same tour where they played with Cheap Trick on July 4 just outside Rockford, Illinois, where Barry Taylor was hit by an exploding M-80.

1979: Summer European *Highway to Hell* Tour

The band played ten dates starting on July 13, in Arnhem, Holland (which could be where Angus first met his wife Ellen) and ended in Nurnberg, Germany on September 1.

1979: *Highway to Hell* Tour (North America)

Playing the Oakland Auditorium in Oakland, California on August 5, the band launched another massive assault on the US, covering forty-seven dates in sixteen states and ending in Columbus, Ohio, on October 21. This would be the last time I saw Bon alive, when they played the Aragon Ballroom in Chicago, Illinois, on October 19.

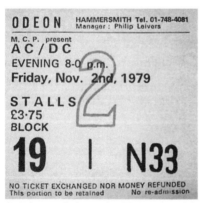

A ticket stub from the Hammersmith Odeon in London dated November, 2, 1979. They became so popular there, that many times they would play two—four nights in a row to accommodate all their fans.

1979: *Highway to Hell* Tour (UK)

Back in the UK, the band started in Newcastle on October 25 and played fourteen dates in Manchester, Glasgow, Stafford, Bridlington, Leicester, and Liverpool, including an unprecedented four nights straight on November 1–4 at the Hammersmith Odeon in London.

1979–80: *Highway to Hell* Tour (Europe)

By November 11, AC/DC traveled back to Europe to play the Forest National in Bruxelles, Belgium and continued through thirty-seven dates in Holland, Germany, and Switzerland, ending in France on December 15 at the Theatre De Verdure in Nice. Their December 30 date in Groppingen, Germany, was cancelled, possibly due to exhaustion.

1980: *Highway to Hell* Tour (Europe/UK)

Somehow between December 17 and January 27, 1980, the band managed to play fourteen dates, starting at the Hammersmith Odeon in London and ending on January 27, 1980, at the Gaumont Theatre in Southhampton, which would be Bon's last live performance with the band.

1980: *Back in Black* Warm-Up Tour (Europe)

After Bon's death and Brian Johnson's hiring, the band played six dates in Belgium and Holland to warm up the band. Brian's official first date with the band was at the Palais Des Expositions in Namur, Belgium on June 29, 1980. Brian told Atlantic Record executive Perry Cooper that he was so scared that night he could feel his knees shaking.

1980: *Back in Black* Tour (North America)

This tour started on July 13, 1980, in Edmonton, AB, Canada, at the Northlands Coliseum Concert Bowl and included sixty-five dates, ending on October 11 at the Orpheum Theater in Boston. On September 14, they played the Dane County Coliseum in Madison, Wisconsin, where I saw AC/DC with Brian Johnson for the first time.

1980: *Back in Black* Tour (UK)

Starting on October 19 at the Colston Hall in Bristol, the band played twenty-four dates, ending at the Hammersmith Odeon in London for six nights between November 10 and November 16.

1980: *Back in Black* Tour (Europe)

On November 20, they appeared at the Gota Lejon in Stockholm, Sweden and continued through Norway, Germany, France, and Switzerland, playing twenty-three dates and ending on December 20 in Lille, France.

1981: *Back in Black* Tour (Europe)

On January 8, 1981, they opened the tour in Metz, France and played 14 dates through France and Spain, ending in Bruxelles, Belgium on January 25.

1981: *Back in Black* Tour (Japan)

It took the band years to finally play Japan, but that they did. On February 1, 1981, they performed in Osaka, February 2 in Nagoya, and February 3 and 4 in Tokyo.

1981: *Back in Black* Tour (Australia)

Returning to perform in Australia for the first time since Bon Scott's death, they opened their tour in Bon's hometown of Perth on February 13, 1981, just days before the first anniversary of his passing. Bon's parents and family members attended. They were all quite moved by how the band and the fans honored his memory.

AC/DC played eight dates in Perth, Adelaide, Sydney, Brisbane, and Melbourne. That summer they also performed at the *Monsters of Rock* festival in Donington on August 22, 1981.

1981: *For Those About to Rock* Tour (North America)

The band was scheduled to play sixty-one dates throughout the States from September through December, but for reasons unknown, the entire tour was cancelled.

1981: *For Those About to Rock* Tour (North America)

By November 11, they were back on stage in Seattle and continued through the US, playing thirty-two dates covering sixteen states and two cities in

Canada. The tour ended with two nights in Landover, Maryland, on December 20 and 21. This tour would mark their debut on December 2 at New York City's Madison Square Garden.

1982: *For Those About to Rock* Tour (North America)

The cannons kept rolling through the States starting in Birmingham, Alabama, on January 17, 1982, and continued through twenty-eight dates, including four nights at the Seattle Coliseum and three nights at the Cow Palace in San Francisco. The tour ended in Phoenix, Arizona, on January 25.

1982: *For Those About to Rock* Tour (Japan)

From June 4–10, 1982, the band played five dates in Osaka, Kyoto, Nagoya, and Tokyo. Atlantic Records released a very rare promotional album to radio DJs in Japan featuring AC/DC songs on one side with songs by Foreigner on the other. Not only is it rare, but ironic, considering Foreigner was AC/DC's least favorite band to share a stage with.

1982: *For Those About to Rock* Tour (Europe)

This tour was scheduled to start in Dortmund, Germany on July 17 and continue through Germany and France for twelve dates, but the entire tour was cancelled. Considering they had never really taken a break after Bon's death, the band was suffering.

As Angus said, Phil took Bon's death harder than anyone else in the band, and had never really slowed down long enough to deal with it. Malcolm and Phil were not getting along, and Phil was fighting substance abuse problems, which led to his departure from the band during the recording of their upcoming album, *Flick of the Switch*.

1982: *For Those About to Rock* Tour (UK)

After a short break, the band started this tour in Birmingham on September 29 and played nineteen dates, ending in Dublin, Ireland on October 22, including four nights at London's Hammersmith Odeon and two nights at London's Wembley Arena.

1982: *For Those About to Rock* Tour (Europe)

AC/DC closed out the year with eleven dates starting in Nuremberg, Germany on November 26 and ending in Zurich, Switzerland on December 12. Three dates in Paris had to be cancelled.

1983: *Flick of the Switch* Tour (North America)

The tour officially started on October 11 in Vancouver and covered fifty-six dates throughout the US. Four dates in Pennsylvania, Ohio, and Illinois were all postponed until later that year. The band made their second

My backstage pass for the *Flick of the Switch* tour in 1983, where I saw them at Madison Square Garden. In six short years, I watched them go from playing a small club in Madison, Wisconsin, to headlining Madison Square Garden in New York City. As Angus used to say, "We may be little, but we make a lot of noise!"

appearance at Madison Square Garden on December 5, 1983, and I was there to see it.

So much had changed since Bon was gone. Phil left, Barry quit working on the road crew, and *People* magazine had just run a full article about AC/DC still making it despite all the obstacles they had faced over the past three years. I remember this being the first time I witnessed the band being given "star treatment" backstage, watching everyone from Gene Simmons of Kiss to actor Matt Dillon trying to get into their dressing room to say hello.

Since Bon's death, Angus had become the real focal point of the band. As *Guitar Player* magazine would state, "Brian Johnson may be AC/DC's leather-throated vocalist, but Angus is the reigning center of attention." Appearing larger than life on stage, Angus once explained how after seeing him perform that most people expect him to be much taller. "Some of the women that used to come looking for me (after concerts) were like Amazons. I'd open the door and say, 'It's okay, I'm just his butler.'" This leg of the tour ended back at Madison Square Garden on December 19.

1984: *Flick of the Switch* Tour (Europe)

Taking time off to complete the new album, the band started in San Sebastian, Spain on August 11, 1984, and played eleven dates through Sweden, Switzerland, Germany, Italy, and France. On August 18, 1984, they were the first band to return as headliners to the fourth *Monsters of Rock* at the Castle Donington. The concert also featured Y&T, Accept, Gary Moore, Mötley Crüe, Van Halen, and Ozzy Osbourne.

As *Circus* magazine pointed out, "Even the mighty Van Halen had to settle for guest-star billing." Angus told *Guitar World* in 1998, "I remember once we were playing the Donington festival in Britain and I went down the day before the show and they had this gadgetry up there—it looked like Space Station #9! Anyway, I think Van Halen were on the bill too and Eddie Van Halen came up and said, 'Jeez, what's all this!' One of the guys who'd built the thing explained it to him and when he was done I said to Eddie, 'Do you like it?' Eddie went, 'Yeah, it's nice,' so I said, 'Do me a favor mate, take the fuckin' thing with ya! I'm sticking with me Marshalls—simple is better.'"

1985: *Rock in Rio*

For two nights the band played the *Rock in Rio* festival at the Rockedome in Rio, Brazil on January 15 and 19.

1985: *Fly on the Wall* Tour (North America)

Starting out in Binghamton, New York, on September 2, 1985, the band played forty-three dates throughout the US, ending in El Paso, Texas, on October 27, 1985.

1985: *Fly on the Wall* Tour (North America)

Working the east coast of the United States, AC/DC started in Lakeland, Florida, at the Civic Center on November 5 and played fourteen dates, finishing up in Portland, Maine, on November 24, 1985.

1986: *Fly on the Wall* Tour (UK)

After taking time off for the holidays, the band continued in the UK, performing only seven dates in Manchester, Whitley Bay, London, Birmingham, and Edinburgh from January 13 through January 23.

1986: *Fly on the Wall* Tour (Europe)

The European leg started back up in Bruxelles, Belgium on January 26 and continued through seventeen dates in Holland, Germany, Switzerland, Sweden, Norway, and Finland, ending in Kobenhavn, Denmark on February 16, 1986.

1986: *Who Made Who* Tour (North America)

Supporting songs from the *Maximum Overdrive* movie soundtrack, the band started in New Orleans, Louisiana on July 31 and played thirty-seven dates throughout the US and five nights in Canada. The tour ended on September 19 in Uniondale, New York.

1988: *Blow Up Your Video* Tour (Australia)

Taking a longer time than usual to record a new album, AC/DC launched the *Blow Up Your Video* tour in Australia on February 1, 1988. Playing the first two nights in Perth, they continued with twelve dates through Melbourne, Sydney, and Adelaide, ending at the Brisbane Entertainment Centre on February 22.

1988: *Blow Up Your Video* Tour (Europe)

Back in Europe on March 7, 1988, this leg of the tour started in Birmingham, UK and went for twenty-seven dates through Holland, Belgium, Germany, Sweden, Norway, Finland, France, and Switzerland, closing back in London on April 13 at the Wembley Arena.

1988: *Blow Up Your Video* Tour (North America)

Launching a forty-seven date tour throughout the US and Canada, the band started this leg in Portland, Maine, on May 2, and finished on June 25, 1988, at the San Diego Sports Arena in San Diego, California.

1988: *Blow Up Your Video* Tour (North America)

Less than a month later, the band was back on the road opening this part of the tour on July 20, 1988, at the Pan American Center in Las Cruces, New Mexico, playing forty-eight dates through the US. I saw them play in Alpine Valley in East Troy, Wisconsin, on September 10. They finished up this leg of the tour in Ottawa, Canada two nights later on September 12 at the Civic Centre.

This was also the only time Malcolm Young did not perform with the band. Angus and Malcolm's nephew, Stevie Young, filled in for Malcolm so he could take a break from touring and address his dependence on alcohol. Stevie looked and played so much like his famous uncle that some of the fans didn't realize it wasn't Malcolm on stage.

1988: *Blow Up Your Video* Tour (North America)

Starting on October 4, in Glens Falls, New York, AC/DC soldiered on through twenty-nine more dates across America. The final date for this tour was on November 13, 1988, at the Great Western Forum in Los Angeles, California.

1990: *Razors Edge* Tour (North America)

Once Malcolm was well and back in the band, the decision was made to switch drummers. Simon Wright took an offer to play with Dio, and Chris Slade accepted the position. After lackluster sales during much of the eighties, the band returned with a vengeance with their new album, *The Razors*

Edge. The tour launched on November 2, in Worcester, Massachusetts, and lasted through thirty-three dates, ending on December 16 in Long Beach, California.

This part of the tour included a date at the Dane County Coliseum in Madison, Wisconsin, on December 1, 1990. That night was my introduction to the new drummer, and held a new treat for the fans, the Angus dollar bill, which would rain down on the audience during the song "Moneytalks." I got to see the band after the show, and was proud of their return to the spotlight with such a spectacular album.

After we had caught up on the last decade, I pulled out prints of the pictures taken of us at Alpine Valley back in August of 1978. I brought along copies for Angus and Malcolm, plus the original pictures for them to sign. I believe this was the first time I had ever asked them for their autographs. When Angus saw the pictures, the first thing he said was, "Oh, those were taken last week!" I'll never forget how he then looked at them for a while, getting tears in his eyes. He looked up at me and said, "Bon really looked great then, didn't he?" And I said, "Bon was at his peak back then, Angus, he looked amazing!" Which made us both smile.

Finally Malcolm walked in, and I got another big hug and lots of laughs. After catching up, I was able to ask them a few questions for my review of the show for the newspaper I was writing for. Just recently, *Guitar Player* had favorably reviewed the new album, claiming that Malcolm's right hand should be declared an Australian national treasure. I asked Malcolm what he thought about that, and he quipped, "That review cost me a lot of money!" I asked Angus what he thought of being called the God of heavy metal. He just sneered at me and said, "I'm not the God, I'm the *monster!*"

1991: *Razors Edge* Tour (North America)

Back to work as soon as the holidays were over, the band started the second leg of the *Razors Edge* tour on January 11 in Vancouver, playing twenty-seven dates and ending on February 22 at the Florida Suncoast Dome in St. Petersburg, Florida. Having played golf in Sarasota, Florida, Brian Johnson fell in love with the area and built a house right outside Sarasota, where he still lives to this day.

1991: *Razors Edge* Tour (Europe)

On March 20, 1991, AC/DC started their European tour for *Razors Edge* in Helsinki, Finland. The band played twenty-six dates through Sweden, Norway, Germany, France, Switzerland, Holland, Ireland, and England. The last date was at Kings Hall in Dublin, Ireland on April 27, 1991.

1991: *Razors Edge* Tour (North America)

Without much of a break, the *Razors Edge* tour landed back in the States on May 24, 1991, in Buffalo, New York, and continued for thirty-six dates, ending on July 14 at the Sea Performing Arts Center in Old Orchard Beach, Maine. This leg included a performance at Alpine Valley in East Troy, Wisconsin, on June 28. Unable to catch an Angus dollar as they flew all over the Coliseum in Madison, Wisconsin, back in December, this time I just happened to be standing right underneath a bundle that literally fell on my head. That night I had fun giving away as many as I could, of course keeping five or six for keepsakes. Backstage after the show, Brian showed me the black eye he had just gotten in "a pub down in Sarasota, where he just bought a house."

1991: *Razors Edge* Tour (Europe)

Starting on August 10 in Denmark, the band toured through Europe, play-ing twenty dates through Hungary, Poland, the UK, Germany, Switzerland,

An AC/DC Angus dollar from the *Razors Edge* tour. I missed getting one when they played in Madison in December of 1990, but was lucky enough to be standing below one of the bundles dropped at their show at Alpine Valley in East Troy, Wisconsin, on June 28, 1991.

Holland, France, Austria, Italy, and Spain. For the first time ever, the band played in Russia, ending the tour in front of over one million people at the Tushino Airfield on September 28, 1991, making that night the largest live concert audience in front of which the band has ever performed.

1991: *Razors Edge* Tour (Australia/New Zealand)

Bringing the *Razors Edge* back home and closing out the tour, AC/DC started in Sydney on October 14, and played fifteen dates through Melbourne, Perth, Adelaide, Brisbane, and for the first time ever, Wellington and Auckland, New Zealand, ending on November 16, 1991.

This is the tour on which the band reunited with Phil Rudd when they performed in New Zealand. Phil asked Malcolm if he could give it another go, and by the time they were ready to record their next album, *Ballbreaker*, Phil Rudd was asked to rejoin the band.

1996: *Ballbreaker* Tour (North America)

After taking one of the longest breaks to date in between albums, AC/DC began the *Ballbreaker* tour on January 4, 1996, playing seven nights at the Thunder Dome in St. Petersburg, Florida. The band continued through the US, Canada, and for the first time, Mexico City, for forty-nine dates, closing that leg at the Reunion Arena in Dallas, Texas on April 4. When the band hit Milwaukee, Wisconsin, on March 5, I had the honor of visiting with them backstage after their show at the Bradley Center. We hadn't seen each other in six years, but as always, it seemed like we had just spoken a week ago.

That night Angus was signing two Gibson SGs to be given to fans who won them through a radio contest. As he was signing them, he joked that the guitars he was signing were better than the ones he plays. It was really exciting to see the band again and be able to welcome Phil back. Malcolm was enjoying the new technology of laptops and was watching a soccer match when I first walked in.

I also met a dedicated fan by the name of Carl Allen, who was following them on tour. As the band packed up and headed for the tour bus, Carl asked Malcolm whatever happened to the Marvel comic book that was supposed to be released. The tour manager was corralling them out the door and Malcolm turned around and looked at Carl and pointed to me and said, "Ask Sue, she goes all the way back, she knows everything."

The band also invited us to stay and eat dinner, so I told Carl all about the call I got from Marvel Comics in the early 1990s. I was publishing a rock 'n' roll newspaper called *Rock Central*, and had run an article about the first night I met the band back in 1977. I always sent my articles to the band through their publicity company, and after they received the newspaper, they called me in search of pictures of Bon Scott.

Considering all the images of Bon on the Internet today, it was very surprising to me that they were having trouble collecting pictures for Marvel Comics. The next day a gentleman from Marvel called me and told me all about the comic book they were designing and that that was why they needed pictures of Bon for drawing reference. He told me that in the comic book, Bon was in Hell with the Devil and Richard Nixon, and he won a card game where the stakes would be to have AC/DC visit him in Hell and let him sing with them one more time.

Being a huge fan of the band's, and a true Bon Scott fanatic, I made no bones about my displeasure of their intended subject matter. I told him that for one thing, I didn't believe Bon Scott was in Hell, and no, it didn't make me feel better that he was running the place! Video games were just catching on, and right after that call, Marvel Comics downsized and the AC/DC comic book was never released. Needless to say, I wasn't disappointed to hear that at all.

1996: *Ballbreaker* Tour (Europe)

Opening in Oslo, Norway on April 19, AC/DC covered Europe, playing fifty-two dates in Sweden, Germany, Austria, the UK, Ireland, Spain, Portugal, France, and Italy. The tour closed in Bordeaux, France on July 13, and marked their first appearance in the Czech Republic, on May 29.

1996: *Ballbreaker* Tour (North America)

Back in the US, AC/DC started in Wantagh, New York, at the Jones Beach Amphitheatre on August 1, 1996, and played thirty dates throughout the US and Canada. The tour ended on September 14 at the World Amphitheatre in Tinley Park, outside of Chicago, Illinois. The best part of that last night was that the band included "Down Payment Blues" in their set, which I hadn't heard them play live since the 1970s.

My backstage pass from the *Ballbreaker* tour in 1996, one of
the many in my collection, which are in photo albums, stuck
to the back of books, and hiding in other places around my
house. My goal was to someday cover a whole wall with them.

1996: *Ballbreaker* Tour (South America)

Returning to South America for five dates, where the band has a massive fol-
lowing, the *Ballbreaker* tour opened in Brazil in Curitiba on October 11, and
Sao Paulo on October 12. Then it went on to Buenos Aires, Argentina on
October 18 and 19, and closed in Santiago de Chile in Chile on October 22.

1996: *Ballbreaker* Tour (Australia/New Zealand)

Returning to Bon's hometown of Perth on November 2, the band played fifteen dates, including shows in Adelaide, Melbourne, Sydney, Brisbane, and
Darwin. The last two nights they performed in New Zealand, in Auckland
on November 27 and Christchurch on November 30.

2000: *Stiff Upper Lip* Tour (North America)

After a four-year break, AC/DC went old school by having their brother George produce their new album, *Stiff Upper Lip*. The tour launched in Grand Rapids, Michigan on July 31, 2000, and continued through the US and Canada for thirty-five dates, ending in Oakland, California, on September 20.

When they performed at the Bradley Center in Milwaukee, Wisconsin, on August 30, I was able to give Angus a copy of the manuscript for my first book, *Rock 'n' Roll Fantasy: My Life and Times with AC/DC, Van Halen, Kiss* . . . . I asked him to read it and let me know if there was anything in it that they would object to. I also told him I hadn't found a publisher yet, and he suggested I publish on my own, à la Stephen King. This was years before authors started publishing themselves, so at first I didn't take him seriously. Of course Angus knew what he was talking about. Angus ended up telling me that my book needed more "dirt," and I took his advice and self-published it as a CD-ROM in 2001.

2000: *Stiff Upper Lip* Tour (Europe)

Once again starting their European tour in Belgium, on October 14, the band played thirty-nine dates, including shows in Germany, Sweden, Norway, Switzerland, Austria, France, Finland, Holland, England, Scotland, and Spain. The tour ended in Barcelona on December 14, just in time to take off for the holidays.

2001: *Stiff Upper Lip* Tour (Australia)

Back in Perth on January 18, AC/DC toured through Australia, playing sixteen dates in Sydney, Melbourne, Brisbane, Adelaide, Hobart, and Canberra. They closed the tour in Sydney on February 15 at the Sydney Entertainment Centre.

2001: *Stiff Upper Lip* Tour (Japan)

Making their third trip to Japan, AC/DC played in Yokohama on February 19 and 20 and Osaka on February 22. Not that they don't have fans in Japan, but the band has never been as huge as in other parts of the world, mainly due to Japan's love affair with cute long-haired boy bands, which AC/DC definitely is not.

2001: *Stiff Upper Lip* Tour (North America)

Returning to the States on March 18 in Fort Lauderdale, Florida, the band performed thirty-five dates in the US and Canada. The last two nights were shows that were postponed in Madison, Wisconsin, and Detroit, Michigan. The original dates were scheduled for May 1 and 2, respectively, but the band ended up closing the tour on May 11 and 12. The day they were scheduled to appear in Madison at the Kohl Center on May 1, I was in touch with their tour manager regarding backstage passes for the show that night. When I gave him a call in the early afternoon, he said it was bad timing and that he had a doctor to deal with. He told me to call him back, but I never got through to him. Frantic that something terrible had happened, it was announced two hours later over the radio that AC/DC were cancelling their show.

At the time I was working for a local radio station, which had a huge promotion in play when that announcement came in. When my boss found out that I knew the band had a doctor come to the hotel and didn't tell anyone until they cancelled, he wasn't too happy with me. Or course that would be the last thing I would do, to say something before the band announced it.

"Pyro" Pete mentioned that they will only postpone a show if they absolutely have to. "I've seen Brian sick, go out and sing, come back and sit down and take his cough medicine. He would have a cup of tea with honey in it, and go right back out on stage and give it one hundred and ten percent intensity. And no one would ever know that right after the show he would be in bed for two days. They're working men. They are clocking in, it's their jobs. If they sold tickets in your town, it's their job to come and play your town. If they got sick, and they had to come back, they would get it in as soon as they could fit in another date."

When they came back on May 11, I found out that Brian was having throat problems and couldn't sing for a couple of nights. Due to the extra days being added to the tour, they were in new buses, making up two dates while their families were waiting for them in Florida to enjoy a short holiday. There were no meet and greets that night, so we all went outside afterwards to watch the buses drive away. I was standing outside with about twenty fans, including Gary Karnes, who had a guitar he wanted Angus to sign.

To our disbelief, as soon as the buses passed us, the first bus stopped and with wet hair and the tour manager in tow, Angus jumped off the bus to sign autographs and take pictures. It was actually quite chilly that night, which isn't unusual for Wisconsin, and he stood there until each and every fan got an autograph or a picture taken. I asked him if he got the CD-ROMs of my book that I had dropped off at their hotel on May 1, and he smiled and said they were on the bus and he was going to read it on the road. I gave him a hug and thanked him for all the years of great music. Little did I know that it would be a full seven years before we would see each other again.

2001: *Stiff Upper Lip* Tour (Europe)

Beginning on June 6 in Milton Keynes, UK, the band played 17 dates through Germany, Sweden, Finland, Switzerland, France, Italy, and the Czech Republic, ending in Koln, Germany on July 8. After the *Stiff Upper Lip* tour ended, AC/DC gave away "the world's greatest lawn ornament." Some lucky fan won a life-size replica of one of their cannons. The cannons, along with several versions of the bell and multiple "Rosies," all rest between tours in a warehouse somewhere in England.

2003: Appearances at the Roseland Ballroom in New York City, the SARS Benefit in Toronto, and Dates with the Rolling Stones

On March 11, the band played a special date at the Roseland Ballroom in New York City for a lucky audience of those who were able to win tickets. The band was in town for their "abduction," as Malcolm would say, into the Rock and Roll Hall of Fame.

That summer, AC/DC played five dates in Germany from June 9–22: two headlining shows, and three supporting the Rolling Stones. Also appearing with them were the Pretenders. There were rumors that the tickets for the Stones weren't selling that well in Europe until they added AC/DC. It would be the first time since 1979 that AC/DC were billed as a supporting act.

On July 30 they co-headlined with the Stones at the Downsview Park in Toronto, Canada for the SARS benefit. The audience was estimated at close to 500,000 people, making it the largest-attended concert in Canada's history. On October 21, the band played one last date that year at the Carling Apollo Hammersmith in London, and then took a five-year break.

During that time, I saw Brian Johnson and Cliff Williams perform on the *Classic Rock Cares* tour in Clearwater, Florida, in July of 2007. The tour featured Brian, Cliff, Robin Zander from Cheap Trick, Rainbow's Joe Lynn Turner, and Eddie Money. It was a short tour up the east coast of the States to raise money for the John Entwistle Foundation. I solicited several rock magazines to see if any of them would like a concert review. Of course, all they wanted to know about was when AC/DC planned on going back into the studio and if there would be a new tour.

Over the years there had been many rumors about the band calling it quits and finally retiring, after touring for almost thirty years. At the time, Brian and Cliff honestly didn't know what was going on. They had heard the same rumors, and until the call came in from the Young brothers, they were waiting right along with the rest of the world. The upside was that I found out Brian's wife loved my book, *The Story of AC/DC: Let There Be Rock*, and I was able to give a copy to Cliff in person. Brian kissed me and told me I did a good job and Cliff called me a few days later to thank me for bringing back a lot of good memories.

The downside was that I came back with only a concert review of the show and no news on AC/DC, much to the horror of three very big editors who shall remain nameless. Two out of three never printed my review, and haven't spoken to me since. I know when to keep my mouth shut. AC/DC surprised the whole world (including Brian and Cliff) when they reunited in Vancouver in the spring of 2008 to record *Black Ice*.

2008: *Black Ice* World Tour (North America)

AC/DC started their new tour with a "dress rehearsal" in Wilkes-Barre, Pennsylvania on October 26, 2008. Fans who won tickets to this special event traveled from all over the world to see AC/DC perform live, up close and personal. Once my publishers found out about the new album and tour, they wisely asked me to write a new chapter to update *The Story of AC/DC: Let There Be Rock*. This tour was set up to be different from their previous way of doing things. This time there would be no meet and greets, and the band gave only a handful of interviews, finally landing on the cover of *Rolling Stone*.

The band officially opened the tour in Wilkes-Barre on October 28, and appeared in Chicago, Illinois, at the Allstate Arena, playing two nights on October 30 and November 1. On twenty-eight dates through the US and Canada, AC/DC tickets were sold out almost as soon as they went up for sale. My fourteen-year-old son had heard about the band his whole life and assumed that I could get him a private meeting with the band. After not seeing Angus or Malcolm for seven years, I wasn't so sure I had that kind of power, but I gave it my best shot.

Asking for an interview for the updated version of my *Let There Be Rock* book, I was turned down by Albert Music, Sony, and the band's business management in New York City. However, they did pass on my request to the tour manager, and he talked it over with Angus. The night before the call came in, I almost paid close to $400 for two tickets to the Allstate Arena in Chicago for their show on November 1. Right before I hit the Buy button, something told me to wait for one more day. It was already Sunday night, and the concert was the following Saturday.

Not wanting to let my son down, I waited and the very next morning at 9:00 a.m., AC/DC's tour manager called me. As he told me that the band wasn't doing press on this tour and there were no meet and greets, I was thinking how very nice it was of him to call me and turn me down in person. And then he said he mentioned it to Angus, and his reply was, "If Sue Masino wants an interview, Sue Masino gets an interview!" Of course I had to ask him to repeat that, because I couldn't believe my own ears. He then went on to inform me that the interview would take place over the phone sometime in the following week, and that they had tickets and backstage passes waiting for me in Chicago. I was so taken aback, I had to ask him a couple of times if I should buy tickets just in case.

That night my son and I got to see AC/DC slay 17,000 people at the Allstate Arena, putting on an incredible show. The new album was fantastic, the band was better than I had ever seen them, and the entire experience was surreal. Here I was, thirty-one years after I had met them, watching a little band that I met back in 1977, now superstars in their own right. They closed the show with two encores, "Highway to Hell" and "Let There Be Rock." Of course during "Highway to Hell," they showed a picture of the band with Bon in it. It brought tears to my eyes to think how proud he would be of them.

Afterwards my son Jamey and I got to spend forty-five minutes alone with Angus and Malcolm in their dressing room, and again, it felt like no time had passed at all. Malcolm told me that his wife loved my book, and Angus teased me that he wanted a signed copy and not just one from the store. Of course we talked about the old days and especially about Bon.

Even after being gone for almost thirty years, Bon was never far from their thoughts. We ended our visit with taking a picture, and Angus gave Jamey a guitar pick. The next day I was able to drop off two signed books for them at their hotel in downtown Chicago, and Angus even came down to the lobby to pick them up, much to the amazement of my two girlfriends who finally got to meet him. The band completed that leg of the tour in Tampa, Florida, on December 21.

2009: *Black Ice* World Tour (North America)

Right after the holidays, on January 5, the band picked back up in Cleveland, Ohio, and played fourteen more dates in the US and Canada. The first leg of the *Black Ice* North American tour ended in Nashville, Tennessee, on January 31 (on New Year's Eve), marking their thirty-sixth anniversary as a band.

2009: *Black Ice* World Tour (Europe)

On February 18, starting in Oslo, Norway, the rock 'n' roll train steamrolled through Europe for twenty-nine shows, including shows in Germany, Sweden, Norway, Belgium, Holland, Switzerland, Italy, Hungary, the Czech Republic, Spain, England, and Ireland. The last night was at the LG Arena on April 23 in Birmingham, England.

2009: *Black Ice* European Open Air Tour

Through the summer of 2009, the band played open-air festivals throughout Europe. Starting in Germany on May 13, they performed twenty-one dates in Austria, Spain, Greece, Portugal, France, Norway, Finland, Denmark, Sweden, Holland, England, and Ireland. Making their debut in Belgrade, Serbia on May 26, the tour wrapped in Angus and Malcolm's birthplace of Glasgow, Scotland on June 30.

2009: *Black Ice* World Tour (North America)

The third leg of the *Black Ice* tour started in Foxboro, Massachusetts, on July 28. The band played thirty-three dates through the US, Canada, and Mexico and ended on November 21 with their debut in San Juan, Puerto Rico. For the second time, I got to see the *Black Ice* tour when they played the United Center in Chicago on August 14, 2009.

By now the band was in full swing and overjoyed by the outpouring of love from millions of dedicated fans. After their show, my sister Lori and I were invited backstage to visit with the whole band. There were friends and family in attendance, including Malcolm's son, Ross, who couldn't be more of a sweetheart. He followed us around to make sure we had our pictures taken with all five band members.

I was able to get autographs for my daughter (who has never met them), and my sister got so many autographs for her sons that I quipped to Angus and Malcolm, "Did you also sign that car loan and the mortgage papers?" which made them both laugh. Starting right after our visit, for a while the band included my book for sale on their official website.

2009: *Black Ice* World Tour (South America)

Ending the year in South America, AC/DC opened their tour in Sao Paolo, Brazil on November 27. Two nights in Peru and Chile were cancelled due to logistical problems, so the band closed the tour with three nights on December 2, 4, and 6 at the Estadio de River Plate in Buenos Aires, Argentina. Those nights were filmed for the release of the double DVD *Live at River Plate*. With the band playing in front of over 200,000 people, counting the three nights combined, that DVD spectacularly shows how tight they had become, and how loved they are in Argentina.

2010: *Black Ice* World Tour (Australia/New Zealand)

Still touring after fourteen months, AC/DC brought *Black Ice* back home starting on January 28, 2010, in Wellington, New Zealand. They played four-teen dates through Auckland, New Zealand, Sydney, Melbourne, Brisbane, and Adelaide, ending the tour with two nights in Perth on March 6 and 8. In attendance at the shows in Perth, was Bon Scott's mother Isa, who saw the band perform every time they came through on tour. She passed away the following year on August 30, 2011, at the age of 94.

2010: *Black Ice* World Tour (Japan)

On their fourth visit to Japan, AC/DC played two nights in Tokyo and one in Osaka between March 12 and March 16.

2010: *Black Ice* Tour (North America)

I never dreamed the band would stay on tour for this long, and this leg of the tour gave me my third opportunity to see the band—another first for me since the 1970s. The last leg of their North American tour only included five nights: Las Vegas on April 9; Kansas City on April 11; Louisville, Kentucky, on April 13; Milwaukee, Wisconsin on April 15; and closing on April 17 in Des Moines, Iowa.

Catching them in Milwaukee was a pure delight, and I had the pleasure of hanging out with Malcolm's son Ross, who watched the show from the sound board. I also realized another dream come true when I made it onto the Jumbotron during "You Shook Me All Night Long," dancing my heart out. Everyone was in high spirits over the success of the *Black Ice* tour, which ended up being the second-biggest selling tour in music history. The biggest selling tour in rock history to date is U2's *360°*, which lasted from 2009–2011 and brought in over 730 million dollars.

2010: *Black Ice* World Tour (Europe)

Closing the *Black Ice* tour after being on the road for nineteen months, the band started in Bulgaria on May 14 and played twenty shows, including dates in Italy, Romania, Poland, Austria, Germany, Norway, Finland, Sweden, Denmark, Spain, and France. They officially closed out the tour in Bilbao, Spain on June 28. For this last leg of the tour, the band set up camp in Vienna and flew to each of these dates in a private jet. Their show in Oslo, Norway, on May 30 was cut short by six songs due to problems with the plane they were using.

On May 19, Phil Rudd's fifty-sixth birthday, they played an outdoor stadium in front of 47,000 fans in Udine, Italy. Since Udine was the only city they played in Italy in 2010, the city took it very personally and the band was celebrated the entire week. Thanks to a dedicated fan, Mario Rimati, who first talked to a local book store, then the promoters, and finally the Tourism Bureau of northern Italy, I was flown over to do a book signing and see AC/DC live at the Stadio Friuli. This was another dream of mine come true, considering I had never been to Italy, and had always wanted to see the band play an open air festival in Europe.

They don't have the same safety restrictions as we do in the States, so during "Shot Down in Flames," the audience actually started a bonfire in the middle of the crowd! I have never seen an audience have so much fun, and the band was in rare form. At the start of "Hell's Bells," as the church bell descended toward the stage, Brian Johnson walked all the way to end of the catwalk, turned around and ran as fast as he could toward the bell. As the band launched into the song, Brian grabbed the bell and swung across the stage as the audience went wild.

I had been in touch with Phil's daughter over Facebook, and she was upset that the band wasn't going to have time to say hello after the show. After seeing them four times and getting tickets in the VIP section for the show, I certainly wasn't going to complain. I told her not to worry, I would be in the audience and I asked her to wish her father a happy birthday from me.

As they started the show, and each band member appeared on the giant screens on either side of the stage, I got the biggest surprise of the night. As most fans know, the whole band always wears black T-shirts with jeans, and Angus of course appears in his schoolboy outfit. That night, Phil Rudd was wearing a Harley Davidson T-shirt, which I'm sure made all the motorcycle enthusiasts in the crowd happy. It was a special hello to me, since Harley Davidson motorcycles are made in Wisconsin. Once the band finished the tour, they were already talking about having enough material for a new album, giving hope to all their fans around the world that the band was coming back. It was just a question of when.

21

The First Single Recorded Under the Name "AC/DC"

One of the Only Recordings That Featured Vocalist Dave Evans

Malcolm and Angus had been playing around the clubs in Sydney with Larry Van Kriedt on bass while Colin Burgess covered the drums. They made their debut as AC/DC on New Year's Eve of 1973. In February they went into EMI Studios to cut their first single, "Can I Sit Next to You Girl," and "Rockin' in the Parlour." George and Harry produced it, with George recording the bass parts and Malcolm playing lead guitar on "Can I Sit Next to You Girl." A week later, when drummer Colin Burgess collapsed on stage at Chequers from what was believed to be too much drink, he was immediately fired. Big brother George once again saved the day and played drums for their second set. Van Kriedt played drums for a while, but was eventually let go, as well.

In June 1974, AC/DC officially signed a deal with Albert Productions with distribution through EMI. On July 22, "Can I Sit Next to You Girl"/"Rockin' in the Parlour" was released in Australia. The single was also released on the Polydor label in New Zealand. It soon became a regional hit in Perth and Adelaide, and eventually reached the top five.

The record received rave reviews from the Australian press, which described AC/DC: "It starts off like rubber bullets, builds right into a power chord structure just bristling with energy, and includes some incredible dynamic effects—like pure fuzz noise echoing from channel to channel, then fading out as a machine gun rhythm guitar fades in, rising to a powerful blast as they scream out the title over and over. Overall, a stunning record."

AC/DC with vocalist Dave Evans from 1974. This vintage shot features the original vocalist Dave Evans, and as you can see by all the spandex, velvet, boots, and bellbottoms, the band were still experimenting with their look.   *Photo by Philip Morris*

Australia got its first look at AC/DC live on film when a clip of the band playing at the Last Picture Show Theater in Cronulla aired on *GTK*—at the time, Australia's only national rock television show. Even though Peter Clack and Rob Bailey didn't record on "Can I Sit Next to You Girl," they do appear in the film.

By the fall of 1974, AC/DC were looking for a new singer. Tensions had been building with Dave Evans, who was often booted off the stage so the band could jam on blues boogies. Malcolm and Angus both thought the band sounded better without him. At times, when they played two to four shows a day, Dave's voice would give out and their manager Dennis Laughlin would fill in for him. Plus, they felt his "glam" image contrasted too much with the rest of the band. An eventual punch up between Dave and Dennis sealed his fate.

They asked Dave to leave after his last concert in Melbourne, and Bon Scott's real debut with the band was at Brighton-Le-Sands Masonic Hall in Sydney on October 5, 1974. (October 5 happens to be Brian Johnson's birthday.) There were no hard feelings between Dave and Bon. After that, Dave ran into Bon on several occasions: "We shook hands, wished each other luck, and had no animosity towards each other."

Dave told *Rock-E-Zine* in September 2000, "At first I was shocked and so was the Sydney audience who were my fans, but Bon made his own character work brilliantly with the band and he endeared himself with his cheekiness and he always seemed to have a twinkle in his eyes. Also his voice was unique and had an unusual quality. Some of my favorite rock songs are ones that Bon sings." Dave went on to find his own success with the band Rabbit, who scored a hit with their song, "Too Much Rock 'n' Roll." Evans now lives in Texas, and continues to record and tour with his band, King of all Badasses.

22

Angus' Image Embroidered on Socks

AC/DC's Merchandise

The first time I met AC/DC, on August 16, 1977, they had no merchandise to sell at their concerts. The only item I obtained that night was one of the first AC/DC buttons that they had produced. Roadie Barry Taylor gave it to me, and I honestly can't tell you how many of them were made at the time.

As the band toured the world over the next three years, the record company produced T-shirts to commemorate each album. However, when they opened for Aerosmith in August of 1978, they still were not selling AC/DC merchandise at the venues. After their set, I asked Angus in the dressing room when they were going to start selling more than T-shirts, like perhaps, guitar picks. Angus turned, and sneering as he threw a guitar pick at me, he said, "Like I'm going to spend money on something I just throw away!"

The back of the Angus dollar bill from the *Razors Edge* tour, caught at Alpine Valley in East Troy, Wisconsin, in June of 1991. Apparently they got in trouble with the Queen of England for passing out fake bills without the Queen's face on them. Maybe if they had featured her in a schoolboy uniform that might have made her happy.

An AC/DC pin from 1977. When I first met the band on August 16, 1977, roadie Barry Taylor gave me this pin, as it was the only piece of merchandise they had at the time. They weren't even selling T-shirts yet.

An AC/DC lighter, one of the many cool items fans send me from around the world. Press down on the side and let there be fire!

An AC/DC set of pool balls, one of the multitude of objects with the AC/DC logo on them that you can buy today. The list of items keeps growing, but luckily they have refrained from condoms and caskets. But you never know.

Backtracks: A collector's box set that contained three CDs, two DVDs, one album of rare cuts, a hardcover book, and memorabilia from AC/DC's early days of touring—all encased in an amplifier that actually worked!

Three decades later, there isn't much you can't buy without the AC/DC logo on it, or Angus' "little devil" caricature, including socks. Now you can purchase clothing, stickers, buttons, tour books, bed linens, dishes, drinkware, lighters, ear plugs, flashing devil horns, baby clothes, hats, backpacks, posters, shot glasses, pool balls, pinball machines, and even a special AC/DC version of the game *Monopoly*. Luckily they have had the good sense to refrain from putting their logo on condoms and caskets, but you never know.

You can find all these items on AC/DC's official website, plus giant retail chain stores like Walmart, Shopko, Sears, and JCPenney all offer AC/DC T-shirts, sweatshirts, and hoodies. Actually, the only piece of AC/DC merchandise I haven't seen for sale yet (as Malcolm once joked) is "AC/DC skid marks on your underpants."

23

Have a Drink On Me

AC/DC Spirits

I t is a documented fact that the band members of AC/DC did some pretty serious drinking back in the early days of the band. Although according to former bassist Mark Evans, he only saw Angus drink three times, and all three times it didn't sit well with him. Hence his love for tea, chocolate, and milk in favor of the harder stuff. Tragically, the heavy drinking took Bon Scott's life and sent Malcolm Young into recovery during the late 1980s. Excessive drinking and other illicit distractions also played a large part of Phil Rudd leaving the band in 1983, not to return until 1995.

When the band broke their seven-year silence and embarked on the *Black Ice* tour in 2008, backstage antics were reduced to Angus and Malcolm sipping tea, and Brian and Cliff enjoying an occasional drink with their friends and family. Now that their struggles were permanently behind them, the band stepped up to endorse a few drinks of their own.

The BBC reported on August 16, 2011 that AC/DC had teamed up with Australian winemaker Warburn Estate to sell a variety of wines named after their biggest hits. The four different bottles that are being sold in stores across

Riff Raff Liquor, entitled Bon Scotch Liquor, aged seven years. They also have their own wine, and there is a German AC/DC beer available, as well.

Australia include a Hell's Bells Sauvignon Blanc, a Cabernet Sauvignon called Highway to Hell, a Back in Black Shiraz, and You Shook Me All Night Long Moscato. Steve Donohue, general manager of buying for the Woolworths Liquor Group, stated, "We wanted to make sure that AC/DC's home fan base could have easy access to their rock icons' wines."

In early 2013, AC/DC Premium Lager became available in Germany and its maker has advertised that the beer is "brewed in accordance with the rock 'n' roll manifesto of 1973 and the German purity law of 1516, producing a consistent 5 percent alcohol lager. Angus Young stated, 'We hope to give beer drinkers the same assurances we give our loyal listeners. They know what they're gonna get every time. There are never any surprises!'"

Aside from endorsing their own spirits, it's hard to say how many drinks have been named after the band. Author Jane Rocca featured a chapter on rock star drinks in her book *The Cocktail*. The Bon Scott includes dark rum, lime, a fig, ginger beer, and brown sugar. Which makes me wonder: after it's mixed, does it taste just like Jack Daniels? Because it should.

24

Back in Black

One of the Biggest-Selling Albums of All Time

T he band had just started working on the new album in London. After the sudden death of Bon Scott and once Brian was hired, instead of recording with Lange in London as they had planned, the band decided to take advantage of the tax benefits of recording in the Bahamas at Compass Studios in Nassau. This recording studio had been built by Chris Blackwell, the owner of Island Records. Not only would it take the band out of the glare of the media, but it would also provide a quiet relaxing place for the band to work Brian in.

I received one of Barry's last letters, written from Hollywood, dated May 5, 1980. He wrote about visiting the band and that they were well and fairly happy. Barry mentioned that their new singer was from Newcastle, which is in Northern England on the Scottish border. He went on to say that the people from that region were known for their hospitality and geniality, which Brian certainly fit. He told me that he had a good voice and apparently wrote good lyrics. He went on to explain that the band were forced to become exiles by choosing to record the new album in the Bahamas, and that even though it was nice to see them, he couldn't imagine going back out on the road. Barry also mentioned that Angus got married the day he left England to move to the States, and Malcolm was looking forward to becoming a father for the first time.

Evidently flying off to a tropical island wasn't all that it was cracked up to be. When the band arrived, violent thunderstorms were thrashing the island. Brian remembered, "It wasn't a tropical paradise. It wasn't all white beaches. It was pissing down, there was flooding and all the electricity went out—nae television." The accommodations weren't exactly secure, either. Brian stated, "This big old black lady ruled the place with a rod of iron. We had to lock the doors at night because she'd warned us about these Haitians who'd come down at night and rob the place. So she bought us all these six-foot fishing spears to keep at the fucking door! It was a bit of a stretch from Newcastle, I can tell you."

Malcolm recalled in *Classic Rock* August 2005, "It was the best place to do that album because there was nothing going on. We'd sit through the night with a couple of bottles of rum with coconut milk in and work. That's where a lot of the lyric ideas come from."

Along with AC/DC, some of rock's biggest stars also paid Mr. Blackwell's studio a visit in 1980. Keith Emerson of Emerson, Lake, and Palmer had recorded there before, and enjoyed it so much he made his home in the Bahamas for several years. "What happened with us, with ELP, is we were recording in Switzerland, and I didn't like the place very much, because there wasn't a lot happening. So ELP moved to the Bahamas in 1978 or 1979, to start work on their *Last Beach* album. The reason why we chose the Bahamas, because it was kind of a tax exile place, which is probably why AC/DC chose it. In England at that time, it was being run by the Labour government, who charged the exorbitant amount for people who were making large amounts of money. I think we paid eighty to ninety percent of our earnings. We all got out of that one. So a lot of British bands were leaving England."

Emerson agrees that Compass Point was a hotbed for rock stars. He remembered running into Grace Jones, who was also working at Compass, right before AC/DC arrived. "Then we came to realize that a band from Australia was coming down. I didn't know much of the history of the band, but there was always an excitement when you knew a band from England was coming. When AC/DC arrived, they had all their English gear on, leather jackets . . . And of course you know what we wore on the island was a pair of shorts and a shirt, if that. Brian was the first guy I spoke to, and he was trying to get used to the weather. It was very hot, and by the time they arrived, I had bought a twenty-one foot sports fisherman boat. It wasn't vastly glamorous, but it enabled me to get out and fish and water ski, scuba dive, it had a stereo onboard, an ice freezer on it, something manageable for one person to skip around the island with.

"When I mentioned this to Brian, he said, 'Oh God, I would love to come out with you!' And most of the other band members said the same thing. I asked them if they wanted to come out with me and fish. They'd arrived somewhere in the spring, and in April the tuna fish were pretty abundant around the islands, as long as you knew where to go. So I had a lot of education in fishing from the locals, so I was pretty confident we'd catch something. I think we left mid-afternoon, and sure enough, all the birds were flying out from the mainland, and were converging on a particular area of the sea, so we just put the rods in, and we had a fish on in about ten minutes! Which of course they got very excited about that. I was relieved because if we didn't catch anything, my credibility as a fisherman is, well it would be like Ernest Hemingway."

Of course I had to ask him who caught the first fish.

> I don't know, we were trolling which is when you put all the lines out and just wait. It could have been Brian who brought the first one in. I think it was a great excitement for them, and kind of introduced them to my way of the Bahamian life. I think they grew to like it, and settled into their recording at Compass Point.
>
> I ran into Brian a while later on the beach, and he told me he had a little bit of difficulty putting his vocals on, after he had been sunbathing. Right after he had been on the beach, he would go directly into Compass Point Studios, which is right across the street from the beach. Wearing his shorts, he'd just put the headphones on, and have to do this rip-roaring vocals, and it just wasn't happening. He was singing his heart away, and it just didn't have that power. So he had this idea. He told them he was going to go back to the hotel, and then he'd be right back. He was gone for about an hour when he came back wearing his stage gear. He walked into the vocal booth and said, "Right now, roll the tape." And of course it came out, like rip-roaring, you know? He just couldn't sing in his shorts, that's what it was.

Back in 1980, Emerson wasn't quite familiar with AC/DC's music, so I asked him what he thought of them as people, since I've always thought they were very down to earth. Laughingly, he replied, "Oh, absolutely! There were no egos, there was no 'Hey, listen, I'm a rock star and I can't get any salt water on me. And I certainly cannot deal with this ballyhoo bait that you got here in this stinking bucket!' Basically all the guys just mucked in, and thoroughly enjoyed the experience. I was just happy to have a bunch of guys on my boat! In other words, there was no 'Don't you know who I am?' attitude. I would have recognized that straight off, and I would not have invited any of them on my boat! They were very keen and very interested, and it was certainly great for me to have their company."

With Mutt Lange once again at the helm, AC/DC embarked on recording their eighth album with a new lead singer. Working with Lange again, Angus told *Classic Rock*, "It was very good—for both us and him, I think. After he made *Highway to Hell* he was in big demand, but I thought it was good for him [to record with AC/DC again]. Especially after what happened to us. It's to Mutt's credit that he still wanted to be involved with us after Bon's death."

Not only did Brian have to fit in with the band, but he also had the daunting task of coming up with his own lyrics. I can just imagine the pressure of joining a band well on their way to superstardom, but I can't fathom the responsibility of writing words for their music! Brian explained in VH1's *Ultimate Albums* that he was paralyzed with fear. Praying for guidance, Brian revealed that he experienced a supernatural event regarding Bon that he was reluctant to go into detail about. He did later admit that one night he was woken up out of a dead sleep, and was inspired to sit and write lyrics down as fast as he could put them on paper.

In memoriam to Bon, the band decided on an all-black cover, with a most fitting title, *Back in Black*. The ten songs included on this historic album were "Hell's Bells," "Shoot to Thrill," "What Do You Do for Money Honey" "Given the Dog a Bone," "Let Me Put My Love Into You," "Back in Black," "You Shook Me All Night Long," "Have a Drink On Me," "Shake a Leg," and "Rock 'n' Roll Ain't Noise Pollution."

The lyrics to "Hell's Bells" were inspired by a comment Mutt Lange made to Brian in the studio one night. Brian recalled in *Ultimate Albums* on VH1, that when he wrote "Hell's Bells," there was a terrible storm booming over the island. Lange suggested, "Rolling thunder," which prompted Brian to continue, "*I'm a rollin' thunder, pourin' rain, I'm comin' on like a hurricane. My lightnin's flashin' across the sky, you're only young but you're gonna die.*" I have heard that all of the lyrics to "You Shook Me" came to Brian while he was sitting in the loo. Luckily, I don't have any details on that one.

Within six weeks, the band had miraculously created an album that would herald the second phase of AC/DC's career. Brian was very relieved when the recording was finished, he told *Classic Rock* in August 2005. "It was about three in the afternoon, it was a beautiful sunny day and I went outside down to where the huts were. I sat on this wall and I got a ciggie out and sat among the trees. I was so happy that I had done it. But I hadn't really heard one song. I'd go in and do a couple of verses, pop back and do a chorus. That's the way Mutt keeps you interested, you know." The only complaint Brian had was about the high notes on "Shake a Leg," claiming, "Oh, that was fucking way up. Some of those notes will never be heard by man again."

For some reason, it took *Creem* magazine until their May issue to acknowledge Bon's death. "At press time, Bon Scott, thirty-year-old [sic] vocalist of AC/DC was reported dead in England. Found in the car of friend Alastair Kinnear, the Australian belter of 'Highway to Hell' and similar screechers

My backstage pass from the *Back in Black* tour from the Rosemont Horizon (now the Allstate Arena), dated September 20, 1980. I had just seen them in Madison, Wisconsin, on September 14, and Phil Rudd invited me down to see them in Chicago six days later.

died of apparent 'alcohol poisoning.' What's especially ironic is the Australian band's career was just taking off in the States after great success in England. As yet, Atlantic Records has had no comment on the incident or the band's future plans, although their next album was in the final mixing stage, and will doubtless be released soon."

Brian once stated that after he joined the band, "I was a bit scared, because I didn't know what to expect. I was more scared of the crew than I was of the lads, because the crew were reeling off names like Yes and Rick Wakeman, these fucking huge bands they've worked for. But the lads made me feel dead comfortable. The band's the fucking best! The biggest bonus about being in the band is the fact that I can get into their gigs without paying for a fucking ticket, and I've got the best seat in the fucking house! Honestly! I could just sit up there and watch that band because they're fucking great. A great band and a great bunch of lads. I know what they were going through when Bon went, wondering about going on and all that—it's only natural." Brian received more assurance when Atlantic Records declared the new album "brilliant." The month of June was spent rehearsing in London, before launching the *Back in Black* tour with six warm-up dates in Belgium and Holland. On June 29, 1980, Brian Johnson appeared with AC/DC for the first time in Namur, Belgium at the Palais Des Expositions. Bon's successor was immediately welcomed with open arms by AC/DC, and especially Bon's fans. Brian was quoted as saying, "That poor boy was loved by thousands of people worldwide. When we did a warm-up gig in Holland, this kid came up to me with a tattoo of Bon on his arm and said, 'This bloke was my hero, but now he's gone, I wish you all the luck in the world.' I just stood there shaking. I mean, what can you say when people are prepared to put their faith in you like that? Since then, I feel like I've been singing for that kid and so many others like him."

Brian also told Tommy Vance from the BBC, "I think Bon Scott had a bit of genius. It annoys me that nobody recognized that before. He used to sing great words, write great words. He had a little twist in everything he said. Nobody ever recognized the man at the time. Oh great, when the man died they were startin' to say, 'Yeah, the man was a genius.' That was too late; it's not fair. I think he was so clever, and I think he had such a distinctive voice as well. He was brilliant."

Even Atlantic's Perry Cooper wasn't so sure they could continue without Bon. "They called me up and said, 'We've got this new singer, and we're going out on the road. We want you to come out and see him.' And I flew out to see them somewhere in Canada, and went on the bus with them from somewhere to Calgary. And I'm sitting there on the bus, and there was Brian.

"He came up to me and said, 'I was told I had to make friends with you. You are the key to Atlantic.' And I said, 'What the fuck are you saying? I can't understand you!' And all he did was tell jokes the whole way, he was so wonderful. He's the best guy in the world!"

In the beginning of July, AC/DC filmed video clips for *Back in Black* in Breda, Holland. From July 13–28, they played eleven dates in Canada before making it back into the States. The new album was released in the US on July 21, in the United Kingdom ten days later, and in Australia eleven days after that. Within six months, *Back in Black* peaked at #4, staying in the *Billboard* Top Ten for five months.

On Sunday, September 14, 1980, AC/DC returned to Madison, Wisconsin, to play a sold-out show at the Dane County Coliseum, with Blackfoot opening. Barry was no longer with the band, but Ian Jeffery generously set me up with tickets and backstage passes. About an hour before showtime, AC/DC were ushered in the back door. As they were taken to their respective dressing rooms, I could see Angus jumping up and down trying to wave at me. He was motioning for me to follow the band, which I did. Once they were settled in, Angus came out and said that he wanted me to meet Ellen, his new wife.

Ellen was taller than Angus (like most of us), about the same height as me. She was very pretty, with long straight blond hair and blue eyes. We had a very pleasant visit talking about Angus and how he didn't fit his stage persona at all. We both laughed when she confessed that she didn't appreciate his mooning the crowd. She seemed more resigned to it when I explained to her that I thought by now, the audience expected it. After mentioning that Angus had been fighting off a cold, she grabbed him by the arm and pulled him out of a chilly draft of air. I smiled to myself when I realized that Angus had finally found what he was looking for: "a blond wife to come out on the road and take care of him."

As they got ready to go on stage, I found a great spot to watch the band on stage right, about thirty feet behind Phil Rudd. Since I hadn't heard anything off the new album yet, I didn't know what to expect. As the sold-out crowd got restless, the lights went down, and the audience started to scream. Piercing the darkness was the mournful wail of a bell chiming a death knell, as a gigantic church bell slowly descended from above the stage. The band broke into the opening phrase of "Hell's Bells" as the lights came up, and the audience exploded into a deafening cheer. To this day, I don't think I have ever witnessed anything like it!

Brian Johnson walked out to the center of the stage wearing a black T-shirt and blue jeans, with his trademark flat cap pulled down over his eyes. After swinging at the bell with a mallet, he started singing, "*Rollin' thunder, pourin' rain, I'm comin' on like a hurricane*" with a gale-like force that has to be seen to be truly appreciated.

With their amazing new songs, mixed with the best of Bon's, the audience wholeheartedly embraced them. Brian sang with every molecule of his being, giving justice to Bon's memory. There was no doubt that the band sounded stronger than ever, but the loss of Bon had deeply impacted them.

After their performance at the Coliseum, Phil invited me to party with him the following weekend when they played the Rosemont Horizon in Chicago with Blackfoot. Seeing AC/DC a few days later at a larger venue was a great treat, but bittersweet as well. Again the audience started going crazy when Hell's Bell made its descent toward the stage. Their new songs, "Back in Black," "Hell's Bells," and "You Shook Me," were becoming rock anthems. Any doubts the band may have had over Brian being the right choice evaporated with the roar of the audience.

Bon's death would propel AC/DC into superstardom, so there would be no worries for their rock 'n' roll dreams. Forever the prophet, Bon always said he wouldn't go until he was famous. *Time* magazine would declare Mutt Lange's production as "genius," in connection with the album's "sonic quality" and "arena anthems of uncorrupted hookiness."

Time magazine counted the album as one of the Top 100 Best Albums of All Time. *Gentleman's Quarterly Australia* ranked the album #1 of the Top 50 Most Influential Australian Albums. Gibson Guitars named the song

"Back in Black" the greatest guitar riff of all time. To date, *Back in Black* has sold over forty-nine million copies, and is second only in sales to Michael Jackson's *Thriller*, making it the second best-selling album ever recorded. The song "Back in Black" was the first song to receive platinum status for a ringtone, earning them a RIAA award for one million downloads.

In 2013, the Grammy Hall of Fame marked its fortieth anniversary, which coincided with AC/DC's fortieth anniversary as a band. The Recording Academy honored the band by inducting their album *Back in Black* into the Grammy Hall of Fame. AC/DC's classic album joined a diverse group of twenty-seven other albums that "are memorable for being both culturally and historically significant."

25

Monuments, Awards, Avenues, and Accolades

AC/DC Honors Continue Around the World

Postage Stamps and Fossils

In commemoration of Australian rock 'n' roll, the Australian Post issued twelve postage stamps featuring various artists. AC/DC were chosen, along with the Easybeats, Billy Thorpe, Skyhooks, and the Masters Apprentices. Angus appears on one of stamps, with the words "It's a Long Way to the Top" written across his schoolbag.

The Young brothers even have fossils named after them. In November of 1998, the Australian Museum reported that the fossils were two species of a "strange joint-legged" animal, which was believed to be related to millipedes or the horseshoe crab. One is named for Malcolm: Maldybulakia malcolmi, and the other is Maldybulakia angusi, for Angus.

Awards and Accolades

Kerrang! magazine honored AC/DC on September 26, 1998, when they presented the band with a Hall of Fame award. Though they rarely show up at such events, Angus and Brian actually made an appearance. Receiving their award, Brian took off his hat, and Angus took off his pants.

On March 16, 1999, the following spring, and reportedly remaining clothed, Brian and Cliff attended an awards presentation at the Roseland Ballroom in New York City to receive the Diamond Award for *Back in Black.*

This was given to them by the RIAA to mark sales in the US of over ten million copies.

AC/DC were immortalized in the Rock Walk in Los Angeles, in front of the Guitar Center on Hollywood Boulevard, on September 16, 2000. Two weeks later, the SFX Radio Network broadcasted a two-hour AC/DC concert to over 175 stations across the country. The show had been recorded in Phoenix, Arizona, on September 13.

Greg Barr reviewed their performance in September of 2000 at the Compaq Center in Houston, Texas: "This is a band that has, over the past twenty-five years, barely varied from a formula of beefy chords, bombastic bass lines, meat-and-potatoes drumming, tongue-in-cheek lyrics, and song titles that are an adolescent boy's wet dream . . . The forty-seven-year-old [Malcolm] Young and his forty-four-year-old brother Angus—the pasty-skinned, elfin chain smokers who are the brains behind AC/DC—are part of a cock rock tour de force that can still kick some serious ass."

In 2000, the RIAA upgraded fourteen of AC/DC's titles to sales of over seventy million, tying the band for ninth place on the RIAA's Top Grossing Artist list. This made them the fifth-highest selling certified band in United State's music history, coming in behind the Beatles, Led Zeppelin, Pink Floyd, and the Eagles. RIAA CEO Hilary Rosen said that "AC/DC is one of rock 'n' roll's greatest assets and has truly earned the right to be called legendary."

Angus and Malcolm received the Ted Albert music achievement award from Albert Music at the 2003 APRA Music Awards in Sydney on March 26. Malcolm sent a taped message from London saying, "On behalf of AC/DC and Bon Scott, especially Bon because he's a big part of this, we're proud of the honor of receiving this award." Ted Albert, the man who started it all by signing the Easybeats, had died of heart failure in 1990.

Black Ice won Best Rock Album and Highest Selling Album at the ARIA Music Awards in 2009. It was also nominated for Album of the Year and the band was nominated for Group of the Year. Their new album was also nominated for Best International Album for the Brit Awards and the Juno Awards. *Black Ice* went on to win for Album of the Year in the 2000 Classic Rock Roll of Honors Award.

The following year, in 2010, Angus and Malcolm won for Songwriters of the Year at the APRA Awards, and "Rock N Roll Train" won for Most Played Australian Work Overseas. At the fifty-first Grammy Awards, the same song was nominated for Best Rock Performance by a Duo or Group with

Vocals, and *Black Ice* was nominated for the Best Rock Album. For the first time in their career, AC/DC won a Grammy that night for Best Hard Rock Performance, for their song "War Machine."

AC/DC, one of the last bands to allow their music to be digitally available on iTunes, released their entire catalog in November of 2012, and sold over 700,000 downloads in the first week. In addition to releasing their album catalog, AC/DC's concert films are now also available on iTunes for sale or rental. These include *Live at Donington, No Bull* (Director's Cut), *Live at River Plate, Live at Circus Krone*, and two compilation collections, *Plug Me In* and *Family Jewels*.

Crossing Genres

Proving George's theory of the basic construction of AC/DC's songs, blue-grass band Hayseed Dixie released an entire album of AC/DC covers called *A Hillbilly Tribute to AC/DC*. The band members included "Einus Younger" and "Barley Scotch." The CD was quite successful, impressing Cliff Williams so much that he hired the band to play an end-of-tour party at his house in the mountains in North Carolina.

For more proof that AC/DC's appeal crosses over many genres, multi-platinum band Green Day's *Dookie* album featured a picture of Angus on its cover. Just look for the guitarist on the roof of the building in the bottom right hand corner—there's Angus, shorts and all.

AC/DC were also featured in a Budweiser beer commercial which included two lizards and a ferret. The ferret is singing, and one of the lizards holds up a lighter while "Back in Black" is playing in the background.

The Atlanta Falcons officially changed their team uniforms to the color black, and declared "Back in Black" their new theme song. It's rare to watch an NFL football game or a European soccer match that doesn't use "Back in Black" or "Thunderstruck" in between plays.

"Back in Black" can also be heard on Walmart television commercials, and many of the band's songs appear in over one hundred television series and movie soundtracks, including those for *Top Gear, The Crazy Ones, Delivery Man, The Avengers, Battleship, Bridesmaids, Megamind, Grown Ups, Private Parts*, and *Rock Star*.

Even in Port Lincoln, South Australia, a tour operator discovered that playing AC/DC's music attracts more sharks than any other tunes. Apparently the vibration draws them to the cages where they rub themselves up against the bars.

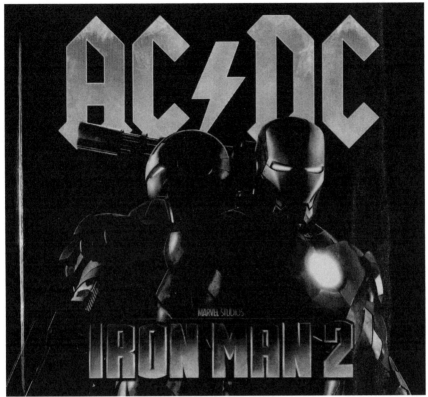

Cover of the soundtrack to *Iron Man*, one of the many movies that feature songs by AC/DC. Their music is also featured in television shows and commercials, and at football and soccer games.   *Jim Johnson Collection*

Statues and Monuments

In time for his birthday in 2001, Bon Scott was honored at the Kirriemuir Gateway to the Glens Museum in Scotland. On display celebrating Bon's life were old photographs and a copy of his birth certificate. Over the years, this display continues to draw thousands of Bon Scott fans from all over the world.

Angus reached a milestone in celebrity when McFarlane Toys released an Angus Young doll in October of 2001. It was timed perfectly to complement the giant statue of Angus that had dominated the stage on the *Stiff Upper Lip* tour. The doll was sixteen inches tall, inspiring some to cheekily describe it as "almost life-size."

In 2006, marking the twenty-sixth anniversary of Bon's death, the National Trust of Australia selected Bon's Fremantle gravesite to be included

Bronze statue of Bon Scott, which now stands near the pier on the ocean in Fremantle, Australia, not far from where Bon worked on the crayfish boats before he became a singer in a rock and roll band.

on the list of classified heritage places. The listing is usually reserved for buildings, but due to the amount of fans who visit the cemetery each year, his resting place was recognized. Next to Bon's gravesite is a stone bench placed by Chick and Isa Scott, Bon's parents.

A plaque was also placed in Cumberland Close and reads, "Ronald Belford 'Bon' Scott, Born Kirriemuir 9th July 1946, Died 19th February 1980, Let There Be Rock, Song Writer and Singer with AC/DC, World's Greatest Rock 'n' Roll Legend."

Dedicated Australian fan Doug Thorncroft, who started his own WA Bon Scott fan club, petitioned the city to erect a bronze statue of Bon in time for the anniversary of his sixtieth birthday in July of 2006. In memory of his passing, that night the AC/DC tribute band Thunderstruck played at Melbourne's Hi Fi Bar. Joining them on stage were former bassist Mark Evans and Bon's ex-wife Irene. Thorncroft also went to work on something similar to a Hollywood Walk of Fame, and has worked to get nearby Short Street renamed Bon Scott Place.

In 2008, a life-size bronze statue of Bon Scott, sculpted by Greg James, was unveiled at Fishing Boat Harbour in Fremantle on February 24. The statue stands not far from where Bon once worked on the crayfish boats.

Streets and Boulevards

Spain honored the band by naming a street in Leganes, right outside Madrid, after them. Malcolm and Angus (clad in his schoolboy suit) were present at the christening of Calle de AC/DC.

Australian fans also successfully petitioned to get a street named after them in Melbourne. Formerly Corporation Lane, on October 1, 2004, it was renamed ACDC Lane. The street runs parallel to Swanston Street, where the video for "It's a Long Way to the Top" was filmed in 1976.

When the city wouldn't allow a lightning bolt to separate the letters, local artist Knifeyard crafted a lightning bolt out of the same metal as the street sign, and bolted it above and below the sign with a hammer drill. To say AC/DC fans are passionate doesn't quite cover it. Angus' comment was, "Welcome to the highway to hell!

Supporting the Troops

AC/DC's music has also been an aid to the American military, helping to flush out Manuel Noriega from Panama's Vatican Embassy after his country was invaded. The blasting of "Highway to Hell" and "Hell's Bells" finally causing the opera lover to surrender. This method of melodic metal torture worked so well it was used again at the 2004 Battle of Fallujah in Iraq to drown out the city's mosques' call to arms.

Museum Exhibits

From April 28 to September 29, 2012, AC/DC's *Australia's Family Jewels* exhibition appeared at the EMP museum in Seattle, Washington. Developed and presented by the Arts Centre Melbourne and Western Australian Museum in association with AC/DC, Albert Music, and Sony Music, this is the first and only fully endorsed exhibition to bring to life the history, creativity, and power of one of the world's greatest rock bands. The exhibition featured more than 400 artifacts including photos, instruments, thirty-five years of show posters from around the world, letters, lyrics, and costumes, including an extremely rare Angus Young schoolboy outfit and his 1975 home sewn "Super Ang" costume, complete with the red and gold satin cape.

By 2014, AC/DC is now the #1 hard rock band in the world, having sold over 220 million albums, outselling Kiss, the Who, Aerosmith, the Rolling Stones and Metallica. With sales of over 71 million albums in the US alone,

AC/DC is one of the ten biggest-selling bands of all time, alongside Michael Jackson, the Eagles, Elvis Presley, Garth Brooks, and the Beatles.

Fellow Australian Joe Matera stated, "Their legacy is their volume of work that defines what is Australian rock. The band took the pub rock of their early beginnings to the world, in turn turning it into what defined stadium rock for the masses. They created a sound that nearly every rock band has tried to emulate in some part ever since. Their sound is distinct, unchanged, and purely unadulterated rock'n'roll of the finest order. And like a fine wine, it gets even better with age."

ACDC Lane in Melbourne, Australia, which used to be called Corporation Lane, was dedicated to AC/DC by the city of Melbourne. It's not far from where the band were filmed on the back of a flatbed truck playing "It's a Long Way to the Top (If You Wanna Rock 'n' Roll)."
Photo by Brian Rasic

26

Always Smiling

Bon Scott and His Antics

Bon Scott was one of those guys—once you met him, you would never forget him. He was constantly joking around, always trying to make you laugh, while the whole time writing things down in his notebook of "dirty ditties." Bon was known as a hard drinker who loved to party, but he was also very serious about his writing, recording, and performing, which he did with such joy, it was infectious. Especially when he was on stage in front of a crowd.

Bon, the oldest in the band, was known for taking off on his own when the band had a break. Once he missed a performance, and sometimes he walked in at the last minute, but up until his untimely death, Bon Scott could be counted on. While searching through all that has been written about him, I thought it would be fun to list a few of his "antics," if you will.

Did you know:

- Bon loved Broadway show tunes and used to sing along to them as he was growing up.
- While on the road, Bon was known for washing his socks and underwear in the sink every night, no matter where they were staying.
- Bon liked a good crease in his jeans, and he would iron his clothes before his performances, sometimes on the bar itself.
- After washing his hair, he used to use Scotch tape on his bangs, so they would dry lying down. This must have been in the days before they had portable hair dryers.
- Once Bon dressed as Tarzan, with a small loincloth and not much else, and decided during a gig to swing on a rope between the stacks of the PA. It worked during rehearsal, but not so much when he tried it during their show. Angus remembered, "These days you've got harnesses and everything, but he just got a rope flung up there and swung across the PA system. He cleared it. Then when we were doing the gig, he swung, but it was a bit like that cat in Bugs Bunny—Sylvester—swinging into

all those dogs. He forgot all the kids were going to be standing on their chairs and he went straight into the crowd. There was a lot of young girls and he crawled back on stage with just his jock strap on. They tore all his clothes off!"

- He also kept notes for future lyric ideas, and when the band went into the studio, he would wait to hear the songs, and then sit and write lyrics—in the earlier days, in the kitchen at Albert Studios.

- Bon was late arriving to the band's first appearance at the Hammersmith Odeon in London on November 10, 1976. Apparently he chose to take the tube to the venue instead of a cab or even a limo. The funniest part is that Michael Browning, their manager, sent someone outside to take pictures of the marquee with the band name up in lights. When the photos came back, one of the shots showed Bon walking up to the stairs of the Odeon with his bag slung over his shoulder, casually showing up for another day at work.

- When Bon leapt off the pulpit in the video for "Let There Be Rock," he landed so hard on the front pews that he tore the ligaments in one of his ankles.

- One of the funniest Bon quotes that I found in my research came from Mark Evans in his book, *Dirty Deeds*. After playing in Paris, Bon and Mark were standing on their hotel balcony royally pissed, watching the sun come up. As Bon was staring off into the distance, where you could see the Eiffel Tower, he said to Mark, "You know, there's a tower just like that in Paris."

- The only time Bon really lost his temper was when they played on the *TV Week King of Pops* awards show. They played live, and Bon had all kinds of problems on stage. When they were done, they went downstairs and broke a lock off a door to get into a bar. Inside was a stack of *TV Week* magazines, with Sherbet's singer, Daryl Braithwaite, on the cover. This enraged Bon, which prompted him to tear up all the magazines. He spent the rest of the night drinking champagne from a frozen turkey. And if you knew Bon, you don't have to ask which end he was drinking it from.

- Bon Scott expressed many times to his closest friends that he was getting tired of the touring and wanted to settle down and raise a family. He once went to a tarot card reader who told him he would meet a blonde, get divorced, meet a dark-haired woman, and have a short life.

- On a dare, Bon dove into the pool from the second floor balcony of the Freeway Gardens Motel in Melbourne in 1975.

- Bon's motorcycle-riding skills were legendary; supposedly he rode around nude, and drove his road bike up a staircase to one of his gigs. Once he even rode from Adelaide to Melbourne, with no protection other than a T-shirt. He got badly sunburned, and froze at night while sleeping in a ditch on the side of the road. His escapades courageously earned him the nickname "Ronnie Roadtest."

- AC/DC made their second appearance on the Australian television show *Countdown* in April, 1975, this time with Angus in his schoolboy uniform, and Bon in blond braids, and a schoolgirl's dress, complete with makeup, earrings, and fake breasts. At the time, men in drag were not all that popular on television, and his cross-dressing caused a flurry of complaints. I'm not sure what was the most upsetting: his outfit or

Volts is one of the CDs included in the Bonfire Boxset, which featured popular AC/DC songs that started out with different titles.   *Jim Johnson Collection*

his rolling around on his back, smoking a cigarette and exposing his knickers to the television audience.

- To enhance that raspy edge to his voice, Bon's morning ritual was to gargle with red wine and honey.
- A fan wrote in to tell me a story of his close encounter with Bon Scott after a show in Portland, Oregon, in the summer of 1978. Bruce didn't see the show that night, but was visiting with a friend who had called and asked him to come over and check out his new motorcycle. Offering his friend a test spin, Bruce was driving down the road when a guy with shaggy dark hair came running toward him, trying to wave him down. When Bruce stopped to see what he wanted, the guy who was wearing an AC/DC T-shirt, pointed at his own face on the shirt and claimed he was Bon Scott. Apparently Bon followed a lady home that night who lived in a sketchy part of Portland, and not having a ride back to his hotel, was rolled by a couple of guys who took his wallet and ran. Bruce gave him a ride back to his hotel, much to Bon's relief.
- My all-time favorite memory of Bon is from the night they played the Riverside Theater in Milwaukee, Wisconsin, on September 12, 1978, where they were opening for UFO. I took my sister Kathy along with me and we arrived early enough to have time to visit with Barry Taylor during the late afternoon and early evening. It was one of the last times I would see the band perform in a smaller venue, and I was really excited to be able to see them up close.
- My sister and I worked out a place right behind the road cases on the back of the stage to watch the band. It was about as close as we could get without getting in their way, or so I thought. The band was amazing, ripping up the audience. Some of them had never seen the band before, and it was always fun to watch their reactions. When it came time for Angus to climb up on Bon's shoulders, they did a huge walkabout, including going up into the balcony of the theater. Bon eventually made it to the stage, but Angus was nowhere in sight. His guitar was still wailing away, but I couldn't spot him anywhere. The audience started looking around and just when I started to wonder where he was, I felt a soft tap on my right elbow. My sister was on my left, so I turned around and crouched down behind me was Angus jamming away! When I turned and looked at him, he smiled and nodded for me to move over to the left, and as I did, he rushed past me back out on stage to a thunderous roar from the audience! I really don't think the crowd knew what hit them, and when UFO came out, they paled in comparison. After the

In my opinion, one of the best shots of Bon Scott on stage, at the Stone Hearth on August 16, 1977. Fans around the world agree that this picture is one of their favorites. I know it is mine.   *Photo by Keith Wessel*

show, my sister, Angus, and I were sitting in one of the small dressing rooms talking during UFO's set. Bon was in rare form that night and we could hear him laughing all the way down the hall. All of a sudden we heard a knock on the door. It was Bon. He came twirling in with a tray in one hand, and a huge smile on his face. He walked directly over to my sister and bent down, shoving the tray under her nose. Then he said, "Would you like an hors d'oeuvre, ma'am?" By now he was giggling non-stop and when we looked at what was on the tray we could see why. Bon had collected up about a dozen small cups of horseradish from the deli tray and apparently someone had cut themselves, so Bon had them squeeze a drop of blood into each cup. I'm sure he was certain that this would horrify my sister and send her screaming out of the room, but he picked the wrong girl. My sister would go onto becoming a sergeant in the army and was way past being grossed out by a few drops of blood. She looked up at Bon and said, "No thanks. Besides, it's coagulating! You're going to need a transfusion." Her dry retort sent Bon into a laughing frenzy and he went reeling out of the room, laughing all the way. I believe that was the last we saw of him that night.

- While performing at the Apollo in Glasgow in November of 1978, Bon got lost during their walkabout, and ended up outside. Since he didn't have a ticket or pass to the show, they wouldn't let him back in until he convinced them that he was indeed in the band! Luckily not having a shirt on in the November cold convinced them to let him back into the venue.

27

What Do They Do When They're Not Playing?

Angus Young

For years, Angus Young has lived in Aalten, Gelderland, in the Netherlands, where his wife Ellen grew up. They just recently built a stately abode which sports Angus gargoyles in stone, complete with horns. He also has a home in Sydney, Australia.

When he is not working on writing or recording music, Angus is an accomplished painter. His landscapes are quite beautiful, and when I asked when he was going to have a proper art showing, Malcolm jokingly replied that "he was saving that for his old age." The late Perry Cooper raved to me about his talents on canvas. "Angus is a brilliant painter. I was in shock, because I've seen some of it, and he is absolutely brilliant! He does watercolors and things, and he is just a great painter! Once when I asked for one of their early computers, Angus drew a bunch of caricatures of us on a note with little devils on it, and sent it to me at Atlantic."

Forever humble, Angus once stated, "I tend to look at the music as a song; it sounds a bit funny talking about it as someplace to play a solo. My brother would beat me up. People tend to see me as a soloist. Poor people. You'd think they'd have something better to do . . . I mean there are solo people who just do that sort of thing. I like it as a band, as a unit. You should hear me on my own. It's horrendous."

Angus is a very private person, and you don't hear much about him in the news. He did cause a stir when he and Ellen built their new home in Aalten, because of the size of it in comparison to the rest of the neighborhood—which means he lived in a small house up until a few years ago. And you never hear about the latest ride he's bought because in his book, Brian Johnson revealed that Angus doesn't have a driver's license!

Malcolm Young

Up until his recent health issues, Malcolm has kept himself busy running all things AC/DC. There wasn't a decision or move made without his approval. When he's not touring, he enjoys the company of his family and working on new music with his brother Angus.

Malcolm commissioned another bell to be made by the John Taylor Bell Founders. It was a copy of the original Hell's Bell, but this one says "Home Bell" and hangs in place of a candelabra at the top of a sweeping staircase at his Hertfordshire home, outside of London. He also has a home in Sydney, Australia.

Proof that there is no rivalry among band members, *Guitar Player* once asked Malcolm if it bothered him that Angus gets more attention. He said, "No, because we all get the same money. If he was getting more money, then it would bother us."

Malcolm, like his brother Angus, has always kept a low profile. Much to Brian Johnson's horror, in 2006 Malcolm sold the Jaguar he had bought brand new in 1992, in favor of a Nissan. He got Brian all excited about the fact that he might buy a Bentley Continental, but then decided to wait until the *Black Ice* tour was finished.

Phil Rudd

In the early days of the band, Phil—"the Charlie Watts of heavy metal," as Martin Popoff called him in *Metal Hammer*—enjoyed building model airplanes, toy boats, and fast cars and capturing everything around him with an old film camera.

While on tour, he was known to fill his hotel room with Scalextric, which were powered race car systems invented in 1952 by B. "Freddie" Francis. Before the band traveled in tour buses, Phil, being a car fanatic, was usually the designated driver. When he's not on tour, he lives in New Zealand, and owns his own recording studio, Mountain Studios, and a restaurant called Phil's Place on the Harbour Bridge Marina in Tauranga, New Zealand.

In January of 2005, Phil sponsored New Zealand's race car driver, Jared Carlyle, who drove a Ford Falcon owned by Phil's Mountain Recording team.

Phil has always had a penchant for driving fast, to which Brian can attest. Brian comically wrote, "You'll usually see Phil driving alone, the reason being everyone is too scared to get in the car with him. You see, Phil thinks all the other cars on the road are there for his entertainment. The rest of the lads would make all kinds of excuses. Mine was, 'Sorry mate, I've got to stay home and rearrange my fridge magnets' . . . Angus' excuse was that he'd forgotten the riff to 'Highway to Hell,' and had to practice it again. Cliff feigned endless nausea attacks, and Mal just said, 'You're fucking joking.'"

Brian Johnson

Brian settled in Sarasota, Florida, in 1991, and is a serious gourmand and an avid race car driver. He owns several cars, and placed in the Daytona 500 in 2003. His wife, Brenda, shares his passion, and gets behind the wheel herself. When at home, they enjoy an exact replica of a Newcastle pub Brian used to go to, called the Queen's Head, which he had built to scale right inside his house.

In 1997, Brian decided to produce Neurotica, a Sarasota band he discovered there in a bar one night. "They're the only band that made me look up from me beer. And it was a good Guinness, too," said Brian, who handled production with Mike Fraser mixing. He also cowrote the opening track, "Deadly Sin," and sang backup vocals for lead singer Kelly Shaefer.

Before Neurotica, Shaefer sang in the band Atheist. Shaefer remembers the first time he heard AC/DC. "My dad turned me onto them when I was about eight years old. He is a longtime AC/DC fan, and he had a jeep with a roll bar, and I remember cruising around listening to 'Let There Be Rock,' and I thought that was so cool!"

Having Brian produce Neurotica's first album, *Seed*, was a dream come true for Shaefer. "Brian had lived here for a few years before this, and we often said how cool it would be if someday he would come out and see us play. The club that we were playing at the first time he saw us, only held about fifty or sixty people, and it was called the Monterey Deli. During the day it was a sandwich shop, at night they cleared away the tables and let us play.

"So we did two sets of original material, and invited all our friends out. It was a really low-profile gig, and Brian had been in a club right around the corner. The guy behind the bar suggested to Brian and Doug Kaye, a local producer he was with, that they should go next door and check out this band. Doug didn't want to come over because he knew me from when I played in the death metal band Atheist. So he reluctantly came over with

Brian, and we watched them walk in. We were in the balcony looking down on the crowd, and when we saw him, we said, 'Oh my God! We gotta throw down!'

"So we went down and played, and this club was so small that Brian was sitting right in front of our amps. I damn near threw sweat on him, he was that close. So we just gave it all we had, and he said, 'Fuckin' hell, buy these lads a round of beer.' So he bought us all a round of Old Speckled Hen. A friend of ours gave Brian our demo on his way out. Two days later I got a call from Doug Kaye, saying Brian was really blown away by our performance and he wanted to hear some more songs." Neurotica's CD, *Seed*, was released on April 14, 1998, on the independent label NMG Entertainment.

Shaefer described Brian: "Of all the things that I can say about Brian, I've never met anybody more humble about who he is. That has always been my fondest memory of Brian, and working with him, it always comes up as a common denominator—that he is a ridiculously humble, mega-icon. He is so unassuming. He still carries his business card from back when he was doing vinyl roofs. There is a picture of him in a Camaro with T-tops with his head sticking out, wearing his trademark hat!"

Brian was a guest vocalist on Jackyl's 1997 album *Cut the Crap* on the song "Locked and Loaded." He returned to duet with lead singer Jesse James Dupree on the song "Kill the Sunshine," in 2002.

In April of 2002, it was announced on MTV News that Brian was working with British composer Brendan Healy and Sarasota Ballet Artistic Director Robert de Warren on a musical called *Helen of Troy*, an action-filled love story based on Greek mythology. He wrote fourteen songs for the play, which was originally scheduled to open at the Van Wezel Performing Arts Hall in Sarasota, Florida, in March, 2003.

The show featured five singing roles, a chorus of fifteen, a dancing troupe of fifteen, acrobats, jugglers, and fire eaters, and cost 1.2 million dollars to produce. Brian's friend, actor Malcolm McDowell (*A Clockwork Orange*) was chosen to play Zeus, who also served as the narrator.

Robert de Warren was quoted in the MTV News in April 2002 regarding Brian's creativity, "It's not all based on rock. It's rather like Gilbert and Sullivan. It's very British, actually. There's a lot of very beautiful melodies, and it's amazing how literate [Brian] is, which is quite unusual for a rock star."

Shaefer also mentioned to me how talented Brian was to write songs for this musical. "Something that most people don't understand is how hard that is to do. He wrote a musical with a composer by mouthing out melodies, and not many people can do that, that I know of. At least not able to write an entire musical!"

Guitarist Rick Derringer organized *Musicians 4 Disaster Relief*, which was held in Orlando, Florida on February 5, 2005. The event was in association with the John Entwistle Foundation, the American Red Cross, and the Florida Hurricane Relief Fund. Brian and Cliff performed, along with Michael Bolton, Dickey Betts from the Allman Brothers, Chuck Negron from Three Dog Night, Loverboy, Robin Zander, Eddie Money, Mark Farner from Grand Funk Railroad, and Dee Snider from Twisted Sister.

Brian made his acting debut in two scenes of the 2005 movie *Goal*, where he appears sitting in a pub as a Newcastle United fan. On July 31, 2004, Brian made a guest appearance in Penrich Derbyshire, England. He joined Twisted Sister during their set for a version of "Whole Lotta Rosie" at the *Rock and Blues Custom Show*. Then on September 6, 2005, Brian joined Velvet Revolver on stage at the Hard Rock Café in Orlando, helping to raise money for the victims of Hurricane Katrina. They jammed on a rendition of Led Zeppelin's "Rock 'n' Roll." Two days later, both Brian and Cliff appeared at the Germain Arena in Estero, Florida benefiting the American Red Cross Hurricane Charley Disaster Relief.

Together, Brian and Cliff played fifteen dates through July of 2007 for the *Classic Rock Cares* tour, set up to raise money for the John Entwistle Foundation. Donating money for instruments and free music education for kids in need, the tour featured Brian; Cliff; vocalists Robin Zander, Joe Lynn Turner, Mark Farner, and Eddie Money; and guitarist Mark Hitt and drummer Steve Luongo.

On December 22, 2008, Brian Johnson dedicated a music room at the Sarasota Memorial Hospital, with

My autographed ticket from the *Classic Rock Cares* tour at the Ruth Eckerd Hall in Clearwater, Florida, on July 3, 2007. Brian Johnson, Cliff Williams, and guitarist Mark Hitt all autographed it for me. The show also featured Joe Lynn Turner from Rainbow, Eddie Money, and Robin Zander from Cheap Trick.

a $20,000 donation from the John Entwistle Foundation. The room includes guitars, a keyboard, an electronic drum kit, and music software for recording.

Brian branched out into movies, and was one of the executive producers of the 2008 movie *Totally Baked*. He also composed three of the songs for the soundtrack: "Who Phoned the Law," "Chase That Tail," and "Chain Gang." All three songs were performed by Brian and Cliff on the *Classic Rock Cares* tour.

In 2011, Brian wrote his first book, *Rockers and Rollers: A Full-Throttle Memoir*, which contains all of his memories of each of the cars he has owned over the years. When he was just a boy, his father built him a headboard for his bed with a steering wheel on it. Brian explained, "So we went off to the local garage and asked them if they had an old steering wheel . . . He got a large stick, pushed it through our headboard, and piled pillows up, like a driving seat. 'Son, there's your first car.' Four legs, iron casters, no brakes, no gas tank, no tax, no insurance . . . I jumped in and drove forever."

His first race was in a Lotus Cortina MK1 that he drove and crashed in a one-hour enduro at Road Atlanta in 1998. He survived without a scratch, but you couldn't say that about the car. Brian claims this incident is what hooked him on racing.

He tells a hilarious story about Cliff visiting Brian in Newcastle before they were to play a gig at the Apollo in Glasgow. Along the way, Cliff decided to buy an Aston Martin from a roadside dealership and drive the band to the gig before having the car checked out. On the way to the show, not only did the windshield wipers not work (and it was raining), but the car blew a gasket, forcing them to call for a cab to drive them the remaining eighty miles. Though he swore off Aston Martins, Cliff eventually gave in and bought another. Most likely a new one.

Brian personally owns sixteen or seventeen cars, including five race cars, a Wolseley (the same model of the one and only car his father ever owned), 1960s Rolls-Royce Phantom, a Triumph Roadster, a Mercedes 300SL Gullwing, an Aston Martin, and a racing-green Bentley. In August of 2012, Brian hosted a six-week radio show on BBC 2 called *Rockers and Rollers*. He also placed first on the BBC's Top Gear in June of 2013.

Later that year, Brian was a guest vocalist on Sting's album *The Last Ship*, and he popped up on stage with the Eagles in Tampa, Florida, on November 26, 2013. In December, Brian placed first in the Sebring 2013, and in the spring of 2014, Brian premiered in his show on Quest TV called *Cars That Rock*.

On March 21, 2014, Brian joined Billy Joel on stage at New York's Madison Square Garden to belt out "You Shook Me All Night Long," much to the delight of Joel's audience. A whole book could be written about what Brian does while he's not recording or touring with AC/DC. To keep up with him, check out his website at brianjohnsonracing.com.

On July 9, 2014 (Bon Scott's birthday, no less), Brian Johnson received an honorary Doctorate in Music from the Northumbria University in Newcastle, alongside students graduating from their Engineering and Environment degree programs. Recipients are nominated for their achievements, links to the university, and their inspirational qualities. Brian once studied engineering at Northumbria before his love of music called him away. His award was in recognition for the "significant contribution he has made to the music industry."

Cliff Williams

Living a few miles south of Brian Johnson's place in Fort Myers, Florida, Cliff fills in occasionally with the rhythm and blues band, the Juice. Cliff played bass and sang backing vocals on Adam Bomb's 1984 song, "I Want My Heavy Metal."

Brian and Cliff continually perform for various charities, including a benefit for the Opera House in Sarasota, Florida, on March 28, 1998. Together with Billy Leverty on guitar, and Jackyl's Jesse Dupree, they played "You Shook Me All Night Long," "Back in Black," "Long Tall Sally," and "I Saw Her Standing There."

Cliff made a guest appearance on *San*, a CD by Bosnian-American musician Emir Bukovica and his band, Frozen Camel. He also played four dates with them in Bosnia, Croatia, and Slovenia.

Brian and Cliff also appeared at the *96 K-Rock For Relief II* benefiting Hurricane Wilma victims. The concert took place at the Germain Arena in Estero, Florida, on December 15, 2005. Also performing were Robin Zander of Cheap Trick (another of Brian's neighbors), Joe Lynn Turner of Deep Purple, Eddie Money, Loverboy, Mark Farner of Grand Funk Railroad, and Buck Dharma of Blue Öyster Cult.

If you're lucky, you might catch Brian and/or Cliff jamming with the Greg Billings band while they are at home in Florida.

28

Albert Productions

George Young and Harry Vanda Help Build a Dynasty

S oon after the Easybeats formed, they signed Mike Vaughan as their manager, and Mike introduced them to Ted Albert, a third-generation publishing mogul of J. Albert and Son, which was founded in the early 1900s and was one of Australia's oldest and most respected music publishing companies. Ted Albert, in turn, formed a production company, which was an offshoot of J. Albert and Son. The first order of business for Albert was to sign the Easybeats.

Throughout the 1960s Ted Albert was managing director and discovering and signing new artists and groups, producing their records and leasing the finished recordings to established record labels, who would then handle the release, promotion, and distribution. Two of their most successful artists were the Easybeats and Billy Thorpe and the Aztecs, whose records were released through EMI Parlophone.

The Easybeats had broken into the international music scene with their single "Friday on My Mind." That song made it to #16 on the US charts and #6 in Britain, which prompted the band to relocate to London. Even though George and Harry had written their biggest hit, "Friday on My Mind," the Easybeats would never repeat the success of that song, constantly chasing their true sound. George believed that a band should stay loyal to their roots, a philosophy he would wholeheartedly teach his younger brothers. The Easybeats did have two more minor hits in 1968, "Good Time" and "St. Louis." In 1969, they would leave England one last time to tour Australia, where they were supported by the Valentines before officially breaking up.

After the Easybeats parted ways, George Young and Harry Vanda spent three years, from 1970 to 1973, honing their recording expertise practically living in their London studio. Since they hadn't yet found a hit band in England, Ted Albert persuaded them to move back to Australia. Together they immediately went to work with an Albert prodigy, John Paul Young

Harry Vanda and Malcolm Young deep in discussion at Albert Studio in Sydney, Australia, back in the day. Harry was the one who gave Malcolm his first Gretsch guitar.   *Photo by Philip Morris*

(no relation). They wrote the song "Pasadena" for him, which almost made it into the Top Ten. This success inspired Ted Albert to finance a record label, including a state-of-the-art recording studio, and Albert Productions was born.

George Young and Harry Vanda became in-house producers for Albert Productions, and it quickly became one of the most successful and longest established music labels in Australia. From the late 1970s to early eighties, George and Harry enjoyed a very successful career recording and writing albums and singles under the pseudonym Flash and the Pan. Their hits included "Hey St. Peter," "Down Among the Dead Men," and "Walking in the Rain," which was covered by Grace Jones. Some of their most notable Albert Production clients include the Easybeats, AC/DC, Stevie Wright, John Paul Young, the Angels, William Shakespeare, Billy Thorpe and the Aztecs, and Rose Tattoo.

Albert has been a major contributor to the Australian music industry, and it's not uncommon to find fans waiting around the entrance to the Albert's King Street studios, hoping to catch a glimpse of one of their idols. J. Albert & Son also own the radio station 2UW in Sydney, and before building their own recording studio, they used to record artists in the 2UW studios as well as EMI's Sydney Studios.

In 2014, Albert Productions celebrated fifty years in the business, and aside from Ted Albert, George Young, and Harry Vanda, another person integral to their success is Fifa Riccobono, who started as a secretary back in 1968, and by the 1990s had become the first female CEO of any Australian music company. Riccobono stated to Bernard Zuel in the *Sydney Morning Herald*, "The key was the trust they had in each other and the desire to work for each other, part of what enabled her to be a groundbreaker for women in the notoriously sexist Australian music industry. 'One of the things that allowed me to do the things that I do and to do them as well as I could do them, was I always had Ted's backing. Having someone back you like that makes you go out and fight as hard as possible. I never wanted to come back and let him down, or fail George and Harry.'"

Mark Opitz apprenticed with George and Harry, and recalled to author Jake Brown in his book, *AC/DC in the Studio*,

> Harry and George ran a very tight little family. While working for Vanda/Young, I learned that, obviously, attitude is a very important thing, but more importantly what I really learned from those guys is you have to be able to tap your foot to it, which is dancing basically. It's got to be able to affect you in that physical sense, whether it's AC/DC or a pop group, you find yourself moving to it. That was one of the prerequisites after you had a melody, which was another one they always emphasized as really important. Melody and feel, probably in that order, is that I really learned from them.

Angus told Jane Albert in her book *House of Hits*, "When we first went out there, we were lucky enough to get a deal with Albert even before we left Australia, so that was good for us. We didn't have to go shopping ourselves, but what was good was that Ted [Albert] advanced us a lot of the money so as we could get out there and tour and back up the records. For him it was a long-term investment, but it paid in the end. It all helped."

29

Gorilla Suits, Super Ang, and Spider-Man

Angus and His Schoolboy Uniform

For a while AC/DC tried several wardrobe ideas. Aside from Angus' schoolboy uniform, he tried dressing as Spider-Man, Zorro, and as Super Ang(us), complete with a fake telephone booth. After he got stuck in it during one of their shows, that idea was scrapped. For a while the drummer dressed as a harlequin clown, Malcolm was a pilot, and the bass player was a motorcycle cop. Dave Evans stuck with what he knew best, and remained a rock god. Deciding to heed George's advice on never forget that they were a rock 'n' roll band, AC/DC dumped the costumes, except of course, for Angus' schoolboy uniform. As a schoolboy, Angus would run home from school and leave directly for band rehearsal without changing his uniform. When the band first started they tried all types of costumes, following the trend of the early 1970s glam rock. When nothing seemed to stick, the band chose to perform in T-shirts and jeans, which they do to this day. Except of course, for Angus.

Glossy of Angus Young used for the cover of the international version of their album *High Voltage*.

Angus Young in his green velvet schoolboy uniform. He also has them custom made in black, brown, burgundy, purple, and blue.

© *Photo Diego Petrussi Udine*

Some of his suits are designed by David Chambers of London. He has worn his velvet uniform in many colors, including black, brown, burgundy, purple, blue, and green. He also has a pair of boxer shorts displaying a flag for every country. One of his original navy blue velvet school uniforms now resides in the Melbourne Museum in the exhibit *The Melbourne Story*, and one is also on display at the Hard Rock Café in Glasgow. Capitalizing on his diminutive stature, the devilish schoolboy run amok was a hit from the beginning, and it would be safe to say this band follows the rule "If it ain't broke, don't fix it."

Angus told journalist Sylvie Simmons, "I was moaning to my sister how you can't move on stage when your jeans are stuck, you know, you get all sweaty up there? So she suggested I wear my school uniform, since I was still going to school and it was easy enough to pinch a few extra ties or whatever I needed. She thought it would be a good gimmick and class it up a bit." Malcolm added, "Up to that point he'd just stand there and play like the rest of us, but as soon as he put on that school uniform he became a monster."

Angus is known to sweat off three to five pounds per performance, and except for some bruises and a few chipped teeth, only once did he require stitches, when he crawled through some broken glass—no doubt in a bar somewhere in Australia.

When Angus was asked by *Guitar* magazine in November of 2013 if he would still be wearing his trademark school uniform at the age of 64, he comically stated, "Have you seen what some of the younger [artists] are wearing nowadays? . . . They look like they've stolen their mothers' skirts! If that's fashionable, then you could say I've maintained a distinctively classic look."

30

Gone for Twelve Years

Drummer Phil Rudd Left the Band in 1983 and Returned in 1995

H aving never really taken time off after Bon died, as Angus said, Phil took Bon's death the hardest. While the band was hard at work on the album *Flick of the Switch*, Phil's problems had gotten steadily worse. Perry Cooper revealed that he had shared a room with Phil while on tour, right before he left the band. Perry was shocked at his behavior, which included hiding things around his room, and seeing people that weren't there. Phil's situation was also compounded by his romantic involvement with one of Malcolm's relatives. Things came to a head with Phil and

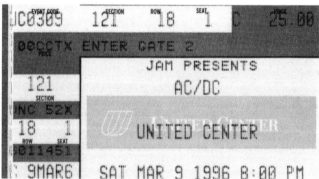

This was Phil's first tour with the band in twelve years. Pictured is my ticket stub from the *Ballbreaker* tour in Chicago on March 9, 1996. That night I had been invited by Angus and given tickets and backstage passes for the show. Despite my invitation, I had trouble getting in to see the band. By the time I saw Angus, he said, "Well, there you are!" We both burst out laughing when I said, "Could you get any more famous? I believe the Pope has got to be easier to see than you!"

Malcolm in a punch-up, and Phil being put on the next available plane back home to Rotorua in New Zealand.

With the addiction he was battling, I'm amazed he kept it together for as long as he did, and was sad to hear that he had left the band. Angus told Mark Putterford in his book *Shock to the System* that Phil hadn't really gotten over Bon's death and that the tightness of their "family" unit had died with him, and Phil was hell-bent on living the high life, whatever the consequences. "If he hadn't stopped, he'd have gone overboard and done something drastic to either himself or someone else."

As soon as the band finished recording *Flick of the Switch*, they flew back to England and placed an anonymous ad in *Sounds* magazine, which read, "Heavy Rock drummer wanted. If you don't hit hard, don't apply." Angus quipped that the ad really said, "Any drummer under 5' 2"." After dozens of auditions at Nomis Studios in London, twenty-year old Simon Wright, who had previously played with Tytan and A to Z, was chosen for the position. For a kid who saw AC/DC and Def Leppard play in Manchester in 1979, this was an ultimate dream come true. As Simon remembers it, "I saw an ad in a British music paper that said, 'Rock group looking for a drummer.' I never dreamed it would be AC/DC. I made a phone call and then I went to a rehearsal, there were Brian, Angus, Malcolm, and Cliff. I couldn't believe my eyes. We went through a first rehearsal, and things went very well. They invited me back, and the second time I was very nervous. But they obviously liked what I played, so I got the job."

Settling in Rotorua, New Zealand, Phil pursued giving helicopter tours, car racing, and shooting competitions. Eventually he built Mountain Studios, where he still records and produces local artists.

Phil told *Drum!* magazine in 2005, "I bought a couple of helicopters. I learned to fly helicopters when I first visited New Zealand. I have some relatives here, and it was an accident that I visited one time . . . and never left. So I started flying helicopters and settling into the local lifestyle, which was great. It was great to not have to be going anywhere. You could plan to do something for a couple of weeks. It was a change. And I did a lot of competitive handgun shooting, I raced cars, I had five kids."

Upon his return to the band for the *Ballbreaker* album and tour, Cliff told *Guitar School* about when Phil came back into the band. "Phil always had a natural feel for what this band does . . . it just fits like a glove with Phil. You can't really put your finger on it—it's just a feel."

In 2001, he opened his own restaurant, Phil's Place, in Tauranga, New Zealand, offering "fresh local food at affordable prices." Many fans grabbed

The cover of Phil Rudd's solo album, *Head Job*, released on August 29, 2014. Phil is the first member of AC/DC to release a solo album. His band is a three-piece with vocalist/bassist Allan Badger and guitarist Geoffrey Martin. Their first single to be debuted in July was "Repo Man."   *Jim Johnson Collection*

up Angus dollars on the *Razors Edge* tour, but now for $13.75, you can find a Phil Rudd dollar for sale on eBay.

After the *Black Ice* tour ended, Phil gifted himself with a Hughes 500 helicopter, which costs close to a half a million dollars. Considering that the *Black Ice* tour of 2010 was the second-largest grossing tour of all time, Phil Rudd deserved a present.

Giving back to his community, on April 15, 2012, Phil hosted *Ferrari Day*, featuring 30 Ferraris (including two of his own) to help raise money for the Look Good Feel Better charity at the Tauranga Bridge Marina, in Tauranga. The event drew a crowd of thousands. Phil was quoted as saying, "The main thing is to get people down here and have a day of fun. Let's make the most of the rest of the summer while it lasts. I didn't want this to be an exclusive event, it's not a pretentious thing, it's a family day that a whole lot of people can enjoy."

On March 19, 2013, Phil appeared at the Farmer Auto Village in Mount Maunganuion to offer a chance to take a spin in one of his luxury cars for a price. Phil showcased eleven of his own cars, seven being "the rarest supercars in the world." The cars on display included a Ferrari F40, a Ferrari 599, a Lamborghini Murcialago, a Lamborghini Gallardo, a 2010 Rolls Royce Ghost, a unique Can Am race car, a Bentley Super Sport, a 2011 Aston Martin DBS, a 2010 Mercedes SLS AMG, an Audi R8 V10, and a 2011 Bentley Mulsanne. Proceeds collected from the car rides (along with some AC/DC memorabilia that was auctioned off) were donated to the Red Cross Christchurch Earthquake Appeal.

In August of 2014, becoming the first AC/DC band member to record and produce a solo album, Phil Rudd released *Head Job*, featuring himself along with bassist/vocalist Alan Badger and guitarist/vocalist Geoffrey Martin. "Repo Man" was the first single to be released and revealed a very straightforward rock 'n' roll sound with heavy guitars and that Phil Rudd signature backbeat.

Less than a month before the release of AC/DC's new album, *Rock or Bust*, the world was shocked by the news of Phil Rudd's arrest on the morning of November 6, 2014. It was reported that his waterfront home in New Zealand was raided, and Phil was taken into custody for "attempting to procure a murder." He was also charged with possession of cannabis and methamphetamine.

On November 26, Phil made no plea in the High Court of Tauranga, New Zealand, and his case was transferred to the Tauranga District Court after the charges were dropped for attempting to procure a murder due to inefficient evidence. His lawyer submitted a plea of not guilty on December 2, excusing Phil from appearing in person. Phil was released on bail, but the day after his lawyer submitted a plea of not guilty, Phil was taken into custody again on December 3 after an altercation with a man outside the Columbus Coffee Café in Gate Pa, Tauranga.

Apparently, a staff member of the café had called the police, and Phil was taken into custody where he was again bailed out. Conditions were added that he refrain from consuming illicit substances and not have contact with any of the people in question or witnesses who were named in the police records. Those conditions were requested by the judge, in regard to Phil's erratic behavior, and a case review hearing was scheduled for February 10, 2015.

Upon hearing the news, the band claimed to have had no prior knowledge of Phil's troubles before his arrest. Later, it was revealed by Angus that Phil had kept them waiting in the studio in Vancouver to the point that producer Brendan O'Brien claimed if Phil Rudd didn't show up, they would be hiring another drummer. When he finally did make it to Vancouver, Angus admitted that he didn't look like the Phil they knew. That he had "let himself go." Then on October 4, 2014, when the band gathered in London to shoot videos for their two singles, "Play Ball" and "Rock or Bust," Phil wasn't there, stating that he had to stay in New Zealand due to family problems. Local drummer Bob Richards, who plays in Celtic Pride and previously in the band Shogun, sat in on the drums for both videos.

As the headlines hit the newswire on Phil's arrest, even Angus claimed that when his wife Ellen told him the news, he literally fell out of bed! Angus also stated to David Fricke of *Rolling Stone* that Phil's arrest "is a big blow to us. . . . But we will definitely be out there. We are committed to this." While promoting their new album, on November 15, 2014, Angus and Cliff participated in a Reddit Ask Me Anything session. One of the first questions was in regard to Phil touring with them. Cliff replied, "Phil has to get himself well. That may take some time."

31

Malcolm and Angus' First Recording

Tales of Old Grand-Daddy

The first time Malcolm and Angus Young ever recorded was on an album that their brother George Young and Harry Vanda were producing called *Tales of Old Grand-Daddy*, by the Marcus Hook Roll Band. It was announced in March of 2014 that the album would be reissued on June 2, 2014, on vinyl, CD, and digital download.

The Marcus Hook Roll Band was formed by George and Harry in 1972. Their first three singles were recorded at Abbey Road Studios in London before they relocated back to Australia. When it came time to record a full-length album in early 1973, George invited his younger brothers to record some tracks.

George Young told *Classic Rock* magazine, "It was the first thing Malcolm and Angus did before AC/DC. We didn't take it very seriously so we thought we'd include them to give them an idea of what recording was all about."

The finished product was a straightforward, hard-driving rock 'n' roll album, which included the three singles that they had recorded in the UK. The songs "Quick Reaction" and "Red Revolution" give a good hint to the beginning sounds of AC/DC.

George stated, "We had Harry, myself, and my kid brothers Malcolm and Angus. We all got rotten—except Angus, who was too young—and we spent a month in the studio boozing it up every night." The band never played a live gig, and then quickly fell apart. Which thankfully made way for Malcolm to continue on to form AC/DC.

The track list on CD and download includes: "Can't Stand the Heat," "Goodbye Jane," "Quick Reaction," "Silver Shoes & Strawberry Wine," "Watch Her Do It Now," "People and the Power," "Red Revolution," "Shot in the Head," "Ape Man," "Cry For Me," "One of These Days," "Natural Man," "Moonshine Blues," "Louisiana Lady," and "Ride Baby Ride."

You can find *Tales of Old Grand-Daddy* on sale at various locations, including Best Buy and Amazon.

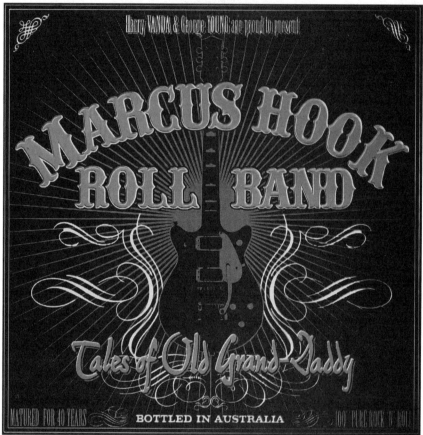

Tales of Old Grand-Daddy was released as a studio project called the Marcus Hook Roll Band in 1973. Led by George Young and Harry Vanda, the band included Angus and Malcolm on guitar, their brother Alex Young and Howard Casey on saxophone, Freddie Smith on bass, and drummers Ian Campbell and John Proud. George brought his little brothers Malcolm and Angus into the studio to give them their first taste of recording.

32

The Only Band Who Were Invited to Play Encores with AC/DC

Cheap Trick

S upporting the *Powerage* album, once again AC/DC traveled south to Atlanta, Jacksonville, and Miami, and then north through Pennsylvania, New Jersey, New York, and Massachusetts. Most of these dates were supported by Cheap Trick, the power pop quartet from Rockford, Illinois, who had just released their first self-titled album.

The two bands got along so well together that Cheap Trick was the only opening act that were welcome to come out on stage at the end of the night to jam with AC/DC. Some of these shows they actually co-headlined, and many were sold out.

Their tour manager Kirk Dyer, also notoriously known as "the Wheel," worked with Cheap Trick for fourteen years. He recalled the first time they played with AC/DC.

> I remember it was someplace in North or South Carolina, [Greensboro, North Carolina on December 18, to be exact], after we finished the Kiss tour, we started co-headlining. I was in the dressing room with the band, and I opened the door and these little squirts went by, and I said, "What the hell?" They were five of the shortest guys I had ever seen. So I couldn't figure out what was going on, what were these guys doing? And I saw they were headed up to the stage, so I walked out to the soundboard. I watched one song and ran back to Cheap Trick's dressing room and dragged them all out to the soundboard to hear these guys. It was the first night of the tour. They just rocked, personally, they just blew me away! They have been my favorite band ever since, still are.
>
> Every night they played together, they would always watch each other's set. We always made sure that we made room for them on

stage when we were playing. By the end of that tour, we were jamming together. Every night there was an encore that involved both bands. At the end of the tour, Bon Scott was becoming famous for putting Angus up on his shoulders, so I got Rick Nielsen up on my shoulders, and we had a chicken fight the last night [that we played with them] in Omaha, at the Music Hall Civic Center. It turned into thirty minutes of pure hell; it was just crazy. It was a real "break your guitars, beat people up" chicken fight. It sort of disintegrated from a song or two into this literal guitar-swinging war, and everybody was just laughing their asses off. I said, "These guys are going to be the next big thing," and sure enough, they were.

AC/DC were scheduled to play on the fourth of July 1979, at the Winnebago County Fairgrounds in Pecatonica, Illinois, which is right outside of Rockford. Naturally, Cheap Trick were the headliners in their hometown, to be supported by AC/DC, Molly Hatchet, and the Babys. Even though I was working for Cheap Trick at the time, I still secured my passes through my friend Barry Taylor. I didn't want to take any chances that I wouldn't be able to roam freely once backstage.

When we arrived, our tickets and passes were there, but no Barry. It was a beautiful Midwestern summer day; sunny skies, and a rowdy crowd ready to raise some Independence Day hell. As the crew was setting up the stage, testing equipment, and getting ready for the show, there were firecrackers and M-80s exploding everywhere. Right before we got there, someone had thrown an M-80 up on stage, which had exploded, injuring one of the road crew. Nothing like a drunken amateur pyro punk with a lit fuse in his hand.

As my boyfriend John and I walked around looking for Barry, the Babys were on stage. You remember them, the Bay City Rollers with better haircuts? Lead singer John Waite went on to enjoy a successful solo career thanks to his hit "Missing You." The more we looked for Barry, the more concerned I became. Once we checked every conceivable place he could be working, I was stricken with a terrifying thought. I told John to stay where he was, and I went running off to the main production trailer. I ran inside and asked if they could explain what the person who was injured in the explosion looked like. To my sheer horror, they described Barry! I found out what hospital they took him to, and went racing out the door. I grabbed John and we ran to the car and drove straight to Rockford Memorial hospital.

What happened was that Barry was underneath Phil's drum riser, adjusting things, when the M-80 came flying up on stage. It bounced off the stage, hit Barry in the chest, and exploded right next to his head. He was bright red from the explosion, and deaf in one ear. They had just given him a shot

My vintage *Highway to Hell* T-shirt surrounded by CDs from the *Bonfire* box set.

Photo by Teal Kozel

of painkillers, and told us to take him back to the tour bus and put him to bed. I was so upset for him, I was in tears. Two groupies had tagged along, so at least someone went with him to the hospital. The band had to go on stage, and didn't have anyone extra who could care for Barry.

We carefully guided him into the car, and put him in the back seat, flanked by two girls we all didn't know. They were at least nice and compassionate, which was much appreciated. When we got Barry to the bus, we thought he was all right to climb the steps, and let go of him. When he reeled backwards towards the ground, we grabbed him and helped him into the bus and put him to bed. By now the band was done with their set. They all came into the bus and gathered around us to see how Barry was doing. Each one of them thanked both John and me profusely for going to the hospital and taking care of him. Of course, it was the least we could do. I was just grateful that we were there to do it. I gave Phil a bag of homemade chocolate chip cookies to give Barry when he felt better, and we left him to sleep.

We were able to enjoy some of Molly Hatchet's set, and got a huge kick out of Cheap Trick's. As I stated before, Cheap Trick and AC/DC got along very well together, especially Bon Scott and Cheap Trick's bassist, Tom

One of my first AC/DC backstage passes from the company Stardate, who booked the band into the Stone Hearth in Madison, Wisconsin, on the first night I met the band.

Petersson. Let's just say the two partying together were a lot like squirting gasoline onto a fire. Right before Cheap Trick went on stage, their tour manager, Kirk Dyer, had quite a time of it getting Tom ready to perform. I marveled at Kirk's calm demeanor while trying to lead Tom up to the stage. It would have been much easier to just throw him over his shoulder, which at six feet five inches tall, he could have easily done. Once Tom was up there, he did a fine job. To be fair to Tom's miraculous recovery and future success, these were the days of pure debauchery, and both Tom and most tragically, Bon, paid a dear price for their indulgence.

At the end of Cheap Trick's set, Bon, Angus, and Malcolm came up on stage, and for their encore joined the band in playing "Sin City," and Chuck Berry's "School Days." This special treat was highlighted by Rick Nielsen climbing up on the shoulders of one of their roadies. Cheap Trick was the only band to share the same stage with AC/DC, who didn't mind following them. When the *Highway to Hell* tour was booked, AC/DC were turned down by Van Halen, Sammy Hagar, and Foreigner. To which Bon stated, "Our aim is to make the headliners work for their money."

The band spent the rest of week supporting Cheap Trick through Kansas, South Dakota, Iowa, and Nebraska. Barry called me from Iowa on the ninth, thanking me for the cookies. He suffers an explosion to the face, and he's thanking me for cookies! He said he was feeling much better, and the doctors assured him his hearing would someday return. Ironically, later that week, while still working for Cheap Trick's manager, I opened a fan letter to Cheap Trick.

It contained the newspaper article with a picture of Barry sitting on the drum riser, holding his ear, and being attended to by paramedics. What a horrible thing to happen to such a sweet person. The *Rockford Register Star* wrote, "In one of three ambulance calls to the concert, Barry Taylor, 24, a 'drum roady,' [sic] for AC/DC, suffered possible ear damage and a possible concussion when an M-80 firecracker exploded behind his head."

On September 1, 1979, AC/DC were honored to open for the Who, along with the Scorpions, Molly Hatchet, and Cheap Trick, at an open-air festival in Nuremberg, Germany. Kirk Dyer, Cheap Trick's ex-tour manager, vividly recalled AC/DC's set that day.

> I remember Nuremberg 1979, we were playing in Hitler's war stadium, where he used to have his war rallies. It was a two-day event, and AC/DC followed us, and then the Who. During our set, all the band guys are watching us play. Pete Townshend and all the AC/DC guys are trying to get us to screw up, that kind of thing. Which is normal, band guys will sit on the sidelines mooning each other, just like a football team or something. Just a bunch of practical jokers.
>
> Anyway, it was time for AC/DC to go on, and no one could find Angus. You can hear him, but no one can tell where he is. All of a sudden you see that he's up on a security guard's shoulders all the way in the back of the crowd—85,000 deep! About a quarter of a mile away from the stage, starting the song. I'm standing on stage with Pete Townshend and Rick Nielsen, right next to them, and they're talking, and Pete was just blown away. He couldn't believe how great they had just rocked. I don't think he had ever seen them before that. They just came out and did a killer set; I mean it was unbelievable. [AC/DC] came out and just blew the crowd away, and the Who guys are looking at each other, and Pete Townshend said to the rest of the band, "How are we going to top this?!"
>
> It was a hell of a memorable weekend. They had put all the bands in the same hotel, and at the bar that night after the gig was like a *Who's Who* of major rock stars. It was Cheap Trick sitting with AC/DC sitting with the Who . . . We took pictures of me, Bon Scott, Bun E., and Robin Zander playing pool.
>
> The next day we're all on the airplane, and it hadn't started to move. We started to pull out, and all of a sudden the plane stopped, and here comes Bon running across the apron of the airport, with no shoes on, half a bottle of Jack Daniels already down his throat at eight o'clock in the morning! He had forgotten his shoes, and was already in the bag the next morning after the show. So all the guys on the plane were razzing him when he got on.

One of the infamous jams between AC/DC and Cheap Trick was actually caught on camera, and Cheap Trick's drummer Bun E. Carlos released a video of it on September 2, 2000. It featured a rendition of "Johnny B.

Goode" at the Sioux Falls Arena in Sioux Falls, South Dakota on July 7, 1979. Three days, actually, after Barry was hit with that M-80 in Rockford.

Dyer has always been impressed with how they handled themselves.

> They always had the goal, no matter what the goal was, in mind. They never lost sight of what they were trying to accomplish, that's the part that I think struck me the most. In just talking to the guys, they always said they wanted to be big, they always wanted to be the best. There is no tighter five-piece band around. The rhythm section is the best in the world, in my opinion. They just blew me away. They don't sit on their laurels, or sit around and rehash old stuff. Sure, everyone puts out a greatest hits album now and then, when they don't have their songs together, but those guys have always managed to come up [with something new]. They take three chords and twist them so many different ways it never gets boring. That's what I love about them, they just rock! I never ever, ever get tired of them.

The only other time someone outside AC/DC were allowed to play with them was when Atlantic Records executive Phil Carson joined them on stage in Brussels. It was January 25, 1981, the last night of their *Back in Black* tour, and Carson got to jam with AC/DC on the Little Richard classic "Lucille."

33

Road Stories

Pranks with Nantucket

Brian's first gig here in the States was on July 30, 1980, at the County Fieldhouse in Erie, Pennsylvania, with Nantucket opening. Guitarist Tommy Redd remembered it very well, saying that Brian was so nervous that night, his knees were literally shaking.

> The first night in Erie, Pennsylvania, we were supposed to be playing with Humble Pie, but they didn't show up. The second night they showed up at the Spectrum [in Philadelphia] and it was sold out. When they showed up they got into a spat over the sound and lights. Steve Marriott, who was a great singer, was drinking really bad. They didn't want to accept that they weren't the headliners and couldn't call the shots on the lights and sound. But that's when their part of the tour came to an end. So Nantucket started out playing just thirty minutes, and that was expanded to an hour.

Over the next four weeks, Nantucket would have the honor of opening many sold-out shows for AC/DC as they traveled through Virginia, North Carolina, Georgia, and Tennessee. Tommy Redd is proud to say that he turned AC/DC onto North Carolina barbecue, which looks white. Tour manager Ian Jeffery originally thought it was tuna. Once the band tried it out, they loved it so much they demanded it everywhere else they went. Or they would have Tommy try to explain to the promoters what kind of barbecue they were looking for.

Angus Young iron-on that came with the *Bonfire* box set. This caricature of Angus as the "Little Devil" was actually drawn by Angus himself.

Tommy also laughed about the wet bar that always stood on stage right behind the curtains. It was called "Hell's Bar." Tommy said, "It had two arms that swung out, like doors, and each door had about three gallons of liquor hanging upside down, so you could get a shot. It had an ice drawer in it, and all these cups, everything you needed to make a mixed drink. We would always run out of our beer, with the radio people, friends, and people coming backstage. We always ran out, and I would end up on stage mixing Brian Johnson drinks. He would come around the corner and say, 'Tommy, got anything?'"

Redd described other stress relievers while on tour: "We used to play dart tournaments after sound check, and everyone put money up. You could win some good money. They were like ace dart players, so you had to be partners with one of those guys to get into the ballpark. One night in Savannah, Georgia, we got into a dart tournament at a happy hour in some bar, and they really killed those guys. The local yuppies had no idea who they were playing against. There were roadies along because they never separated themselves from the road crew."

Nantucket also has the honor of being the only supporting band that was given, by George Young no less, an AC/DC song to cover. It ended up being their title song for their third album, released in 1980. Not only did they cover "It's a Long Way to the Top (If You Wanna Rock 'n' Roll)," but they actually performed it while opening for AC/DC. Which must have been a very scary experience.

Tommy explained to me,

> Their brother George brought this song to Epic as a suggestion for us to record it. It came off good, and they hadn't yet released that song in America. We were real hardcore AC/DC fans, and it went over. The only time we had a rough time playing that song was at the Cow Palace in San Francisco. That was the roughest. We played it on the rest of the tour. One time Angus came back to the dressing room and we played it for him. We asked him if it was all right for us to perform and Angus said, "It's OK with me mate, but you don't have any bagpipes!"
>
> Redd still has great affection for the band, especially the Young brothers.
>
> Angus was always drinking a big glass of chocolate milk or coffee, and Malcolm used to walk around with Jack Daniels in a bottle that was as big as he was. You know they're both about four feet tall.
>
> When we played in Lake Charles, Louisiana, Angus mooned the crowd and a local cop (who looked like Jackie Gleason) didn't take kindly to this, and they got into a spat and told them it was time to

leave town. Someone came backstage and told Malcolm that Angus was in trouble. Malcolm showed up and told the police to "Piss off." The police, not knowing who he was, treated him like some little boy who came backstage from the crowd.

Nantucket was traveling around in an old bus we bought from a gospel band, which had to be started with a screwdriver. AC/DC used to really laugh at us riding around in this . . . One time when the windshield wipers wouldn't work, we had to take the panel off in the front of the dash. When we did, we found about ten bags of pot, and I mean, really old bags of pot. That must have been the "get rid of it!" spot on the bus. And we're talking southern Baptist gospel band!

AC/DC had two buses, one of them called "the worm." It was two buses that had a link in the middle like you see on a train. It was made in Belgium or something, and they hated it. We were coming up from West Palm Beach and we stopped at the bar called the Kiki, where we auditioned for Epic. So we were like an hour or so behind AC/DC, who took off on Highway 95. Way out in the middle of Florida, somewhere around Daytona, we saw these lights flashing on the shoulder of the road, they had broken down. Here we were with an old 1960-something bus, it looked like the bus Marilyn Monroe was on in the movie *Some Like It Hot.* It had a big round back, and a huge steering wheel like Ralph Kramden's bus on *The Honeymooners.* So we pulled up and opened the doors, and Ian [Jeffery] and everyone was jumping up and down. It was like stopping at a school bus stop full of kids. We said, 'Well this old bus looks pretty good now, huh?' We took them to the next exit and they made some phone calls. Then they rode with us up to Jacksonville. Here they were riding on this old bus, the one that they always wondered if it was going to make the tour at all.

The color version of Angus the "Little Devil" from the back, appropriately entitled "The End."

Larry Uzzell gives Tommy Redd a dose of his favorite drink while the rest of Nantucket and AC/DC enjoy a good laugh.   *Photo by Bruce Kessler*

The last night Nantucket got to open for AC/DC is one of Tommy's favorite memories.

> I remember that it was someone's birthday, or anniversary, so we knew
> something was up. While performing, we understood why we had
> been forewarned. The drummer's drumsticks had all the tips sawed
> in two, so when he hit the drum heads, the sticks immediately broke
> apart. They [AC/DC] also filled his high hat with shaving cream, so
> the first time he hit that, the cream sprayed everywhere. If that wasn't
> enough, the bass drum had two-sided duct tape on it, so eventually
> the drum pedal just stuck to the drum. I guess there was also a huge
> cake they wanted to drop on my head, but I never did look up!

While Nantucket fought to get through their set, Phil Rudd and some of the road crew were on the side of the stage, doubled over with laughter.

34

Strange but True

Obscure Facts About the Band

AC/DC Plays a Wedding

The most bizarre gig that AC/DC has ever played had to be for a friend's wedding. The brother of the bride was a good friend of the band's and had lent them PA equipment when they needed it. The band got quite a laugh when they realized they were playing in a backyard, with no stage.

Dave Evans told Peter Hoysted of *Axs* magazine in October 1998, "We did a set—a bit of Chuck Berry, a bit of the Rolling Stones. The father of the bride came up to me and asked us if we could play 'Zorba The Greek.' I said, 'Mate, we're a rock 'n' roll band. There's no way.' Then Malcolm said, 'Give me a minute.' He went away and practiced for a while, all from ear. Then Malcolm said, 'Tell him, yeah. We'll do it.' The band went back and played following Malcolm's lead. The people danced and cheered. I hope they all remember that day. The one and only time AC/DC ever played 'Zorba The Greek.'"

It's a Long Way to the Top (If You Wanna Rock 'n' Roll)

Even though Bon Scott grew up playing a drum alongside his father, who played with the Kirriemuir Pipe Band, he never played the bagpipes himself until George Young talked him into it. Bon learned to play the bagpipes for the opening of the song "It's a Long Way to the Top (If You Wanna Rock 'n' Roll), which first appeared on their second album, *T.N.T.* and was also included on the international release of their album *High Voltage.*

Bon continued to play the bagpipes live until 1976, when he set them down at the side of the stage one night and the audience ended up destroying them. After that, the band used a taped version for their live

Bon Scott with his bagpipes in 1976. Bon actually had to learn how to play the bagpipes, as he started out as a drummer that would follow his father's pipe band around in their homeland of Scotland and later after they settled in Australia.

Photo by Philip Morris

performances. The studio recording actually features a synthesized sound of a bagpipe, which couldn't really be played on a real set of bagpipes.

Bagpipers played the song on October 1, 2004, when Corporation Lane in Melbourne, Australia, was officially renamed ACDC Lane. The original video for the song, which was shot on February 23, 1976, features the band playing on the back of a flatbed truck driving down Swanston Street, which is near ACDC Lane.

The song itself has been covered by everyone from W.A.S.P., the Wiggles, Lucinda Williams, Motörhead, the Dropkick Murphys, and Nantucket, to, believe it or not, the 1950s crooner Pat Boone. Boone included the song on his 1997 album, *In a Metal Mood: No More Mr. Nice Guy.*

Cyber Attack: AC/DC Style

On August 7, 2014, it was reported that computer hackers got into the Iranian nuclear computer system and blasted the song "Thunderstruck" in the middle of the night. The incident happened between 2009 and 2010 when the nuclear program in Iran was the target of some devastating attacks, reportedly developed by Israeli and the American governments.

The virus, known as Stuxnet, took control of nuclear facilities across the country and caused thousands of machines to break down. The hackers also chose to not only mess with the systems, but decided to program the computers to play AC/DC's song "Thunderstruck" at very high volumes.

Speaking at the Black Hat security conference, Finnish computer security expert Mikko Hypponen recalled an email he received from an Iranian scientist at the time of the Stuxnet attacks. *VentureBeat* quotes from the correspondence: "There was also some music playing randomly on several of the workstations during the middle of the night with the volume maxed out. I believe it was the American band AC/DC, "Thunderstruck." It was all very strange and happened very quickly. The attackers also managed to gain root access to the machine they entered from and removed all the logs."

After the attack, President Obama spoke out about not using cyber weapons on other countries, for fear they could be turned and used against the United States. He refrained from commenting on the power of deploying AC/DC.

Backstage pass and tickets from the *Razors Edge* tour at Alpine Valley in East Troy, Wisconsin, on June 28, 1991. That was the same night Brian showed us a shiner he had received in a scuffle in a bar in Sarasota, Florida, where he had just built a house.

Vanishing Guides and Mystery Background Vocals

Over the years I've heard many AC/DC stories from fans around the world. The two that I have never forgotten involve a vanishing guide and mysterious background vocals. The first story involves an AC/DC fan who traveled all the way to Australia to visit Bon Scott's grave. This was years ago, before his grave had any special markers or a special gate like it does today. The fan not only traveled to Bon's hometown of Perth and ran into Bon's parents, but he also went to visit Bon's gravesite in Fremantle, which is about twelve miles from Perth.

As he roamed around the cemetery looking for Bon's grave on a bright sunny day, he came across a man dressed in a beekeeper's outfit, including the netting that covered his face. Since he had no idea which way to walk to find Bon's grave, he asked the man if he could help him out. The man in the beekeeper's outfit never said a word, but just pointed in the direction of Bon's grave. Not only was it really hot that day, but there were no bees swarming around anywhere that he could see. So he took off in the direction the man pointed in, and quickly turned around to thank him, to find nobody there. The "beekeeper" had simply vanished into thin air.

The second story also involves an AC/DC fan, who was following the band around Europe on the *Razors Edge* tour. While traveling by train between concerts, he just happened to be on the same train as Angus and Ellen Young. He chatted with them that evening and then Angus excused himself to retire for the night. The fan sat up talking to Ellen and she told him the most incredible story. She explained that while the band was in the studio recording the album *The Razors Edge*, one day they came in to find backing vocals that no one in the band had yet recorded.

Not only was that in itself very strange, but according to everyone who had a listen, the background vocals sounded exactly like Bon Scott. Even though at the time Bon had been gone for over ten years.

35

MTV Breathes New Life into AC/DC

Thanks to *Beavis and Butthead*

Beavis and Butthead, an animated television show created by Mike Judge, debuted on MTV in March of 1993. It featured two amusing metal slackers who had a field day critiquing rock videos, most of which always "sucked, heh, heh, heh." Beavis first appeared wearing a Slayer T-shirt, but wound up wearing one that said "Metallica." Butthead, Beavis's intellectually challenged sidekick, got the honor of wearing a shirt that boasted the hallowed initials "AC/DC." Thanks to pre-teens to twenty-somethings, the cartoon was an instant hit for MTV. Beavis and Butthead's attire made a direct statement on who the real kings of metal were in the early nineties–rock royalty, who all future bands would bow down to.

That summer, AC/DC were invited to record a new song for the soundtrack to the Arnold Schwarzenegger movie *Last Action Hero*. The song "Big Gun" was produced by Rick Rubin. The video for the song was shot at the Van Nuys Airport in Los Angeles, in Hanger 104 E, and was directed by David Mallet. It featured Arnold himself, dressed up as Angus running around the stage while the band plays on. Just the difference in size between Arnold and Angus is hilarious to see.

The soundtrack to *Last Action Hero*, which included songs by Alice in Chains, Anthrax, Queensrÿche, Def Leppard, Megadeth, Tesla, Fishbone, and Cypress Hill, was released in July by Atco. The incredibly expensive film flopped at the box office, but the soundtrack album did rather well. AC/DC's single "Big Gun" debuted at #23 in the UK, and made it to #65 in the States.

By the fall of 1993, AC/DC's album *Live* had reached the two million mark, *High Voltage* had also sold two million copies, and *Who Made Who* had just surpassed three million in sales. In addition, a long-form video titled *For Those About to Rock We Salute You* was released. It was an eighty-four

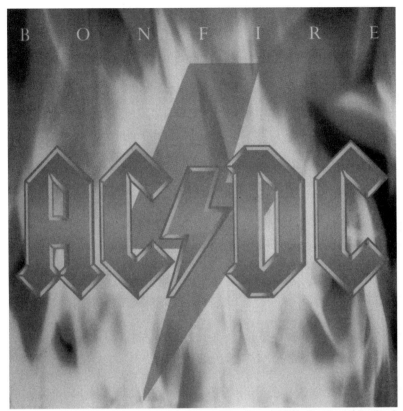

The cover of the *Bonfire* box set, with flames. Thanks to MTV's *Beavis and Butthead*, a whole new generation was more than ready for the *Bonfire* box set once it was released in 1997, catapulting Bon Scott's legacy to a whole new level. *Jim Johnson Collection*

minute recording of their momentous appearance in Moscow. The footage featured AC/DC, Metallica, the Black Crowes, Pantera, and E.S.T. Their label Atco also rereleased the band's pre-1985 catalog in Europe and the US, completely remastered.

At the end of the *Razors Edge* tour, Phil Rudd had caught their show in Auckland, New Zealand, which was the first time he had seen the band since his departure in 1983. Phil spent several hours visiting with them after the show, and in May of the following year, AC/DC invited him back into the studio to record songs for their new album. Having left the music business behind, he seriously had to consider taking up the rock 'n' roll life again. Rumors started to fly that he was back in the band, but his official return wasn't announced until after the album was due to be released.

36

Imitation Is the Sincerest Form of Flattery

AC/DC Tribute Bands, Fans, and Conventions

There is no doubt that AC/DC has some of the best, most loyal fans in the world. After taking a seven-year break and coming out with *Black Ice* in 2008, it was quickly evident that the band was as popular as ever. Not only did the new album hit #1 in thirty-one countries simultaneously, but their ticket sales to the *Black Ice* tour also broke records.

To celebrate their love for AC/DC, every year fans gather from all over the world to attend AC/DC conventions. The largest, called The Big Ball, in 2005, featured Hayseed Dixie and Simon Wright playing in the tribute band Dirty/DC. Some of the funniest AC/DC tribute band names are Seedy DC, Fat Angus Band, Hells Balls, and my personal favorite, the all-female band from San Francisco called AC/DSHE. Band members include Agnes and Mallory Young, Riff Williams, Phyllis Rudd, and Bonny Scott.

Every year there is a Bon Fest held in Bon's birthplace of Kirriemuir, Scotland at the Town Hall. In 2014, it took place over three nights from August 15–17 and featured the all-girl tribute band Back:N:Black. To commemorate the date of Bon Scott's death, there is an annual BonFest Long Way To The Top held in Perth by Doug Thorncroft's Let There Be Rock Productions. In 2014, the event was held on Febuary 15 at the Astor Theatre and featured ex-AC/DC vocalist Dave Evans, supported by the tribute band Hells Bells.

For the love of Bon, projects are constantly being produced, including a show at the Theatre Royal in Hobart, Tasmania on September 11 and 12, 2014, *Hell Ain't a Bad Place to Be: The Story of Bon Scott* starring Nick Barker.

One of the best tribute bands that I have had the pleasure of seeing in person is BandX, from Belgrade, Serbia. Lead vocalist Billy has an uncanny way of channeling both Brian Johnson and Bon Scott. Along with Darko on lead guitar, Dragan on rhythm, Darko on bass, and Igor on drums, live, they come very close to the ever-elusive sound of AC/DC.

According to Mat Croft in *Metal Hammer* Special 2005, two of the best AC/DC covers are Quiet Riot's "Highway to Hell," on the album *Thunderbolt*, and Motörhead covering "It's a Long Way to the Top," with Lemmy "sounding so hoarse you expect a bloody lung to come flying out of your speakers."

The love that the fans of AC/DC have shows no boundaries when it comes to fan websites, Facebook pages, Facebook fan pages, and countless AC/DC blogs. Every day, no matter where the AC/DC news is released, anyone on the Internet can immediately be alerted to the band's every move.

Just as the Beatles did in the sixties, and Led Zeppelin in the seventies, AC/DC defined the eighties, influencing hundreds of bands around the world, such as Australia's Rose Tattoo, Silvertide, Jet, and the Angels;

An AC/DC poster covered with AC/DC buttons belonging to Jim Johnson, a dedicated fan who has a collection of all things AC/DC. As you can see on the Internet every day, there are hundreds of pictures of rooms, man caves, bedrooms, and houses decorated in honor of one of the world's greatest bands.   *Photo by Jim Johnson*

Switzerland's Krokus; Spain's Baron Rojo; France's Trust; and Germany's TNT. In America and the United Kingdom, the list includes Guns N' Roses, Mötley Crüe, Def Leppard, Quiet Riot, Twisted Sister, Kix, Danger Danger, the Cult, Buckcherry, the Darkness, and Rhino Bucket.

Autographs from the *Classic Rock Cares* tour in Clearwater, Florida, on July 3, 2007. The best signature was Brian Johnson's, which was his kind opinion of my book, *The Story of AC/DC: Let There Be Rock*. It reads, "A crackin' roller coaster of a read!"

37

Founder, Creator, Riffmaster, Brains Behind AC/DC

Malcolm Young Retires

Malcolm Young formed AC/DC at the end of 1973, and their first performance was at a small club called Chequers at 79 Goulburn Street in Sydney on New Year's Eve. The only time Malcom took a break from the band was on the North American leg of the *Blow Up Your Video* tour. His nephew Stevie Young filled in for him, and it was stated at the time that Malcolm was taking time off for personal reasons.

The real reason why he left the tour for a short time was to get over his dependency on alcohol, Later, Malcolm candidly stated,

> Just a case of rock 'n' roll. The lifestyle, I'm just a little guy, like five foot three, you know? I was trying to keep up with the big guys. It just got to me. People can't depend on you anymore. So it was just a matter of cutting it right out. When you've got an alcohol problem, you don't see it like . . . Of course, when you're sobered up [and thinking more clearly], lots of thoughts would go through your head like Bon and lots of other things you might have messed up here and there. It was a combination at the end where you just need help, basically. You can't do it yourself. Especially when you've done everything yourself in the past and along comes this little thing that's snuck up on you. It's a whole different thing.

Angus eventually disclosed that "he wanted to get rid of his booze problem, and clean himself up. I think if you can do that on your own free will it's great; and having been through that situation with Bon, I don't think I could have gone through it again."

While at home in Australia, Malcolm spent time with his wife Linda and their two kids. He even bought a horse and dabbled in racing. Although during his recuperation he never put the guitar down for long, and was already working on ideas for their next album.

Of course Angus noticed a huge difference being on tour without Malcolm. He remarked to *Hit Parader*, "He's an incredible songwriter, and an amazing rhythm guitarist. Playing that kind of guitar takes a special person, and Malcolm has just the right feel for it. He's been willing to live a little bit in my shadow over the years, but [touring] without him just reinforced what I already knew—he's a very important member of the band."

During the *Black Ice* tour, the band had been saying they had enough material for a new album, and would at some point go back into the studio. That tour officially ended in 2010, and over the next couple of years, Brian Johnson was quoted as saying that they were planning on going back into the studio to record a new album, and the band intended on playing forty dates to celebrate their fortieth anniversary in 2013.

Between 2012 and 2013, rumors circulated on the Internet pertaining to the health of one of the band members, and in April of 2014, it was finally revealed that Malcolm Young was suffering from some serious health issues. Reportedly he had gone into the studio to rehearse to record a new album, and wasn't able to play like he used to. Allegedly, he had suffered a stroke a few weeks before, and they found a blood clot on his brain. Though he lived most of the time in London, he relocated back to Sydney, to be near family and give him a place to recover.

The following statement appeared on AC/DC's Facebook page on April 16, 2014:

"After forty years of life dedicated to AC/DC, guitarist and founding member Malcolm Young is taking a break from the band due to ill health. Malcolm would like to thank the group's diehard legions of fans worldwide for their never-ending love and support. In light of this news, AC/DC asks that Malcolm and his family's privacy be respected during this time. The band will continue to make music."

True to their word, on May 1, 2014, AC/DC reconvened at the Warehouse Studio in Vancouver to begin recording new material with producer Brendan O'Brien, this time accompanied by Angus and Malcolm's nephew, Stevie Young.

In the fall of 2014, Brian Johnson did confirm that there would most likely be a tour; however, it remains to be seen how many dates they will commit to. The band has toured before without Malcolm, but under such different circumstances. It's hard to envision Angus doing an entire tour without his brother standing stage right.

Malcolm, Jamey, Angus, and me backstage on the *Black Ice* tour at the Allstate Arena in Chicago, Illinois, on November 1, 2008. The best part of this picture was when Angus turned to Malcolm and said, "Put the kid in the middle!" By the look on my son's face, you could say he was very happy to be there.

Australian guitarist Joe Matera agrees that Malcolm's stepping down "is very sad, as he is one of the greatest rhythm guitar players ever. Period. He is a large part, if not the vital core, of the engine room that drives the band and allows Angus to do his thing. The chemistry between the two brothers is an integral part of the band and its sound, without the other, it can never be the same."

Brian Johnson told *Rolling Stone*, "It's been forty years of the band's existence," he continued. "So I think we're gonna try to do forty gigs, forty shows, to thank the fans for their undying loyalty. I mean, honestly, our fans are just the best in the world, and we appreciate every one of them. So, like I said, we'll have to go out, even though we're getting a bit long in the tooth. You know what?! It's been four years [since we last went out on the road] and I'm really looking forward to it."

As "Pyro" Pete told me, "They've toured without Malcolm before, but it was under very different circumstances. Malcolm is like a metronome, he and Cliff have been keeping the rhythm for years, and on top of that, he's really, really good and a really, really nice guy."

Mike Fraser is also amazed by Malcolm's playing. He leads the band by just standing beside the drums, although the whole band watches him for cutoffs, whether it's a nod of his head, or a swift hand signal. Even Angus, while constantly moving around the stage, keeps an eye on him.

Brian Johnson stated to *Metal Injection* on July 9, 2014, "We're done. I'm very excited and we've got some great songs. We miss Malcolm obviously. He's a fighter. He's in hospital but he's a fighter. We've got our fingers crossed that he'll get strong again. Stevie, Malcolm's nephew, was magnificent, but when you're recording with this thing hanging over you and your work mate isn't well, it's difficult. But I'm sure he was rooting for us. He's such a strong man. He's a small guy but he's very strong. He's proud and he's very private so we can't say too much. But fingers crossed he'll be back." It was eventually revealed that, after the *Black Ice* tour ended, Malcolm had successful surgery for lung cancer and received a pacemaker after suffering a heart attack. Now in the hospital with dementia, he would not be rejoining the band. Angus later admitted that Malcolm started showing signs of memory loss during the *Black Ice* tour. Angus sadly stated that his normally very organized brother had to relearn songs that he had played for years and some nights on stage were actually confusing for him. The loss of Malcolm as Angus' muse is heartbreaking. The loss of Malcolm's contribution to AC/DC is most certainly the end of an era. Considering the musical genius he truly is, this news shocked and saddened millions of fans around the world. There will never be a greater rhythm guitar player/songwriter/riffmaster than Malcolm Young.

They just marked their fortieth anniversary, and forty years from now, AC/DC's music will still sound as vital as it does today. With or without Malcolm by their side, AC/DC will continue to do what they do best, which is write, record, and perform some of the best rock 'n' roll music ever created.

The founder and, in my opinion, the heart and soul of AC/DC, Malcolm Young, said it best on their official website. "We've always been a true band. You won't find one any truer. AC/DC will always be AC/DC." And for that, Malcolm, your fans couldn't love you more or thank you enough.

Selected Bibliography

I ncluded in this book are conversations, interviews, and personal encounters that I have had with the band over a thirty-seven year period. In addition to my own material and firsthand experiences, I relied on numerous sources, listed below, in my research for this book. All were very helpful, interesting, and are highly recommended.

Books

AC/DC: Hard Rock Band by Heather Miller
AC/DC: High-Voltage Rock 'n' Roll: The Ultimate Illustrated History by Phil Sutcliffe
AC/DC in the Studio by Jake Brown
AC/DC: Maximum Rock & Roll by Murray Engleheart with Arnaud Durieux
AC/DC: The Encyclopaedia by Malcolm Dome and Jerry Ewing
AC/DC: The World's Heaviest Rock by Martin Huxley
Bonfire AC/DC Boxed Set Band Biography by Murray Engleheart
Dirty Deeds: My Life Inside & Outside of AC/DC by Mark Evans
Encyclopedia of Rock Stars by Dafydd Rees and Luke Crampton
Glad All Over: The Countdown Years 1974–1987 by Peter Wilmoth
Guitar Legends: Guitar World, February 2005
Highway to Hell: The Life and Times of AC/DC Legend Bon Scott by Clinton Walker
House of Hits by Jane Albert
Popular Rock Superstars of Yesterday and Today Pop Rock: AC/DC by Ethan Schlesinger
Rock 'n' Roll Fantasy: My Life and Times with AC/DC, Van Halen, Kiss . . . by Susan Masino
Rockers and Rollers: A Full Throttle Memoir by Brian Johnson
Shock to the System by Mark Putterford
Singing in the Dark by Barry Taylor and Dan Wooding
The Story of AC/DC: Let There Be Rock by Susan Masino
Two Sides to Every Glory: AC/DC, The Complete Biography by Paul Stenning
Why AC/DC Matters by Anthony Bozza

Magazine Articles

Axs, "High Voltage History" by Peter Hoysted, October 1998

Bay of Plenty Times, "Rudd Will Defend Charges," by Sandra Conchie, December 3, 2014

Billboard, quote from Glenn A. Baker found in the article "Angus Young: Seriously" by Jas Obrecht

Billboard, "Spotlight," September 22, 1990

Blabbermouth, "Deep Purple Frontman Recalls AC/DC Booting" by Andrew Tijs, January 2007

Chicago Tribune, "A New Era in Rock: It's Brutal" by Al Rudis, November 1977

Chicago Tribune, "AC/DC Lights It Up" by Greg Kot, January 20, 1991

Circus, "AC/DC: Wired for Success, There's No Keeping a Live Band Down" by David Fricke, January 16, 1979, pages 26–27

Circus, "AC/DC Only Stops for Tea on the 'Highway to Hell,' Thank You Kindly," by David Fricke, November, 1979, pages 30–31

Circus, "May–June 1981 Year End Report," pages 53–54

Circus, "AC/DC Salutes the Stadium Circuit" by Richard Hogan, 1982

Circus, "Photo Journal" by Richard Hogan, December 31, 1982

Circus, "Stage Pass: AC/DC Flick the Switch at Philadelphia's Spectrum" by Dan Hedges, January 31, 1984, page 29

Classic Rock, "Hear AC/DC's 'Play Ball' and Check Out 'Rock or Bust' Cover Art" by Jeff Giles, October 7, 2014

Classic Rock, "Brian Johnson Says It was Difficult Making New AC/DC Album Without Malcolm Young" by Nick DeRiso, October 2, 2014

Classic Rock, "Scott a Touch Too Much" by Geoff Barton, February 2005, pages 37–43

Classic Rock, "For Whom the Bell Tolls," August 2005, pages 40–49

Classic Rock, "Experts Left Thunderstruck by Cost of AC/DC Song" by Scott Munro, August 15, 2014

Creem, "AC/DC's Short Circuit the Angus and the Ecstasy: 'You Can't Tie These Kangaroos Down, Sport!'" by Brad Balfour, September 28, 1978, pages 23–24

Creem, "Satan's Pigeons" by Sylvie Simmons, 1984

Creem, "Close-Up Metal," May 1984

Creem, "Rock 'n' Roll News," May 1980

Cyber Drum, Interview with Phil Rudd by Steven Scott Fyfe, August 15, 2000

Drum!, "Phil Rudd of AC/DC" by Don Zulaica, June 2005

East Kilbride News, November 11, 1976

Electric Basement, with Brian Coles, September 2000

Emerald City Chronicle, "AC/DC Spreading Sparks" by Susan Severson Masino, January 1978

Guitar Player, "Angus Young: Seriously" by Jas Obrecht, February 1984, pages 76–78, 94–104

Guitar Player, "Malcolm Young, Heavy Metal Rhythm Specialist," February 1984, pages 82–92

Guitar School, "Cover story with Angus Young," September 1992

Guitar School "Cliff Notes: Interview with Cliff Williams" by Michael Duclos, March 1995, pages 32–33

Guitar World, "Let There Be Rock: AC/DC's Angus Young on the Rhythm Playing of Malcolm Young" by Nick Bowcott, January 6, 2014

Guitar World Special Collector's Issue, "Dirty Deeds Re-Done" by Richard Bienstock, April 2003, pages 10–17

Guitar World Special Collector's Issue, "Bon Voyage" by Tom Beaujour, January 1998, pages 19–25

Guitar World Special Collector's Issue, "Hard as a Rock" by Alan DiPerna, January 1993, pages 26–33

Guitar World Special Collector's Issue, "Young at Heart" by Steve Rosen, March 1984, pages 34–40

Guitar World Special Collector's Issue, "Let There Be Rock" by Nick Bowcott, May 2000

Guitar World Special Collector's Issue, "Live Wire" by Joe Lalaina, March 1986, pages 46–52

Guitar World, "Young Lust" by Alan di Perna, November 1995

Guitar World, "Sixty Minutes with Angus Young" by Vic Garbarini, August 1996, page 188

Guitar World, "Let There Be Rock: If It Ain't Broke, Don't Fix It!" by Nick Bowcott, July 1998, page 124

Hard Radio, "Hell Ain't a Bad Place to Be!" by Tim Henderson

Hard Rock Mag HS2, December 1996

High Vaultage, "A Delirious Delve into the AC/DC Album Archives" by Mark Putterford, pages 24–26

Hit Parader, by Jodi Summers Dorland, Winter 1985, page 59

Hit Parader Legends of Metal AC/DC, "Angus Young and the Boys Take Us All on the Highway to Hell," Winter 1989

Hit Parader, "AC/DC: End of the Line?" by Winston Cummings, 1995, pages 64–65

Hit Parader, "AC/DC: Lightning Strikes Angus and the Boys Sell Out Arenas from Coast to Coast As *Razors Edge* Reaches the Top" by Winston Cummings

Houston Press, "The Riff Factory," by Greg Barr, September 2000

Kerrang!, "Angus Beefed Up! Or: Dirty Deeds Redone Rather Expensively!" by Paul Elliott

Kerrang!, "Thunder from Down Under No. 11," March 11–24, 1982

Live Design Online, "For Those About to Rock" by Marian Sandberg, January 27, 2009

Louisville, Kentucky Courier Journal, by John Finley, December 13, 1977

Metal CD, "Double Decade of Dirty Deeds," Vol. 1 No. 1, 1992, pages 44–49

Metal CD, "Stage-Struck!" by Mark Blake, 1992, page 42

Metal Edge, "AC/DC: The Big Crunch" by Jim Farber, Fall 1985, pages 46–48

Metal Edge, "AC/DC: Certified Legends" by Bryan Reesman, 2000, pages 14–17

Metal Hammer & Classic Rock, "Hometown Heroes" by Joe Matera, page 9

Metal Hammer & Classic Rock, "Whole Lotta Tributes" by Mat Croft, pages 18–19

Metal Hammer & Classic Rock Special 2005, "Duck-Walkin' All Over You" by Martin Popoff, page 29

Metal Hammer & Classic Rock Special 2005, "Brother's Got Rhythm" by Geoff Barton, pages 32–35

Metal Hammer & Classic Rock Special 2005, "A Touch Too Much" by Geoff Barton, pages 64–70

Metal Hammer & Classic Rock Special 2005, "What Really Happened to Bon Scott?", page 71

Metal Hammer & Classic Rock Special 2005, "Who Made Who?" by Martin Popoff, pages 100–101

Metal Hammer & Classic Rock Special 2005, "Hell on Two Legs" by Jerry Ewing, page 122

Metal Hammer & Classic Rock Special 2005, "It's Electric" by John Doran, page 124

Metal Hammer & Classic Rock Special 2005, "Down and Dirty" by John Doran, page 131

Metal Hammer & Classic Rock Special 2005 "Present AC/DC For Those About to Rock We Salute You," by Martin Popoff, pages 134–135

Metal Injection, "AC/DC's Brian Johnson: "We're Done (With the New Album)" by Robert Pasbani, July 9, 2014

Mobile Production, "AC/DC *Black Ice* Tour: A Good Old-Fashioned Rock Show," by Bill Abner and Michael A. Beck, Volume 2 Issue 7, 2009

Mojo, "AC/DC Celebrate Their Quarter Century" by Sylvie Simmons, December 2004

National RockStar, "Front Row Reviews" by Stuart Hoggard, February 26, 1977

National RockStar, "Front Row Reviews" by Ian Flavin, March 5, 1977

New York Rock, "AC/DC: Still Stiff After All These Years" by Spyder Darling, April 2000

New Zealand Herald, "AC/DC Drummer Phil Rudd Involved in Aggressive Fracas," by David Fisher, December 4, 2014

No Nonsense, AC/DC Website Interview with Colin Abrahams, August 22, 2013

People, "With a Flick of the Switch, AC/DC Stays Current and Powers into a Tenth Anniversary" by Richard Hogan, December 1983, pages 42–44

Record Collector, "Bonfire! The Genesis of AC/DC" by Mick Wall, No. 222, February 1998, pages 102–104

Record Mirror, "AC/DC, Glasgow University" by Eric Wishart, February 26, 1977

Record Mirror, "Boy Wonder Canes 'Em!" by John Howe, October 22, 1977

Record Mirror, "Roadshows" by Selma Boddy, October 22, 1977

Request, "Speak For Yourself: AC/DC," June 2000, page 18

Rock-E-Zine, by Johan Godschalk, September 2000

Rockford Register Star, "Cheap Trick Rocks Filled Fairgrounds," July 5, 1979

Rolling Stone, "Hard Rock, Harder Times: AC/DC Return Without Two Key Members," by David Fricke, November 14, 2014

Rolling Stone, "AC/DC Heading Into the Studio This Spring" by Miriam Coleman, February 16, 2014

Rolling Stone, "Review of *Blow Up Your Video*" by Jim Farber, April 7, 1988

Rolling Stone, "Random Notes," October 1, 1992

Q, "Blackened Sabbath: The Official Account of Events," from the insert inside the AC/DC bootleg called *Swedish Neurotica*

Sarasota Downtown, "Jerry & Brian: Two Rocks on a Sarasota Roll" by Steve Rabow, Summer 1998, pages 56–57

Select, "Review of *Razors Edge*" by Mark Putterford, October 1990

Sounds, "Body Music from Wagga Wagga," October 22, 1977

Sounds, "Sex, Snot, Sweat, and Schoolkids (Or: AC/DC Are Back in Town)" by Phil Sutcliffe, October 29, 1977

Super Polly, "High Voltage (& AC/DC!) Makes 'Gig of the Year'!" by Polly, October 1977

The Sydney Morning Herald, "Albert Productions: The Label Behind AC/DC Rocks up 50 Years," by Bernard Zuel, August 10, 2014

TPI-Total Production, March 2009, Issue 115

Trouser Press, "AC/DC: Young-Fast" by Marc Mayco, November 1977, pages 6–7

Ultimate Classic Rock, "Angus and Malcolm's First Recording to Be Reissued by Dave Swanson"

Undercover Media, by Paul Cashmere

Wisconsin State Journal, "AC/DC Plugs into Its Roots" by Gene Stout, April 26, 2001, page 3

DVDs

And Then There Was Rock: Life Before Brian, November 2005

Let There Be Rock

Live at Donington

Live at River Plate

No Bull AC/DC Live, Plaza De Toros, Madrid

Index

THE FAQ SERIES

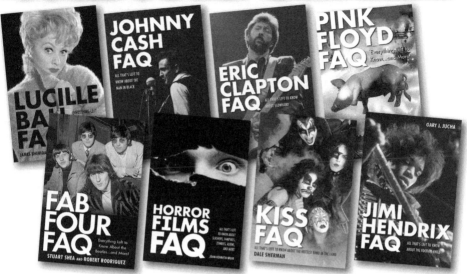

HAL•LEONARD®
PERFORMING ARTS
PUBLISHING GROUP

FAQ.halleonardbooks.com